Lidgate's

THE MEAT COOKBOOK

Lidgate's

THE MEAT COOKBOOK

Danny Lidgate & Hattie Ellis

MITCHELL BEAZLEY

To David Lidgate and the Lidgate family,
past, present and future

An Hachette UK Company
www.hachette.co.uk

First published in Great Britain in 2016 by
Mitchell Beazley, a division of Octopus Publishing Group Ltd
Carmelite House
50 Victoria Embankment
London EC4Y 0DZ
www.octopusbooks.co.uk

Distributed in the US by
Hachette Book Group
1290 Avenue of the Americas
4th and 5th Floors
New York, NY 10020

Distributed in Canada by
Canadian Manda Group
664 Annette St
Toronto, Ontario,
Canada M6S 2C8

ISBN 978 1 78472 049 0

A CIP catalogue record for this book is available from the British
Library.

Printed and bound in China

10 9 8 7 6 5 4 3 2 1

Senior Commissiong Editor Eleanor Maxfield
Senior Editor Alex Stetter
Art Director Juliette Norsworthy
Designer Geoff Fennell
Photographer Andy Sewell (except p21, Danny Lidgate)
Illustrator Grace Helmer
Copy Editor Trish Burgess
Home Economist & Food Stylist Laura Fyfe
Props Stylists Laura Fyfe, Liz Belton
Production Controller Sarah Kramer

Contents

Introduction

Lidgate's is a fifth-generation butcher's shop in the leafy streets of Holland Park, west London. As part of the proud tradition of British family butchers, it is a magnet for cooks, chefs and dedicated carnivores, who come in search of anything from a lunchtime sausage roll to a magnificent rib of grass-fed beef for a dinner party.

We've written this book to share Lidgate's specialist knowledge with meat-eaters everywhere. It's a collection of recipes, often developed in our own kitchen, that suit every occasion, from a midweek supper to a Sunday lunch, from a casual barbecue to a special celebration. It will also help you to discern a good butcher, choose the best meat, find out how to cook it and learn how to cut and carve it.

From past to present

Alexander Lidgate founded the family business in 1850, and was succeeded by his son Charles. It was hard work and the hours were long, but butchery is a sociable business. The family story goes that Charles would buy from Smithfield, London's wholesale meat market, have a few beers afterwards with colleagues, and his horse could lead the meat-laden cart back to the shop unaided.

The business opened a new chapter in 1959 when 19-year old David Lidgate was thrown in at the deep end, having to manage the shop after his father retired due to ill health and then died young. David was a passionate rugby player, but suddenly had to focus his energy on the family shop – indeed, to ensure it survived. It's said that an instinct for good meat is in the blood and he quickly developed a sense for good quality. He also studied the fine meat traditions on the Continent, and had an epiphany whilst visiting a village in Austria. Here he found a tiny shop run by an immaculately dressed butcher with gleaming knives. Pieces of meat were carefully set out on a wooden block, like items of jewellery, and behind the shop he discovered £10,000-worth of the latest butchery equipment. Nothing was wasted: every scrap of meat was turned into an astonishing range of high-class sausages. The days of spit and sawdust were over.

Once back home, David converted a room above the shop into a well-equipped kitchen, and Lidgate's started to make sausages, pies, charcuterie and ready-to-eat dishes. Within a week of employing a cook to undertake some of this work, the shop display changed to ensure that passers-by stopped and shopped.

The rise of Lidgate's as a modern butcher came at the time when meat-graders cared more about size and standardization than flavour. From 1981, beef had to be priced according to a European grading system that favoured fast-growing Continental breeds fed on cereals, rather than British cattle nurtured on grass that provided high-quality meat with relatively little maintenance. David thought this trend as ridiculous as pricing wine according to its bottle. A marker of this trend was that the renowned Perth Bull Sale went from selling nearly all native breeds to virtually none.

As farming and retailers headed largely in one direction, Lidgate's went in another, deciding to prioritize the breed, feed and slaughter of the animal, how the meat was hung and cut, and all the other details that go into acquiring the best possible quality. Taste was all important – a standard they upheld in a retailing world that favoured quantity over quality. Now the pendulum has swung back, with chefs and meat fans also favouring native breeds, grass-fed animals and top-notch quality. Discerning shoppers are once again appreciating what they can get from a specialist independent outlet.

Danny Lidgate, David's oldest son, now heads the business. Like his father, he regards meat not just as raw cuts, but as food on a plate. As boys, he and his brother Ben glazed hams, helped carry customers' bags to their cars, and handed out mince pies and mulled wine to the long Christmas queue. From the age of 17, he trained for four years in the Smithfield Unit of Walthamstow College, and worked in different places, from a cheap-and-cheerful London shop to Denmark's first organic butcher. He went back to the family shop with a broad perspective and took over the reins from David in 2009, at the age of 30, with Ben as company secretary – the fifth generation of Lidgate butchers.

Go into Lidgate's today and you will see many signs of the traditional business it has always been: an old-fashioned clock above the door, a framed horseshoe from the days when Lidgate's salesmen took a horse-and-cart around the neighbourhood to drum up business, customers being served by butchers sporting boaters and deliveries made by drivers wearing ties. People still pay for their purchases at a separate cash desk at the end of the narrow shop, and here they can ask yet more questions about how to cook their meat. Yet there's a youthful energy from all the comings and goings in this early Victorian building, with its warren of rooms. There is the larkiness of butchers, but also serious craftsmanship and a great respect for their meat.

In the main cutting room behind the shop, a rotation of some 20 butchers uses the latest kit to turn carcasses into cuts that are ready to cook. In the kitchen above the shop, three or four cooks develop and cook recipes that make the most of the cuts and offcuts, including Lidgate's versions of classics such as chicken and ham pie and Cornish pasties. A specialist sausage-maker turns out more than 20 different varieties of banger, all made freshly each day. Downstairs, the butchers think up new ways of making the most of meat, such as unusual kebabs and specially stuffed and tied roasts.

Some of the skills being passed down to apprentices go back to the old traditions of high-quality butchery established in the West End. Then as now, butchers learnt from working in a number of shops, and some Italian and French butchers put down roots in London and introduced their Continental practices.

A spirit of cooperation and learning is fostered today by Lidgate's membership of the Q-Guild, a group of UK craft butchers that strives to uphold standards and encourages visits to other shops. David Lidgate was instrumental in starting this organization in 1987 because he noticed how skills and knowledge were haemorrhaging from the trade as fewer family butchery shops were passing from father to son.

Like London itself, Lidgate's is cosmopolitan and a hub of world food. The shop's 34 staff come from many different places, including Brazil, Japan, France and Eastern Europe, and each brings his or her own particular crafts, ideas and recipes into the mix. As a specialist retailer, Lidgate's must move with the times to survive and thrive.

The butcher's trade

It is commonly said that a butcher is only as good as his customer's last meal, and reputation is key. That's why Lidgate's places top priority on quality – they want to satisfy their customers and keep them coming back for more. They also have to get them into the shop in the first place, so every morning, a fresh window display spreads out a feast of chops, pies, trussed birds and handsome roasting joints. Head-butcher Alan dresses the window using not just meat but top-quality fresh vegetables from Michanicou Bros, the greengrocer around the corner. He's been nicknamed 'the Art Director' by one of the customers, and his flair for detail makes as much difference to a window as a designer does on a page. Customers bring questions and shopping lists. Vans drop off meat from a network of family farms; delivery boxes are packed for customers around London and Britain. As people sit down to eat that evening, the shop is cleared and swept, and the process starts again the next morning.

Selecting meat

The first job of a good butcher is to choose the meat. The quality will vary according to how each animal has been fed and exercised, as well as its breed and genetic make-up. This choice, made a long way from the plate, is crucial to the success of good food.

Every Monday, Danny Lidgate goes to Smithfield wholesale meat market as early as 4am to select beef,

lamb and veal. Here he judges by touch as much as sight, using his decades of experience to choose the best. This meat is delivered before the shop opens at 7am.

Other beef and lamb, plus pork and poultry, is sourced from farms all around the country and delivered throughout the week, with game (when in season) coming from specialist dealers. The butcher and the farmer have a direct relationship: some meat may be rejected if there is not enough fat, or too much, or the meat isn't up to scratch in any other way. The on-going conversations mean that both butcher and farmer understand how the eating quality of meat is affected by such factors as feed and this helps to maintain standards.

Hanging and ageing
The period of time during which carcasses are left to mature before being eaten is known as 'hanging'. Meat is 75 per cent water, and maturation is done so that some of the moisture evaporates. It also develops and concentrates the flavour, as well as making the muscles more tender. Lidgate's has its own hanging and dry-ageing rooms, where the meat is kept at the right temperature and humidity. The rows of prime beef darken with age, the outside forming a seal as the meat ages within. Long lines of lamb, each carcass subtly individual, mature in a separate room.

The dry-ageing aspect of hanging is crucial. There has been a tendency over the last 30 years to vacuum-pack meat, both carcasses and cuts, as it makes for easier transportation, handling and storage. Craft butchers, however, dislike it because 'vac-pac' sucks the juice, including the sugars, out of the meat. The subtle sweetness is part of the magic of the meat's flavour, so losing that can lead to a slightly bitter, metallic taste.

The beef at Lidgate's tends to be hung for around 28 days, and the lamb for 7–14 days. Pork and chicken are eaten fresher, and game birds are no longer hung until 'high', but all undergo some degree of development so that they are at their best by the time they are sold.

Cutting
Dividing a carcass into different pieces is as skilful as a tailor cutting cloth for a suit. Lidgate's butchers use super-sharp knives and a bandsaw to get the cleanest

of cuts with no bone splinters. They also cut for tenderness, to make the meat the best it can be on the plate. The tenderest parts come from the centre and hindquarters of the animal, and these are divided into roasting joints and quick-cooking pieces, such as steaks and chops. The rest of the animal, mostly the tougher forequarter, will go into cheaper joints and cuts suited to slow cooking, such as stewing steak. Nothing is wasted; offcuts go into mince and sausages.

Allied to cutting are other specialist skills, such as boning birds so that they can be stuffed and carved easily, and French-trimming racks of lamb so that they are free from scrappy bits of fat and meat, and everything found on the plate is tender and delicious. Given notice, a craft butcher will gladly do these things for you – they are all part of their service.

How a butcher helps the cook
A well-arranged butcher's counter gives you the chance to look at all the meat properly and to ask advice about what is best on the day or for a particular dish. The two most common questions at Lidgate's are: 'How much do I need?' and 'How long do I cook it?' Both quantity and cooking time will vary according to your budget and preferences, and the appetite of those you are feeding. As a general rule, we allow 200–220g (7–8oz) per person, and more if the meat is cooked on the bone. Some may want less than this; others will want more, particularly if catering for guests who might like seconds. Remember that leftovers can always make another meal, and some of the most delicious dishes come about that way.

A butcher can always suggest alternative cuts if you want to buy more meat for less money. Throughout this book we highlight butcher's favourites, which are often the cheaper cuts, and not just because they are generally what the butcher takes home, having sold the prime meat. Buying from a butcher's counter makes it easier to ask advice about how to eat your way around an animal, discovering how to get good value from tasty, lesser-known pieces.

Then there's all the preparation that a butcher can do for you, such as mincing particular fresh cuts for you, which makes a real difference to taste. They can make roasts look neater and easier to carve by careful trimming and tying. Such meat may be slightly more expensive but there's less wastage. Similarly, they can butterfly a leg of lamb, which involves removing the bone and opening out the meat, which makes it good for marinating and quick cooking (see page 230). There's a wealth of things a good butcher can do for you, some of which are described in this book so that you can have a go yourself.

Many butchers now sell ready-to-eat dishes. If they are made in the shop, the meat in pasties, pies, sausages, marinated stir-fries and other preparations will come from the same animals that are also being sold as premium steaks and roasts. In fact, the best dishes are made with the same ingredients that you might use in your own kitchen; Lidgate's uses Maldon sea salt, for example, because it has a subtler flavour than standard cooking salt.

The cooking advice you get from a butcher depends on who you talk to. Just as some farmers do not give a great deal of thought to the eating quality of the meat they produce, so some butchers don't necessarily translate their craft to the table. Lidgate's view is that the next generation of successful butchers will increasingly tend to be cooks, who will have a real enthusiasm for what's on offer and a sound first-hand knowledge how to cook particular pieces of meat. In the shop, we find that the younger butchers cook at home, watch food shows on television and get tips from YouTube. Some of them are trained chefs with several years' experience in professional kitchens and are full of ideas that find their way to the counter.

Meat-buying basics

At a butcher's counter you're looking not just for the best standards of cleanliness, but for meat that has a fresh and supple appearance, free of dryness or cracks. Meat kept on the bone retains its freshness for longer. Once it has been cut off into pieces, it begins to dry out, so a butcher is trying to get a good throughflow of customers and to have enough meat to fill the counter but to cut as much as possible fresh each day. (That's why butchers make other food products, such as pies and sausages – its allows us to use up what we don't sell quickly.) When buying chops or steaks, also look for meat that has been cut evenly so that it cooks evenly.

Like everything we eat, meat has its seasonal aspect.

Animals grow and change, and certain meat recipes suit different times of year. In springtime small, rosy cutlets of new-season lamb appear in Lidgate's counter display. Summer brings a wide variety of kebabs and marinades for the barbecue. From the arrival of the first grouse in August onwards, game birds sit among a display of feathers. From November, when some of our customers celebrate Thanksgiving, through to Christmas and New Year, the shop window is resplendent with turkeys and magnificent eight-bone ribs of beef. It's good to notice and celebrate the way meat changes in this way. Page 98, for example, outlines the way lamb varies over the year and according to its age.

It also makes sense to buy meat that is going to suit a particular recipe or method of cooking. For a quick supper, for example, get a tender piece of meat that can be fried quickly, or one that has been minced or cut thinly, such as an escalope or minute steak. Prime cuts, such as muscles from the loin or back of the animal, are also good for fast cooking but tend to cost more. These are the most celebrated pieces of meat, such as fillet, loin and leg. Some cheaper cuts can be used in quickly cooked dishes as long as the meat is minced or cut across the grain, which shortens the meat fibres and makes them easier to chew. Again, a good butcher will advise you.

To choose the right cut for a recipe, it is helpful to know what the muscles are used for and to have a basic grasp of the relationship between exercise, texture and flavour. With four-legged animals, such as cattle, sheep and pigs, the muscles in the forequarter get the most exercise, just as a human does when crawling, pulling themselves along on their arms rather than their legs. The muscles that do the most work tend to be tougher, so are much cheaper than the more tender muscles on the back. However, the more worked muscles also have loads of flavour, which can be harnessed by careful cooking that also tenderizes them. 'The nearer the ground, the sweeter the meat' is a butcher's saying, and cuts such as lamb shank and beef shin at the end of the forelegs and back legs are especially tasty. Again, the lower leg does more work – think of the whiplash power that comes from a sprinter's leg.

For the most part, tougher cuts are best cooked low and slow so that the connective tissue melts into succulence, and the fat adds even more flavour. Quite often, these tougher muscles have a distinctive texture when cooked, which is looser, and more skein-like than, for example, the meat on the shoulder and belly. This texture carries sauces and flavours very well, making it successful in braises, stews and pies. Such slow-cooked dishes can be made in advance and quickly reheated, making them convenient as well as delicious.

All meat, be it a roasting joint, chops or a côte de boeuf steak is better for being bought and cooked on the bone because extra taste and juiciness is imparted ('The nearer the bone, the sweeter the meat' is another butcher's saying). A butcher will also sell you bones for stock, or marrowbones for roasting to make a form of 'bone butter' to go with steak (see page 64).

Fat has been regarded as a nutritional no-no, but recent studies have shown that natural animal fat, particularly from grass-fed animals, gives not just energy but also useful nutrition. We need some fat in our diet, and the higher quality it is, the better. A good proportion of meat's flavour is found in the fat, which has a subtle sweetness. Furthermore, external fat and internal fat marbling baste the meat during cooking and protect it from dryness, making it even more delicious on the plate. If you want to minimize your fat intake, you can always cook the meat with the fat on, then cut it off before eating. Similarly, if you cook a stew and leave it overnight, the fat will solidify on the surface and can be easily lifted off before the dish is reheated.

Storage & hygiene

The principles of meat hygiene are the same as for any good food: buy it fresh, store it well and don't let it sit around for too long.

On the whole, it is good to eat unpackaged meat within a couple of days. Butchers often use special wrapping paper that allows the meat to 'breathe' so it doesn't become slimy, and that doesn't let liquid seep out. If your meat isn't in butcher's paper, take the meat out of its packaging when you get home, place in a dish, cover with clingfilm or greaseproof paper and put it in the fridge. You want to keep it dry and away from the air to decrease the risk of dryness and spoilage. (Pre-packaged meat has what is called 'modified atmosphere storage', which means the oxgygen around

it is replaced by nitrogen and carbon dioxide. This reduces the growth of bacteria, so the meat lasts longer without taking the steps just mentioned.)

Some customers buy a lot of meat at one time and freeze a proportion of it. We don't advise doing this, particularly if the meat is bought for a special meal, as we think freezing causes a slight deterioration in quality. This is due partly to the loss of blood sugars as it thaws, and therefore a loss of the subtle sweetness and flavour they otherwise give. On the other hand, freezing can be very convenient as it stops meat from going off and means you can always have some to hand. For the best results, don't freeze meat for more than three months, and always thaw it slowly in the fridge.

Meat has a distinctive aroma but it shouldn't smell tainted or off. You can use your senses to decide if meat that has been in the fridge for a while is past it. In traditional French markets, poultry sellers used to offer the buyer a sniff of the back of a bird before they bought it, to show that the bird is fresh and good quality, as this is where it first starts to decay.

To avoid any risk of contamination, it is best to store raw meat at the bottom of the fridge, which is the coldest part, and on a different shelf from cooked meat and food that will be eaten raw. The fridge temperature should be below 5°C (40°F), so cool leftovers quickly and store them in the fridge.

All types of food can cause food poisoning, but there are particular issues to be aware of with meat because it carries bacteria that can be harmful if they are allowed to grow fast for a long time and are not then killed by heat. Storing meat in the fridge and cooking it properly are the basic principles of food hygiene. The UK government's Food Standards Agency (www.food. gov.uk) advises that to kill bacteria the core of the meat should reach 70°C (160°F) for at least 2 minutes. Rare or even medium-rare beef and lamb are cooked to a lower temperature than this, as you'll see if you use a probe thermometer (see page 16). If you are feeding the elderly, the very young or anyone with a weak immune system, you might want to cook meat well done.

The greatest risk of food poisoning comes from cross-contamination, when raw meat comes into contact with food that isn't going to be cooked, especially if it is sitting in a warm kitchen where the

bacteria can multiply. Poultry commonly has campylobacter, so you need to take extra care and ensure the meat is thoroughly cooked. The advice is not to wash meat, as has long been a tradition in some households, because it will actually spread the bacteria.

Even in the midst of cooking a meal, do wash the chopping board, knives and other utensils used for raw meat straight away, or put them to one side, so that there is no risk of using them for cooked items, or food that is to be eaten raw, such as salad. It's all too easy to chop up your chicken and then use the same board and knife to chop some herbs for stirring into the end dish.

One of the main risks for food poisoning comes at barbecues. Keep separate utensils and plates for raw meat and cooked and plan this beforehand so it doesn't get muddled up amidst the smoke and beer.

As for stuffing, in recent years, the advice has been not to put lots of bready stuffing inside birds. It warms up, but doesn't cook as quickly or as well as the outside of the bird and can cause a problem. The moisture inside the cavity also encourages the growth of bacteria that may already be present in your stuffing ingredients.

Home butchery

To understand more about meat, it's good to get stuck in yourself. There are a number of optional step-by-steps in this book that range from simply turning a chicken breast or thigh into a thin escalope to more elaborate techniques, such as preparing a Pesto saddle of lamb (see page 76). For most of these, you'll need just a knife and a chopping board, plus perhaps some skewers, string and a butcher's needle.

Butchery can involve cutting between joints, removing a bone, or tying or skewering a piece of meat. Our step-by-step pictures are a guide, but it only really starts to make sense once you handle the meat. With practice, you will get neater and quicker. Take it slowly and carefully at first and always use a sharp knife.

There are several reasons for having a go at home butchery. The first is cost, as meat can be less expensive if you do some of the pre-cooking preparation. For example, it is often cheaper to buy a whole chicken and joint it yourself (see page 136) than to buy it as pieces, and you also end up with the carcass, which is great for making stock. Cheaper cuts, such as flank steak and lamb breast, can be transformed into dinner party centrepieces by adding a bit of stuffing, then rolling and tying them (see pages 30 and 94).

Certain preparation techniques also make meat quicker and easier to cook and carve. A boned and butterflied leg of lamb, for instance (see page 230), can be cooked in just 30 minutes or so, rested for about 15 minutes, and is then a cinch to carve. A spatchcocked poussin or chicken (see page 152) employs a similar flattening technique so that the bird cooks quickly and carves easily. Even the simple technique of taking pheasant breasts off the bone (see page 172) makes the meat much easier for you and your guests to eat.

Among the more complex step-by-steps in this book is a technique for cutting the middle of a pig to make a porchetta joint (see page 274). This can require a saw, though you can also ask a butcher to prepare the meat up to this point and then carry on with the rest yourself.

Home butchery is really satisfying, and the more complex preparations are an interesting challenge that get easier with practice. Even if you rarely joint a chicken or bone a leg of lamb again, trying to do so will give you a better understanding of the structure of meat. It will also make you more confident about ordering prepared meat from your butcher.

Whatever degree of butchery you do, don't be afraid to make a mess, and always remember that nothing beats hands-on experience. Whenever you are learning something, it doesn't matter if it takes five minutes or an hour: take your time and all will be well.

Equipment
It is not necessary to spend a lot of money on home-butchery equipment, but it is a good investment to buy the best you can afford. Here are what we consider the essentials, listed in approximate order of importance.

Knives
A good set of knives lasts a lifetime and is easier to handle and use than old implements that have been rattling around in the kitchen drawer for years. That said, you don't need to break the bank when investing in decent knives. Many butchers use Victorinox, a good brand that isn't especially pricey. The best knives are made from a single piece of metal so that blade continues into the handle, which makes them stronger and more durable than those simply attached to a handle. Plastic or metal handles last longer than wood.

Butchers tend to use steel knives as these are excellent quality and easy to look after. Some people prefer carbon steel as it stays sharper for a bit longer, but these knives must be washed and dried straight after use or they rust. Ceramic knives also keep their edge for longer.

There are two particularly useful knives to have in your kitchen. The first is a large, well-weighted cook's knife with a blade about 20–25cm (8–10in) long. This is a useful knife for chopping bones and cutting up meat, and preferable to a chopper, which tends to splinter bone. The second is a rigid boning knife, which gives good control when slicing flesh away from bones. At Lidgate's we favour butcher's knives with a slightly curved tip and a 13–15cm (5–6in) blade. This is used to follow lines in the meat with the same sense of touch as a pointed finger.

The best way to hold a boning knife is in a closed fist, like a dagger. This gives you more control and force, but should be used with a small, stroking action rather than big slashing movements. As you work, turn the chopping board or meat around so you can get the best angle for cutting.

Sharpeners
Keeping knives sharp is crucial. A blunt knife is much more dangerous than a sharp one because you need to apply more pressure and the blade can then slip and

cut where it shouldn't. A sharp knife will slide through the meat and make your task much easier.

It is a good habit always to sharpen a knife on a steel before using it to ensure the edge is keen. A steel is a metal rod that you run the knife over at an angle of about 15–20 degrees, going downwards and backwards. Among the different kinds, the most common is a ridged steel, though ceramic steels are excellent and worth considering if you are a keen meat cook. Diamond-coated steels are also very good but need to be used properly or can damage the knives. Note that all steels lose their effectiveness over time, and eventually need to be replaced.

If a blade is used for too long without being sharpened, it will lose its edge and need to be brought back by using a grinder or whetstone. If you don't have one of these at home, you can take your knives into a butcher, who will restore their sharpness for a small charge. It's a good idea to get knives sharpened from time to time, but this does take life off the knife so it is better to maintain the edge as much as possible by using a steel. In addition, butchers are fussy about using knives just for meat rather than for chopping vegetables and other kitchen tasks as we think this helps maintain their sharpness.

Carving fork

Control is essential when wielding knives around meat, and a carving fork definitely gives you more control. It holds the meat steady, allowing you to cut neat, thin and even slices rather than ungainly chunks. Ultimately, it also means you get better value for money, as well-carved meat goes further.

Needle and string

Boned and rolled joints need to be held together firmly yet neatly, and a butcher's needle helps to do this. It has a big eye that can be easily threaded with string. You can simply just tie up a joint with string, but if you use a needle to sew up the meat in a seam on the underside, you get a neater appearance on the table and there is less string to cut through. It doesn't matter if you do a less-than-beautiful job, or don't do it at all; this is part of a butcher's craft and they can do it for you. Roasting bands, skewers and cocktail sticks are alternative ways of holding meat together. Skewers are also useful for keeping flattened meat in shape.

Thermometer

Digital temperature probes have long been used by chefs, but are now becoming popular for home use as well. They are particularly helpful when trying to assess whether meat is rare or medium rare. We've given temperature guides in recipes where you may well want the meat to be cooked in this way. It's important to put the probe into the thickest part of the meat and to leave it there until the temperature reading settles. Be careful not to push the probe through towards the roasting tray, or take the reading near the hotter outside of the meat; both these will skew the reading.

Butcher's Plastic

We use special plastic to cover the meat when we are doing such work as flattening chicken breasts into escalopes, in order to stop the meat sticking and becoming untidy. You can use good clingfilm or greaseproof paper instead.

Poultry shears

If you are preparing a lot of birds, poultry shears make easy work of cutting through small bones and skin, but knives and good kitchen scissors will also do the job.

Tenderizer

Butchers have a small, pronged piece of kit called a tenderizer, which is used for making holes in pieces of meat that you want to marinate and cook relatively quickly, such as kebabs. Alternatively, you can use the tip of a small sharp knife.

Mallet

Butchers call this piece of kit a 'fat-basher'. It's a wide-headed plastic mallet that is used to flatten fat and also meat so it is thin and even. You can use a rolling pin or even a heavy-based saucepan instead.

Food-grade saw

If you get really into home-butchery and start to buy half or whole carcasses, you'll need to buy a saw to deal with bones.

Equipment

1 Meat thermometer
2 Food-grade saw
3 Meat tenderizer
4 Wood and bamboo
 skewers
5 Sharpening steel

6 Large cook's knife
7 Small boning knife
8 Mallet
9 Roasting bands
10 Burger press
11 String

12 Butcher's needle
13 Butcher's plastic

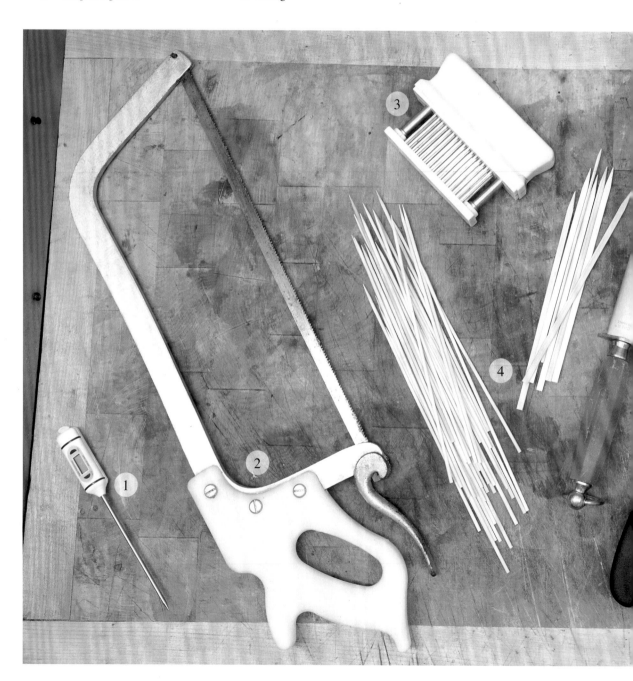

Traditional breeds & pasture-fed meat

Despite market trends, Lidgate's has kept faith with traditional farming methods and the meat produced by people whose priorities are good stockmanship and the eating quality of meat.

Before taking on suppliers, we ask detailed questions, and within five sentences can tell if we're on the same page or not. We're not just looking for really tight operations that offer consistency, but also for people with a thought-through ethos of quality. In general, butchers are good friends to British farmers. They appreciate the care taken over their meat and the feedback on its eating quality, and we act as a buffer between them and the vulnerabilities of increasingly international markets.

Amongst the many things we ask farmers is what they feed their animals, as it makes a huge difference to the quality of the meat. To arrive at the best feed takes years of understanding and patient work; there isn't a silver bullet or single magic ingredient. The work put into improving the pasture itself is painstaking, involving analysis of the soil and time and effort spent getting the most from nature.

Some of our farmers raise their cattle and sheep almost entirely on natural pasture, perhaps with some additional natural feed in the winter before the grass starts to grow again; a handful of good hay or sileage can smell like summer – no wonder when unploughed pastureland can contain as many as 70 types of plant. Such a diverse diet is as good for animals as it is for humans, and leads not just to better-tasting meat, but to better health and less need for medication.

Natural pasture farming is one of Britain's great strengths. We've got a long, narrow island and the sea blows over it in such a maritime climate, giving the best circumstances to grow good grass. British pastureland is a treasure trove, and it's not easy to replicate, which is why Britain has long been famous for meat. If you look at our island from above, you'll see it scattered with 'jewels', such as water meadows that are regularly flushed with fresh nutrients from rivers or streams. Some of these are used for grazing, just as they have been in centuries past; some are neglected, and it's sad that we don't always use our best assets.

The trend towards grain-fed, fast-growing breeds has taken a grip of the marketplace, but good butchers still stock pasture-fed beef and lamb, chickens that have roamed outside and eaten plants and bugs as well as chicken feed, and pork from pigs that have been allowed to lead a natural life rather than being intensively farmed.

The breeds farmers raise are a good indicator of quality. British cattle breeds, such as Aberdeen Angus, Herefords, Dexters and others have it in their bones to know how to take the most nutrition from grass; they cover the ground better than the Continentals, such as Charolais, which were developed to finish their days on grain. The best native beef animal on the hoof looks as though it has 'a leg on each corner' – a solidity and low, four-square shape like a table. The fat of pasture-fed beef tends to be a creamy yellow rather than white, and the meat is full of rich flavours and better nutrition. Breed alone is not enough to ensure the best meat. The crucial combination is breed plus feed. The same is true for sheep. These creatures have mostly resisted the worst of intensive farming, but some have a much more varied diet than others, especially uplands breeds and those that feed on heather and other wild plants, including those on salt marshes.

Pasture-fed meat is now seen as nutritionally superior. We've done a comparative analysis between standard beef and Lidgate's organic, grass-fed beef, from both Judith Freane's Perridge Farm in Somerset and from HRH The Prince of Wales' farm at Highgrove, managed by David Wilson, and the organic meat was found to have higher levels of micronutrients – 37% more iron, 65% more omega-3 fatty acids – and the same has been shown for lamb. Meat is a powerful food, with plenty of minerals that are important to health. There is an ever-growing awareness of the nutritional element of food, and towards school exam time we get more parents than ever coming in to buy good-quality meat for family suppers. Clearly, health as well as taste is part of the shopper's agenda. To understand the source of this, you need to go back to the farm and the farmer; and to access this sort of meat, you can go to a traditional butcher's.

1 Beef

Many customers go to a butcher's specifically for the beef, whether to get the best possible steaks from a well-hung carcass, or a Sunday roast that is second to none. Richly satisfying and with a wide variety of textures, from butter-soft fillet to juicy rump, beef is one of our most interesting, delicious and versatile of meats.

This chapter includes recipes for some of the classic beef dishes, such as Beef & Burgundy pie, Cottage pie, Steak & kidney pudding, Cornish pasties and Lasagne. Then there are recipes for dishes that are gaining in popularity, such as US-style Shortribs, Japanese Beef teriyaki and Brazilian salt-roasted Picanha.

Beef can be pricey, so this chapter focuses mostly on how to make the best use of cheaper cuts to serve family and friends. Prime cuts are covered in more detail in the guide to steaks on page 60, and there are further recipes for them in the Special Occasions chapter (see page 246).

Over recent decades, when retailing and farming increasingly favoured lean, large Continental breeds, at Lidgate's we kept faith with native breeds. Their fat – sweet from the varied plants they graze on traditional pasture – keeps the meat moist, and their slower growth means plenty of flavour and texture. In particular, we favour the often jet-black Aberdeen Angus that hailed originally from the counties of Aberdeenshire and Angus in the east of Scotland, both noted as areas of outstanding grass-fed beef production. Many of the pure breeds of Aberdeen Angus went abroad to countries such as Canada, where their qualities were appreciated. Now they are coming back to the mainstream of British farming.

Other natives, such as Hereford, Sussex, Dexter, Belted Galloways, Devon Red Ruby and Highland cattle, have also made a comeback. In recognition of this, supermarkets, as well as butchers, name beef by its breed. However, be aware that breed alone is not a guarantee of quality; it depends also on how the animals are kept and fed, and how the meat is hung.

Another kind of beef Lidgate's favours is British grass-fed Wagyu. This Japanese breed is genetically predisposed to have meat that is instensely marbled. When cooked, the soft fat melts to create a luscious flavour and texture. Our Wagyu comes from Earl Stonham farm in Suffolk. The animals live mostly outdoors, feeding on grass, before being finished with a cereal mix that the farmer came up with after visiting top-notch producers in the USA.

Young beef, known as veal, is particularly popular with many of our Continental and American customers, who are fond of its subtle flavour and fine texture. It is altogether more delicate than meat from older animals, so needs to be eaten fresh. For a real treat, try our recipe for ossobucco with blood oranges (see page 43), or our melt-in-the-mouth veal meatballs with Gruyère cheese (see page 55).

Beef Cuts

Bones – an advantage of going to a traditional butcher is that you can get a variety of bones for making stock (see page 287). Oxtail, with the meat on, will give superb deeply flavoured stock. The same is true of shin bones, especially with some meat, and the marrow within provides extra flavour. Lengths of marrowbone can be roasted just until the marrow has melted, and it can then be eaten with steak (page 64). You can also serve the roasted marrowbone with a sharply dressed salad.

Brisket – this breast muscle, underneath the neck, has a unique texture that is flaky and tender when cooked long and low. Brisket is sold mainly off the bone and either flat or rolled. It is great slow-cooked (or even slow-barbecued) in one large piece, and is often cured and thinly sliced for deli-style salt beef sandwiches. Salt brisket is often trimmed of fat, but we prefer to keep this on for the flavour.

Cheek – muscle that develops a superb fall-apart texture when used in slow-cooked dishes.

Chuck – a continuation of the rib-eye muscle, this is the best part of the shoulder, with excellent flavour when cooked long and slow in pot-roasts and stews. You can ask your butcher to cut big slabs rather than small cubes because they are easier to brown for a stew and, once cooked, can simply be pushed apart with a spoon. Some chefs like their burger mince to be a half and half mixture of chuck combined with perhaps brisket, featherblade or steak offcuts to get a variety of flavours.

Featherblade – delicious and good-value meat from the shoulder, which has some of the gelatinous qualities of shin. Although it may be trimmed of fat, we think it's best to leave some on. The meat can be cut into flat iron or feather steaks, cubed for stewing, or braised in one piece to a beautiful skeiny texture (see page 46).

Fillet – a cylinder of meat that runs along the back inside the ribcage, this part of the animal gets little exercise, so is the tenderest piece of beef. Cook a piece wrapped in pastry for Beef Wellington (see page 258), fry as steaks, or briefly sear and then cook a larger piece whole in the oven until rare. The tapering end of the cut is the wrong shape for steaks, so can sometimes be bought relatively cheaply for cutting into strips and quick cooking.

Flank – also known as 'skirt', this cut comes from the lower part of the animal. With a distinctive long-grained texture, the meat can be flash-fried for a cheap steak, or cooked long and slow for a tasty pie filling. The forequarter section is also cut as 'bavette' steak, but the rear quarter is cut specifically as flank, especially for our American customers who ask for flank steak.

Neck – known to butchers as 'clod and sticking', this tough and cheap muscle is best slow-cooked, so goes into mince or generic stewing steak.

Offal – liver and kidneys vary in flavour, depending on the type and age of the animal they come from. Beef offal is more strongly flavoured than offal from smaller animals, such as chickens, and is most often used in pâtés and pies. Calves liver is more delicate, and popular with our customers for fast frying.

Oxtail – this multi-jointed part of the animal is chopped between the joints and the pieces are good for slow cooking. The meat falls off the bones, providing a distinctive texture and taste in stews and soups.

Rib or forerib – a prime roasting joint (see page 198), rib can also be cut into one of the butcher's best steaks, either off the bone, or on the bone as a côte de boeuf. It runs along five rib bones, though you can extend this into the sirloin region for an extra large joint (what is called a wing rib is really the sirloin with the bones left on). Rib has a superb combination of muscles and fat, making it one of the picks of the butcher's counter for many meat-lovers.

Rump – this is composed of different muscles: the top 'rump cap' or 'point end', now sometimes called by its Brazilian name 'picanha', has a layer of fat and is excellent cooked whole (see page 58). Rump is eaten as steaks and also tied for a roast (page 206). The thinner end of the rump, near the sirloin, is the tenderest part and a bit of a butcher's secret.

Shin – beautiful, unctuous meat from the lower part of the leg, this is a lovely cut to cook long and slow, either off or on the bone, in a stew or pie (see pages 43 and 50).

Shortribs – the lower end of the ribs, towards the stomach, this cut used to be sold in the UK as Jacob's ladder. It has now become popular thanks to American influence (see page 47). Cook long and slow for superb taste and big meaty bones.

Silverside and thick flank – part of the leg with a shiny membrane covering it that gives the cut its name. This muscle does the most work in the leg, so is a less tender and cheaper lean roasting joint for cold cuts, but we think it's best for pot-roasts and other slow-cooked dishes (page 261). We use silverside (and the lower muscle in the leg, known as thick flank or simply 'thick') for lean mince.

Sirloin – tender, prime meat at the end of the ribs, sirloin is often cut into steaks (see page 37) or left whole as a magnificent roasting joint.

Topside – the beef animal's leg consists of three main muscles, topside being the equivalent of the human front thigh. While it is tender enough to be used as a roasting joint once the butcher has tied some fat around the outside, we often roast it rare and sell it cold for slicing at the counter. Topside, especially the more tender veal topside, which we use for escalopes and kebabs, can also be thinly cut and flash-fried or quickly cooked in other ways (see page 240).

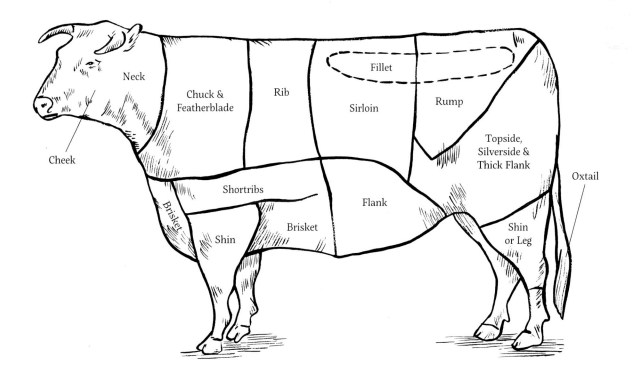

Beef Cuts

1 Marrowbone
2 Featherblade
3 Silverside
4 Oxtail
5 Neck
6 Brisket
7 Shortribs
8 Topside
9 Mince
10 Shin
11 Chuck

Flank steak is a secret of butchers and meat lovers – a tasty cut that's relatively inexpensive. As it can be tough, however, take care not to overcook flank and to cut against the grain to make pieces that are easier to eat. Head butcher Alan came up with this multi-award-winning way to make the most of this lesser-known cut. The meat is basted from the inside with a stuffing of garlic butter that keeps it nice and juicy.

Flank steak pockets with herbs, horseradish & garlic butter

Serves 4

1 thick flank steak, about 500g (1lb), trimmed (ask the butcher for one as thick as possible)

2 tablespoons freshly grated horseradish root

4 whole or halved sunblush tomatoes

salt and freshly ground black pepper

For the garlic butter
150g (5oz) unsalted butter, at room temperature

2 garlic cloves, crushed

1 tablespoon finely chopped flat leaf parsley

For the herb topping
large handful of flat leaf parsley, finely chopped

2 tablespoons finely chopped marjoram

10 medium sage leaves, finely chopped

12 sunblush tomato halves, each cut into 6 small chunks

1½ tablespoons olive oil

Set out six 10-cm (4-in) skewers and prepare the meat as shown in the step-by-step instructions on the following page. You can do this a few hours in advance and keep the stuffed flank in the fridge, covered. Take it out of the fridge 15 minutes before cooking so it isn't fridge-cold.

When you are ready to cook the meat, preheat the oven to 190°C/375°F/Gas Mark 5.

Cook the stuffed flank in the oven for 15 minutes, basting once with the garlicky juices that come out. Cover loosely with foil and set aside to rest for 5 minutes.

Cut the stuffed flank into thick wedges, following the slashes you made earlier. This ensures you cut across the grain and makes the meat less chewy.

Serve with potatoes (chips would be perfect), a green salad and a tomato salad.

→

I First make the garlic butter. Put the butter in a bowl and use a fork to mash in the garlic, parsley and a good seasoning of salt and pepper. Shape into a wide rectangle, about 10 x 2.5cm (4 x 1in). Wrap in greaseproof paper and place in the fridge. Combine all the herb topping ingredients in a bowl. Season with salt and pepper, then set aside.

2 Lay the flank steak flat on a chopping board. Trim off the ends to get a rectangular piece of meat. (You can cut the trimmed pieces into thin strips across the grain and use them in a stir-fry.

3 Use a small sharp knife to cut a pocket about 7cm (3in) deep in one of the shorter ends of your rectangle. Turn the steak around and cut a pocket the same size at the other end. Use a longer knife to carefully join these two pockets together, gently laying your hand on top of the steak to help keep the knife horizontal. Take care not to cut through the sides or top or bottom of the meat: the idea is to have a continuous incision through the centre of the steak so it becomes a flat tube of meat, ready to stuff.

4 Unwrap the chilled garlic butter and sprinkle 1½ tablespoons of the grated horseradish over the top. Now gently push the butter into the pocket in the steak so that it reaches nearly to the other end.

5 Use a sharp knife to make slashes through the top of the stuffed flank about 2.5mm (⅛in) deep at 2.5-cm (1-in) intervals. This will help the steak to cook through evenly and show you where to cut for serving.

6 Roll the meat into a more compact shape by tucking the long sides underneath.

7 Insert the skewers at regular intervals through the meat, going diagonally from the top of one side to the bottom of the other. This helps the meat keep its shape as it cooks.

8 Place the meat on a baking tray. Spread the herb mixture in a line along the top of the meat.

9 Place the sunblush tomatoes on top. Season the meat with salt and pepper and scatter the final ½ tablespoon grated horseradish over the top.

The filling in this classic Lidgate's pie is our version of beef bourguignon. Customers buy the pie in different sizes – anywhere from two to sixteen portions – to heat up at home. As with all pies, the filling is best made in advance so that the flavour develops overnight and becomes wonderfully rich. It is also excellent eaten as a stew with mashed or baked potatoes.

Beef & Burgundy pie

Serves 6

2 tablespoons beef dripping or olive/vegetable oil

1.2kg (2½lb) stewing steak, cut into 2.5-cm (1-in) chunks

3 medium onions, chopped

1 tablespoon plain white flour, plus extra for dusting

150ml (¼ pint) hot beef or chicken stock

200ml (7fl oz) red wine

60ml (2¼fl oz) dry or medium sherry (or extra red wine)

2 tablespoons redcurrant jelly

½ teaspoon freshly ground black pepper

2 medium leeks, sliced

100g (3½oz) mushrooms, sliced

500g (1lb) puff pastry

1 egg mixed with 2 tablespoons milk, for glazing

salt

Put half the dripping or oil in a large casserole dish over a medium-high heat. When hot, brown the meat in two or three batches until well coloured. Set aside.

Add the remaining dripping or oil to the pan along with the onions and a pinch of salt. Cook over a low heat until soft (about 10–15 minutes), stirring occasionally.

Sprinkle the flour over the onions and stir for a minute. Gradually add the hot stock, stirring as you go. Pour in the red wine and sherry, if using. Bring to the boil and allow to bubble away until the sauce has reduced and thickened slightly.

Return the meat to the pan. Stir in the redcurrant jelly and black pepper, then add more salt to taste. Cover with a lid and simmer on a medium-low heat for 45 minutes. Stir the leeks and mushrooms into the pan and continue to simmer for another 45 minutes, or until the meat is tender.

Preheat the oven to 220°C/425°F/Gas Mark 7. Tip the meat into a 30 x 20-cm (12 x 8-in) pie dish. On a lightly floured work surface, roll out the pastry so it is about 5cm (2in) larger than the pie dish. Cut a 2.5-cm (1-in) strip from each edge of the pastry. Press these on to the rim of the pie dish and brush with the glaze. Press the pastry lid firmly on top of the pastry rim and trim off the excess. Crimp the edges together to form a seal. If you wish to decorate the lid, reroll the pastry trimmings, cut out shapes (leaves, stars or cow horns, for example) and stick them on the top with the glaze. Finally, brush the top of the pie with glaze.

Bake the pie for 30 minutes, or until nice and brown. Serve with mashed potato and a seasonal vegetable or two; buttered carrots and cabbage go especially well with this pie.

Rossella is a great part of the Lidgate team, making pies and other dishes in our kitchen upstairs. Every summer she goes back to Naples, reappearing in the autumn and ready to weave her Italian magic once again. When we developed a lasagne recipe, we used her native expertise, and the result is richly layered with goodies. It's very much a treat for supper with family or friends.

Rossella's lasagne

Serves 6–8

225g (8oz) dried lasagne sheets (12 standard sheets)
200g (7oz) medium-sliced ham, cut into thick strips
250g (8oz) mozzarella, cut into large dice
3 tablespoons finely grated Parmesan cheese

For the meat sauce
2 tablespoons olive oil
500g (1lb) lean minced beef
1 large carrot
2 medium onions
2 garlic cloves
1 x 400-g (14-oz) can tomatoes
2 tablespoons tomato purée
1 teaspoon dried oregano
salt and freshly ground black pepper

For the white sauce
80g (2¾ oz) unsalted butter, cut into small pieces
80g (2¾ oz) plain flour
1 litre (1¾ pints) full-fat milk
¼ teaspoon finely grated nutmeg
sea salt flakes

First make the meat sauce. Pour 1 tablespoon of the oil into a frying pan over a medium-high heat. When hot, brown the beef in it.

Meanwhile, pour the remaining tablespoon of oil into a large saucepan over a medium-low heat. When hot, add the carrot, onions and garlic and cook until soft.

Stir the tomatoes into the beef, scraping up the tasty bits stuck to the bottom of the pan. Add this mixture to the vegetables. Stir in the tomato purée and oregano, and season with salt and pepper. Mix well and leave to simmer for about 15 minutes, until the sauce has reduced slightly.

Meanwhile, make the white sauce. Put all the ingredients into a pan and bring slowly to the boil, whisking as you do so to stop lumps forming. The sauce will thicken right at the end to make a thick coating consistency. Season with half a teaspoon of flaky sea salt.

Preheat the oven to 180°C/350°F/Gas Mark 4 while you assemble the lasagne in a 20 x 30-cm (8 x 12-in) baking dish.

Spread a quarter of the meat sauce over the base of the dish; cover with a third of the pasta, followed by a third of the white sauce, half the ham and a third of the mozzarella.

Cover with another quarter of the meat sauce, followed by another third of the pasta and a third of the white sauce.

Top with a quarter of the meat sauce, the remaining ham and another third of the mozzarella. Cover with the remaining pasta and white sauce.

Finally, spread the remaining meat sauce over the top, dot with the remaining mozzarella and sprinkle with the Parmesan.

Bake the lasagne for 1 hour, until patched with brown on top. Serve it with a sharply dressed green salad.

This is a slight adaptation of a great recipe by a Lidgate customer, the Japanese food writer Kimiko Barber. Quickly seared top-notch beef is cut into thin pieces and seasoned with a Japanese dressing that adds no extra fat. As a special treat, use Wagyu beef, which is beautifully marbled with fat and wonderfully tender. Ours comes from Earl Stonham farm in Suffolk, where the animals are grass-fed, then finished on a special diet to give the meat the right texture and flavour. The accompanying salad of refreshing grapefruit, peppery watercress and bitter chicory cuts through the beef's richness, so the recipe is typical of the Japanese diet in the way it uses relatively little meat and plenty of vegetables.

Seared beef salad with watercress, chicory & pink grapefruit

Serves 2–4, depending on appetite

200g (7oz) sirloin steak, cut about 2.5–3.5cm (1–1½in) thick

1 teaspoon beef dripping or vegetable oil

1 pink grapefruit, segmented

100g (3½oz) watercress, trimmed

50g (2oz) red chicory, leaves separated and cut into long shards

1½ tablespoons rice vinegar

salt and freshly ground black pepper

For the dressing

½ small garlic clove, finely grated

½ teaspoon grated fresh root ginger

1 teaspoon caster sugar

4 tablespoons Japanese soy sauce

Take the meat out of the fridge 30 minutes before cooking to take the chill off.

Rub the meat with salt and pepper. Place a heavy-based frying pan over a high heat. When really hot, add the beef dripping and let it melt. Alternatively, brush the meat with vegetable oil. Quickly sear the meat for just 1–1½ minutes on each side (Wagyu or well-hung sirloin is tender enough to eat very rare, but you can cook it for longer if you prefer to have it medium or medium-rare). Transfer the meat to a chopping board for a couple of minutes, until cool enough to handle.

Meanwhile, make the dressing by combining all the ingredients for it in a small bowl. Put the grapefruit and salad leaves on a large serving platter but do not dress yet.

Cut the meat into slices 5mm (¼in) thick and sprinkle with the rice vinegar. Arrange the meat on top of the salad, drizzle with the dressing, then toss and serve.

→

Every family has a version of this time-honoured favourite. After some experimentation, we decided to keep ours pretty simple, with just a few herbs and splashes of sauce for seasoning, as we think good meat should speak for itself. Kids love this pie – and so do their parents.

Cottage or shepherd's pie

Serves 6–8

2 tablespoons olive or vegetable oil

2 medium onions, finely chopped

1 garlic clove, finely chopped

1.5kg (3lb) minced beef (for Cottage Pie) or minced lamb (for Shepherd's Pie)

2 medium carrots, finely chopped

600ml (1 pint) beef stock (for Cottage Pie) or lamb stock (for Shepherd's Pie)

1 tablespoon plain flour

3 tablespoons tomato purée

½ tablespoon Worcestershire sauce

1 tablespoon mustard powder

½ teaspoon dried oregano

1 tablespoon finely chopped sage

1 tablespoon soy sauce

salt and freshly ground black pepper

For the topping

1kg (2lb) baking or floury potatoes (e.g. King Edward), peeled and chopped into medium chunks

50g (2oz) unsalted butter, cubed, plus 15g (½oz) for the top

350ml (12fl oz) milk

Pour 1 tablespoon of the oil into a large pan over a medium-low heat and add the onions and garlic. Cook gently for 10 minutes, or until soft. Set aside on a plate.

Pour the remaining oil into the pan and brown the mince (in two batches) over a high heat, stirring after 3 minutes or so.

Whilst the meat is browning, put the carrots and stock in a pan, bring to the boil, then simmer until the carrots are tender. Set the pan aside.

Sprinkle the flour over the mince and cook for 1 minute, stirring. Add the carrots and stock and bring back to the boil. Stir in the cooked onion and remaining ingredients, mixing well. Season with black pepper, then simmer for about 30 minutes, stirring often.

Whilst the meat is cooking, preheat the oven to 190°C/375°F/Gas Mark 5 and make the topping. Cook the potatoes in a pan of boiling salted water until tender. Drain well. Return the potatoes to the pan, add the cubed butter and milk, and mash until smooth.

Put the cooked meat in a 30 x 20-cm (12 x 8-in) dish. Place dollops of the mashed potato on top and spread it out with a fork, making a ridged pattern all over it. Dot with the extra butter and grind over a little more pepper.

Bake for 30 minutes, or until the top is nice and brown and the meat is bubbling hot. Peas are a favourite accompaniment.

Oxtail's superbly rich, beefy flavour is enhanced by cooking it in cider. Part of the pleasure of eating this meat is picking the tasty chunks off the puzzle-shaped bones, and the amount listed is enough to serve each person a large bone and a smaller one.

Oxtail in cider

Serves 6

2kg (4lb 8oz) oxtail, chopped into joints (your butcher will do this)

3 tablespoons olive oil

2 onions, sliced

2 celery sticks, sliced

3 garlic cloves, finely chopped

1 teaspoon sea salt flakes

2 tablespoons plain flour

1 litre (1¾ pints) hot beef stock (see page 287)

500ml (18fl oz) dry cider

6 carrots, cut into large chunks

2 bay leaves

2 sprigs of thyme

freshly ground black pepper

Preheat the oven to 220°C/425°F/Gas Mark 7.

Arrange the oxtail in a large roasting tray in a single layer. Toss with 1 tablespoon of the oil and place in the oven for 30 minutes, until browned.

Meanwhile, pour the remaining 2 tablespoons oil into a large flameproof casserole dish. Add the onions, celery, garlic and salt, a few twists of pepper and cook over a medium-low heat for 15 minutes, or until the vegetables have softened.

Sprinkle over the flour and stir for 30 seconds. Gradually pour in the hot beef stock, stirring constantly to keep it free of lumps. Add the cider, carrots, bay leaves and thyme and bring to the boil.

Turn the oven down to 160°C/325°F/Gas Mark 3. Add the cooked oxtail to the pan and bring back to the boil. Cover and place in the oven for 4½–5 hours, stirring every now and then, and adding a splash more water if it gets too dry. Some oxtail will become tender before the cooking time is up (like all meat, this cut varies according to the animal), but it's always worth leaving in the oven for longer as the texture becomes ever more unctuous and delicious.

Serve the meat on the bone, with mashed potato and green vegetables. Any leftover meat can be used to make a superb pasta sauce.

Ossobuco (braised shin of veal) is a tremendous late-winter dish, and the blood oranges then in season make this a vibrantly colourful stew. We use the hindquarter shin as it is less tough than the forequarter and cooks a little more quickly. Ask the butcher to cut it to size. The traditional Italian garnish for slow-cooked meat is gremolata, a delicious combination of garlic, parsley and lemon zest.

Blood orange ossobuco with gremolata

Serves 4

3 tablespoons plain flour

1 veal shin (hind is best), cut into 4 pieces about 5cm (2in) long

3 tablespoons olive oil

1 large carrot, finely chopped

1 large bulb of fennel, finely chopped

1 large onion or 2 banana shallots, finely chopped

50ml (2fl oz) balsamic vinegar

400ml (14fl oz) fresh orange juice

400ml (14fl oz) veal or chicken stock

1 blood orange (if unavailable, use an ordinary orange)

salt and freshly ground black pepper

For the gremolata

1 small garlic clove, very finely chopped

finely grated zest of 1 lemon

3 tablespoons finely chopped flat leaf parsley

1 tablespoon extra virgin olive oil

Preheat the oven to 160°C/325°F/Gas Mark 3.

Put the flour in a shallow bowl and season with salt and pepper. Carefully turn each piece of shin in the seasoned flour to coat on all sides. Reserve the flour left in the dish.

Pour the oil into a flameproof casserole dish over a high heat. When hot, add the pieces of veal shin and brown on both sides. (You might need to do this in two batches.) Remove the browned meat and set aside.

Tip the chopped vegetables into the pan, lower the heat and fry gently for 10 minutes, stirring occasionally, until soft. Sprinkle in the reserved flour and cook, stirring, for 1 minute.

Turn up the heat slightly. Add the vinegar and stir well, scraping up the browned bits on the bottom of the pan. Stir in the orange juice and the stock. Return the meat to the pan, bring to the boil, then cover and place in the oven for 1 hour. Remove the lid and cook for another hour, then taste to see if the veal is tender. If not, continue to cook, covered, until it is (veal varies in its tenderness).

While the veal is cooking, mix the gremolata ingredients together in a bowl. Set aside.

Peel the orange and cut into segments between the membrane, removing any pips and pith.

Once the meat is tender, gently stir in the orange segments and sprinkle the gremolata over the top. Serve with mashed potatoes and a green vegetable such as kale or chard.

A forgotten cut from the shoulder of the animal, featherblade has fine, long strands of meat, hence the name. It's a cut with a quiet charisma, and is usually just cut up as stewing steak. Cooked slowly in one or two large pieces, it keeps all its succulence and melts into its beautiful characteristic texture. This recipe is sophisticated enough to serve to friends for supper, perhaps finished with Gremolata or with Buttery Mash (see page 290). Any leftovers are great stirred into a pasta sauce.

Slow-cooked featherblade

Serves 6

2 tablespoons beef dripping or olive oil

1.5–1.75kg (3–3½lb) featherblade, cut into two large pieces

knob of butter

1 onion, roughly chopped

1 carrot, finely chopped

1 celery stick, finely chopped

4–5 garlic cloves, finely chopped

200g (7oz) mushrooms, finely chopped

1 tablespoon tomato purée

1½ tablespoons plain flour

300ml (½ pint) red wine

2 tablespoons red wine vinegar

600ml (1 pint) beef or chicken stock

2 bay leaves

sea salt flakes and freshly ground black pepper

2 tablespoons roughly chopped flat leaf parsley, to finish

For the extra vegetables

12 shallots, peeled

3 celery sticks, cut diagonally into 5-cm (2-in) slices

3 medium carrots, cut diagonally into large chunks

200g (7oz) mushrooms, quartered or halved

Preheat the oven to 160°C/325°F/Gas Mark 3.

Put a tablespoon of the dripping or oil into a large flameproof casserole dish over a high heat. When hot, brown the meat on both sides to a good dark colour. Transfer to a plate. Season with salt and pepper.

Lower the heat under the pan. Add the butter and remaining tablespoon dripping or oil. When hot, add the onion, carrot and celery and cook over a medium-low heat for about 10 minutes, or until soft. Add the garlic and mushrooms and cook for another 5 minutes or so, until the mushrooms start to release their juices.

Stir in the tomato purée and sprinkle over the flour. Cook for a minute or so, stirring to prevent the mixture sticking. Turn up the heat, pour in the wine and stir well, letting it bubble away for a minute to burn off the alcohol. Pour in the vinegar and bubble to reduce slightly. Add the stock and bay leaves. Bring to the boil, covered, then transfer to the oven for 2 hours.

Add the extra vegetables to the part-cooked stew, then return the dish, uncovered, to the oven for another 1½ hours, or until the meat is tender, turning it over halfway through so it browns more on both sides as the liquid reduces.

Before serving, scatter the parsley over the top. The casserole is great with buttery mashed potatoes.

A sheet of ribs is a magnificent sight and a great dish to set on a table. Going way back, shortribs were a cut known as a Jacob's Ladder, and eaten as a poor man's roast. The Americans have made ribs a star turn, and this dish gives the cut the Texan treatment, slathering it with lashings of classic barbecue sauce that's a mixture of sweet, hot, sharp and tangy. You sometimes see beef ribs sold as trimmed-out offcuts. Make sure your get the real deal with a good amount of meat on the bone.

Texan barbecue shortribs

Serves 4–5 (1 rib each, or 1 extra to fight over)

5 shortribs in a sheet (about 1.75kg/3½lb)

For the marinade/sauce
1 tablespoon dried oregano

1 tablespoon Spanish smoked paprika

½–1 teaspoon chilli powder

1 tablespoon flaky sea salt

2 garlic cloves, finely chopped

2 tablespoons olive oil

150ml (¼ pint) apple juice

300ml (½ pint) water

2 tablespoons tomato ketchup

1 tablespoon soft brown sugar

Combine the marinade ingredients in a large bowl. Add the meat and massage the marinade into it. Transfer to a large Ziploc bag and place in the fridge for 24–48 hours, meat-side down, so that it sits in the marinade.

Preheat the oven to 160°C/325°F/Gas Mark 3. Tip the ribs and marinade into a roasting tray and cook for 3 hours, or until the meat becomes tender. After 2–2½ hours, cover with foil if the meat is browning too much, and also add a little more water if the marinade is becoming too thick and starting to burn.

To serve, divide the meat into single ribs, spoon over the sauce and serve with a good slaw and potato salad (see page 291).

→

Danny's Uncle John grew up in a butcher's family, and his steak and kidney pie filling, made with good beef and ox kidney, is much loved by family and friends. Sometimes he adds mushrooms, sometimes chopped parsley, but never both. In this version we've used lamb kidneys, added a hint of nutmeg and enclosed the filling in a traditional suet crust. You could use a quicker-cooking cut of beef than shin, but it does have superb flavour and beefiness.

Uncle John's steak & kidney pudding

Serves 5–6

1 tablespoon dripping, olive oil or vegetable oil

2 onions, finely chopped

150g (5oz) mushrooms, finely chopped

1½ tablespoons plain flour

400ml (14fl oz) hot beef stock

½ teaspoon finely grated nutmeg

1kg (2lb) shin of beef, cut into 2.5-cm (1-in) chunks

250g (8oz) lamb kidneys

knob of butter, for greasing

Worcestershire sauce (optional)

sea salt flakes and freshly ground black pepper

For the pastry

400g (13oz) self-raising flour, plus extra for dusting

200g (7oz) shredded suet

about 220-240ml (8–9fl oz) water

fine sea salt

Melt the dripping or heat the oil in a large, flameproof casserole over a medium heat. When hot, add the onions, ½ teaspoon sea salt flakes and a good amount of black pepper and fry until the onions are soft (about 10 minutes). Add the mushrooms, increase the heat slightly, and cook until they have released their juice (5–10 minutes). Sprinkle over the flour and mix into the juices. Gradually stir in the hot stock, then add the nutmeg. Bring to the boil and boil for a couple of minutes to thicken slightly. Add the beef to the pan, cover and cook on a medium-low heat for 1 hour, stirring occasionally.

Meanwhile, cut the kidneys into quarters and use scissors to snip out the white core. Put in the fridge until needed.

About 20 minutes before the filling is ready, butter a 2-litre (3½-pint) pudding basin, being especially generous on the bottom, and make the pastry. Put the flour, suet and a pinch of salt into a mixing bowl and mix together with your hands. Make a well in the centre, pour in the water and mix it in roughly using a table knife. Once the water is incorporated, use the splayed fingers of one hand to thoroughly combine the ingredients and bring them together into a ball of dough.

Dust the work surface with flour and knead the dough for 30 seconds or so to make it come together more cohesively. Flour a rolling pin and roll the dough into a thick circle. Scatter a little more flour on top, turn it over and roll it out some more. Turn the dough by a quarter every few rolls to help keep the thickness even. You want to end up with a circle about 30cm (12in) in diameter.

Cut a quarter out of your circle of dough and put to one side. Lower the remainder into your prepared basin and press the two cut edges together to seal, rolling them over towards the centre to make a neater join.

Check the seasoning of the meat mixture. The flavour will intensify further as it cooks in the pudding, but you can, if you like, add a shake or two of Worcestershire sauce plus more salt and pepper. When seasoned to your liking, put the meat and two-thirds of the gravy into the pastry-lined basin.

Roll out the reserved quarter of pastry to form a circle large enough to cover the filling. Lift it using the rolling pin and roll it over the top of the basin. Trim off the excess, then pinch the edges together to make a good seal. Cover with foil, tying it with string just under the rim of the basin.

Put the pudding in a steamer (or sit it on a trivet or metal pastry cutter in a large saucepan half-filled with boiling water). Cover with a lid and steam for 3 hours, adding more hot water as necessary to stop the pan drying out.

When the pudding is ready, heat up the reserved gravy and place in a gravy boat. Remove the foil from the basin and slide a knife around the pudding to loosen it. Place a serving plate over the top, then invert both plate and bowl to turn out the pudding.

Serve at the table, cutting open the suet crust, spooning out the innards and pouring over the rich gravy.

Being the most tender part of the animal, fillet is also the most expensive; but fillet tail – exactly the same meat, just the end of the cut and therefore a different shape – is much cheaper, sometimes half the price. That's because it's generally unsuitable for cutting into steaks (though you can bash it flat for a quick-cooking minute steak). This version of Japanese teriyaki makes the most of fillet tail by cooking it just briefly at the end in order to preserve the cut's beautiful silky texture. As an alternative, you can use tasty rump tail, another bargain butcher's cut; just cook it for slightly longer.

Fillet-tail teriyaki

Serves 4

400g (13oz) beef fillet tail, cut into 1.5-cm (¾-in) strips

½ tablespoon vegetable oil

1 medium red onion, sliced

1 red pepper, cut into 1-cm (½-in) strips

1 green pepper, cut into 1-cm (½-in) strips

100g (3½oz) mushrooms, preferably shiitake, cut into 1-cm (½-in) slices

1 medium courgette, cut into 1-cm (½-in) slices

100g (3½oz) mangetout

For the teriyaki sauce

2.5-cm (1-in) piece of fresh root ginger, grated or finely chopped

2 garlic cloves, crushed

1 teaspoon light brown sugar

75ml (3fl oz) Japanese soy sauce

3 tablespoons mirin

2 tablespoons sake or dry sherry, or white wine or water

First make the teriyaki sauce by mixing the ingredients for it in a large bowl. Add the meat, mix well and set aside to marinate for no longer than 15 minutes or it becomes too salty.

Meanwhile, pour the oil into a wok and place over a high heat. When hot, add the onion and stir-fry for a couple of minutes, until slightly softened. Add the peppers, mushrooms and courgette and continue to stir-fry for 4–6 minutes, until softened. Add the mangetout and stir-fry for another minute.

Drain the marinade off the meat and pour it into the vegetable pan. Let the liquid bubble and reduce for 1 minute. Add the meat, stir for 1 minute, then cover and simmer for another minute or so, until the meat is nearly cooked through but still pink in the middle. Serve hot or warm with white rice.

Grass-fed beef is the tip of the top, and in Britain we're blessed with enough rainfall to create rich pastures for feeding livestock. Little wonder, then, that we have a tradition of good breeding and stockmanship. Some of our best beef comes from Highgrove, the organic farm belonging to HRH Prince Charles in Gloucestershire. Such superb British beef needs just a touch of seasoning because there is so much flavour in the meat itself. We played around with what to add and found that a dash of oyster sauce worked brilliantly. No salt, no pepper, no herbs: just meat and a touch of Chinese 'umami' as the secret ingredient. Try this trick with the best meat you can find. If the main ingredient is top class, great food really can be this simple.

Highgrove burgers

Makes 4

500g (1lb) best-quality, reasonably fatty minced beef (chuck, or a mixture of chuck and brisket is good; or, for a very posh burger, ask your butcher for rib or other steak offcuts)

20g (1 tablespoon) oyster sauce

1 egg white or egg yolk (optional)

olive or vegetable oil, for frying

To serve
butter

4 burger buns (or brioches for extra class)

lettuce

tomato slices

red onion rings

sauces, such as ketchup or relish (optional)

gherkins (optional)

Put the mince in a mixing bowl, add the oyster sauce and mix with your hands. If the mince has enough fat, the mixture will hold together well when formed into burgers. If your mince is leaner, add an egg white or yolk as a binder.

Tip the mixture on to a chopping board and divide into 4 equal pieces. Shape each one into a burger about 9 x 2.5cm (3½ x 1in). Put on a plate, cover and chill for 30 minutes to firm up. You can do this up to a couple of hours in advance of cooking.

Pour ½ tablespoon oil into a frying pan and place over a high heat. When hot, add the burgers and cook for about 2 minutes on each side, pressing down occasionally with a spatula. After this, cook for another minute on each side to ensure even cooking. Unless you have a big pan, do the frying in 2 batches to keep the temperature in the pan constantly high.

Transfer the burgers to a board or plate and leave to rest for 1 minute. Cut one open and check it is done to your liking. If not, return it to the pan and cook for a little longer.

Serve the burgers in buttered buns with lettuce, sliced tomato and onion rings. You can also add the usual sauces and gherkins if you wish, but, depending on the meat, this can be an especially delicious burger and doesn't necessarily need further embellishment.

Using veal for these tasty meatballs lifts them into a different class because it has an especially fine flavour and texture, but minced beef or pork can be used if you prefer. The meat is seasoned with finely grated, well-flavoured cheese: Gruyère suits this French recipe, or you can use Parmesan instead if you wish.

Veal & Gruyère meatballs in tomato sauce

Serves 4

500g (1lb) minced veal

50g (2oz) Gruyère or Parmesan cheese, finely grated

3 tablespoons finely chopped flat leaf parsley

1 medium egg, beaten

25g (1oz) dry white breadcrumbs

2 tablespoons olive oil

fine sea salt and freshly ground black pepper

For the sauce

2 x 400-g (14-oz) cans chopped tomatoes

50ml (2fl oz) red wine

1 garlic clove, crushed

pinch or more of caster sugar, to taste

1 sprig of rosemary

2 teaspoons drained capers

Put the veal into a mixing bowl with the cheese and parsley. Season with ¼ teaspoon salt and a good few twists of pepper. Add the egg and mix thoroughly using your hands. Form into 24 walnut-sized balls, place on a plate and chill for 30 minutes.

Meanwhile, put all the sauce ingredients into a large saucepan. Season with a pinch of salt and black pepper. Bring to the boil, then simmer, half-covered, for 1 hour. (If you are in a hurry, you can leave the pan uncovered and the sauce will be ready to eat in 20 minutes, but it tastes better if allowed to cook longer so that the flavours meld and mellow.)

Place the breadcrumbs on a plate and roll the chilled meatballs in them. Heat the oil in a large pan and fry the meatballs in 2 batches, turning them so that they brown all over. Carefully add the meatballs to the tomato sauce. Cover with a lid and cook for another 10 minutes. Remove the lid, turn up the heat and allow the sauce to bubble away if you want to reduce it slightly. Taste and adjust the seasoning, remembering that the meatballs are already seasoned with the salty cheese. Serve with pasta, or boiled or sautéd potatoes.

Rump tail is the slightly tougher end of the rump, but still full of flavour and relatively inexpensive, making it a great choice for pasties. Once cut into small pieces, it cooks quickly and releases plenty of rich juiciness. Danny's Cornish grandmother used to use beef skirt in her pasties. It has great texture, but these days tends to be eaten as bavette steak instead.

Cornish pasties

Makes 6

knob of butter

½ tablespoon olive oil

1 medium onion, finely chopped

75ml (3fl oz) strong beef stock, or ½ teaspoon Marmite in 75ml (3fl oz) hot water

1 tablespoon tomato purée

1 tablespoon Worcestershire sauce

250g (8 oz) beef rump tail or steak offcuts (sometimes a butcher will have trimmings from sirloin or rib-eye steak), cut into 1.5-cm ¾-in) dice

175g (6oz) swede, trimmed and cut into 5-mm (¼-in) dice

175g baking potato, cut into 1-cm (½-in) dice

1 medium carrot, finely chopped

1–2 teaspoons coarsely ground black pepper

plain flour, for dusting

2 x 500-g (1-lb) packets of puff pastry

1 egg mixed with 2 tablespoons milk, for glazing

sea salt flakes

Preheat the oven to 200°C/400°F/Gas Mark 6. Line 2 baking trays with baking parchment.

Melt the butter with the oil in a frying pan over a medium-low heat. Add the onion and a pinch of salt and cook for 15 minutes, stirring occasionally, until sweet and translucent. A little colour is fine, but do not brown.

Add the beef stock and tomato purée, bring to the boil and bubble briefly so it is thick enough to coat the meat and vegetables. Stir in the Worcestershire sauce, then the beef, swede, potato and carrot. Season to taste with the pepper, adding more salt according to the saltiness of the stock. Make sure everything is well mixed.

Lightly flour a work surface and roll out the pastry so each piece is 42 x 22cm (16½ x 8½in). Place a tea plate about 20cm (8in) in diameter upside down on the pastry and cut out 4 pastry circles. Reroll the scraps and cut out another 2 circles.

Place about one-sixth of the meat filling in the centre of each pastry circle. Brush some egg wash around the edge of the circle. Bring the sides up, press together along the top, then crimp so they are securely closed.

Place the pasties on the prepared baking trays. Brush with the eggwash, then bake for 15 minutes. Lower the heat to 180°C/350°F/Gas Mark 4 and bake for another 45 minutes. Serve hot or warm.

A rump is composed of three muscles that lie at different angles from each other and have slightly different textures. Usually, slices of rump steak are taken by cutting through two or three of the muscles, which is why one part of a rump steak can eat differently from another. The long, domed muscle on top of the rump has a layer of succulent fat and is the butcher's choice. In Britain, this is known as the 'point end'. The cut is much valued by the Brazilians and other South Americans, who call it picanha, and it has become something of a 'cult cut' in London restaurants. The cooking method below was suggested by Richard Santos, the Brazilian who makes sausages at Lidgate's. Brazilians are keen on salted meats, and this cooking method captures all the juices and makes a stunning piece of meat even better.

Thyme & rock salt-roasted picanha

Serves 4–6

2kg (4lb) rock salt

2 large handfuls of thyme sprigs, roughly chopped

2 eggs

875g–1kg (1¾–2lb) picanha/point end rump

Preheat the oven to 220°C/425°F/Gas Mark 7.

Mix the rock salt with the thyme in a bowl. Break in the eggs and stir well to make a firm crust.

Cover a baking tray with about two-fifths of the rock salt mixture. Place the picanha rump on top of it, flat-side down, and cover with the remaining salt mixture, patting it to make an even layer (this feels a bit like building a sandcastle on the beach).

Transfer to the oven and cook for 45 minutes. Remove the meat from the oven and leave to rest for 10 minutes (you can leave it for up to 30 minutes if this is more convenient). Crack open the salt crust by firmly tapping it with the blade of a large knife, lift out the meat and place on a chopping board. Brush off any salt still clinging to it with a wad of damp kitchen paper.

Cut the picanha rump into slices at an angle of 45 degrees. Serve with salad and potatoes, the latter perhaps baked in the oven as the beef cooks. If boiling or mashing the potatoes, it is important not to salt the water as the meat is slightly saltier than usual, and this seasons the rest of the plateful.

Steaks & Sauces

A good, juicy steak is one of the real treats of the table, and an important part of any butcher's trade. At Lidgate's we have regular steak tastings in our kitchen to assess the quality of the meat from the different farms that supply us because a steak can only be as good as the animal it comes from.

Different steaks have different qualities, and everyone has their favourite. That's why we've extended our range to include cuts that are popular with our American customers. However, certain fundamentals apply because everyone wants tenderness and taste. Some prime steaks unfailingly deliver these qualities, which is why they cost more. But if you have well-hung, carefully butchered beef, especially from grass-fed animals, all types of steak will deliver both qualities to some degree.

The Big Five
Ideally, prime steak should be thickly cut so that you can brown the outside well but still get pink meat within. We suggest serving 200–250g (7–8oz) per person, but sometimes it's worth cooking and dividing a large steak of decent thickness into individual portions rather than cooking a greater number of thin steaks.

Côte de boeuf – *see* Rib-eye

Fillet – this is the most expensive cut on the animal because it is the most tender. It is best cut no thinner than 5–6cm (2–2½in) to make a steak of about 200g (7oz), although this does make it even more expensive. Its intrinsic tenderness means that fillet can be cooked very rare and still be easy to eat. It has no fat and a more subtle flavour than other steaks, so can benefit from a tasty sauce.

Sirloin – less expensive than fillet, sirloin is about the same price as rib-eye. It is best cut no less than 2.5–3cm (1–1¼in) thick. We think the most delicious sirloin steaks of all come from near the rib end, as they have slightly more fat inside the meat, which makes the steak more succulent.

T-bone – this steak comes from the less fancy part of the sirloin, towards the rump, with the fillet on the other side of the bone. The two kinds of meat cook at slightly different rates, but cooking the fillet on the bone does improve its flavour. It is best cut about 5cm (2in) thick, and it's hard to cut one under 450g (1lb), so it makes a large serving for one, or can be shared between two.

Rib-eye – is one of the tastiest steaks because it has some internal fat, as well as marbling, which bastes the meat from the inside. It is best cut 4–5cm (1½–2in) thick, which will weigh 250–300g (9–10½oz). Watch out that you don't get a rib-eye cut at a slight angle and therefore not the same thickness all the way through, as it won't cook so evenly.

Rib-eye on the bone is called a côte de boeuf. It is cut 6–8cm (2½–3¼in) thick and will serve 2–3 people. This handsome piece of meat is best browned on the hob, then finished in the oven at 180°C/350°F/Gas Mark 4 (see opposite page). Cut the cooked steak almost perpendicular to the bone so that each slice has a piece of the curved outside muscle, a piece of fat and a piece of the central 'eye' muscle, including some from near the bone.

Sometimes you see this steak cut with a longer piece of rib bone and called a Tomahawk steak.

Rump – if the meat is well hung, rump is best cut at least 4cm (1½in) thick; if not well hung, rump can be tough, so is best cut thinly and cooked fast as a 'minute' steak. To cook a large, thick rump to share, brown the outside on the hob, then cook the whole steak in the oven until done to your liking (see below), and slice at an angle.

How to cook a prime steak

Take your steak out of the fridge about 30–60 minutes before cooking so it is at room temperature.

Brush or wipe the outside of the steak with olive or vegetable oil. Season well with flaky sea salt and freshly ground black pepper.

Place a griddle or frying pan over a high heat until really hot (a thick-based pan will take 5 minutes or more, a thin pan just a couple of minutes). The oiled meat should hiss on contact with the pan.

If the steak has fat on the outside (e.g. sirloin, rib or rump), it is best to brown the fat first, holding the steak on its side with a pair of tongs. This renders a little of the tasty fat into the pan and gives the fat a nicely browned surface.

Now cook the steak on both sides. What you're after is a well-browned outside with a pink interior that is as rare or well cooked as you wish (see below).

Thickness	Cooking time per side
3–4cm (1¼–1½in)	2–3 minutes rare
	3–4 minutes medium-rare
	4–5 minutes medium
5cm (2in)	3½ minutes rare
	4 minutes medium-rare
	4½ minutes medium

These timing are guidelines. How long to cook steak depends on the heat of your hob, your pan, whether there's a window open near the cooker, and so on. Cook a certain kind of steak a few times and you soon acquire a sense of when it's done to your liking.

When cooking steak, leave it in the pan without disturbing it for about 1 minute. At that point it will come away from the pan easily and be nicely browned.

A thick steak of 4cm (1½in) or over will need turning a couple of times so it cooks evenly on both sides. Alternatively, brown the meat on the outside, then put it into an oven preheated to 180°C/350°F/Gas Mark 4. Allow 7–8 minutes for a steak 5–6cm (2–2½in) thick, or until a meat thermometer inserted into the thickest part reaches the right temperature, as follows:

> 45–47°C (113–117°F) for rare
> 50–52°C (122–126°F) for medium-rare
> 55–60°C (131–140°F) for medium
> 65–70°C (149–158°F) for well done

Whether cooking the meat on the hob or in the oven, leave it to rest on a warm plate or in a warm place for 5 minutes in order for the juices to redistribute themselves evenly. If unsure whether your steak is done correctly, you can cut into it after resting it for a shorter time and put it back in the pan for 30 seconds or so to cook it further if necessary.

Other tasty steaks

There are a number of old-fashioned steaks that are becoming popular again as cheap and tasty options, but you might need to request them in advance from your butcher. When from good animals, such steaks can be a special treat, but they do need a bit more attention in cooking and cutting to make them delicious, which is why they cost less.

Bavette or Skirt – technically a flank steak, this cut comes from the forequarter and has longer, stringier fibres. Generally slow-cooked and eaten in pies, it can also make a cheap and tasty steak, especially if marinated to make it more tender. Flash-fry, rest and slice thinly across the grain at a 25-degree angle.

→

Steaks

1 & 2 Rump
3 Fillet
4 & 5 Sirloin
6 Rib-eye / Côte de Boeuf

7 Flank
8 Bavette
9 T-bone

Chuck-eye – often requested by our American customers, this cut comes from the front part of the rib-eye, where it meets the chuck, and is sometimes sold as a couple of separate and slightly cheaper steaks. We tend to do our chuck-eyes from wagyu, which is extremely tender and suits this kind of steak.

Featherblade or Flat iron – from a shoulder muscle, these steaks may be cut down through the whole muscle, leaving a line of gristle in the middle, so it looks like a feather. It can also be cut flat, off the gristle, as a flat iron steak. The meat is best cut 2–3cm (¾–1¼in) thick, should be pan-fried quickly and left to rest for 10 minutes before eating. Slice thinly, across the grain.

Flank – sometimes known as goose skirt, flank comes from the hindquarter and is a reasonably compact muscle that can be cut into thin minute steaks that should be flash-fried (cook them too long and they become tough). We also stuff a whole flank with garlic butter and cook it for slicing (see page 30).

Onglet or Hanger – hanging from the bottom of the fillet near the kidneys, this cut can have a slight taste of offal, which some people love. The size varies from animal to animal, but the whole piece is generally around 15cm (6in) long, 8–10cm (3¼–4in) wide and 2.5cm (1in) thick. Most butchers take out the central gristle to get two cylindrical pieces of about 200–250g (7–9oz). One is fine for one generous or two small portions, as the meat is quite rich in flavour. This is a good steak to marinate before cooking to help tenderize the meat (you can also butterfly it open in advance). Pan-fry quickly, keeping it rare, or it can become tough. Once cooked, slice across the grain at a 25-degree angle to make it less chewy.

Good steak sauces

Wine, cream and mustard
Fry your steaks and set them aside to rest. Deglaze the pan with a splash of red wine, pour in double or whipping cream, flavour with a little mustard and boil to reduce to the desired consistency.

Flavoured butters
Allow 15–20g (½–¾oz) room-temperature butter per person and mix in flavourings such as mustard or fresh horseradish, chopped herbs, mashed garlic or crushed peppercorns. Roll into a cylinder, wrap in greaseproof paper and chill until firm. Cut off slices to melt on your cooked steaks.

Chimmichurri
For 6 steaks, combine the following in a screwtop jar:

1 red chilli, deseeded and finely chopped
2 garlic cloves, finely chopped
leaves from a 25-g (1-oz) bunch of flat leaf parsley, finely chopped
1 teaspoon dried oregano
1 teaspoon sea salt flakes
2 tablespoons red wine vinegar
6 tablespoons olive oil

Shake well, and store in the fridge for up to a week.

Roasted bone marrow & garlic bone marrow stuffing
Preheat the oven to 200°C/400°F/Gas Mark 6. Place a 15cm (6in) length of marrowbone per person in a baking tray and roast until the marrow is soft (about 15–20 minutes). Season with salt and pepper and serve a bone alongside each steak for people to spoon out the luscious 'bone butter'.

Alternatively, scoop the raw bone marrow into a bowl, chop it up and mix with finely chopped garlic and parsley, plus salt and pepper. Roll into 1-cm (½-in) 'sausages', wrap in greaseproof paper and freeze. Cut a horizontal slit in the middle of a steak that's at least 4cm (1½in) thick. Insert a stick of frozen marrow and let the steak come to room temperature. Fry as usual, and the marrow will baste and flavour the steak.

2

Lamb

Sweet-tasting lamb is one of our most popular meats, and British
lamb is arguably the best in the world, whether for a Sunday roast,
shepherd's pie or a wealth of other recipes.

At Lidgate's we sell whole legs for roasting, but also
divide other muscles for cooking in different ways.
We cut a wide variety of chops, for instance, including
tender cutlets from the loin, and big and juicy chump
chops – a butcher's favourite.

Lamb can be cooked fast and eaten pink, or slowly
until falling off the bone. It can be grilled, stewed,
roasted and baked. Lamb's rich flavour means that it
combines well with vibrant ingredients, such as dried
fruit, yoghurt, sheep's cheese, pesto, smoked paprika
and curry spices, and our recipes explore many of these
combinations. The minced lamb samosas (see page 89),
for example, make a sweet-and-spicy lunch or supper
dish, while our Middle Eastern koftas (see page 93) are
both tasty and economical, and can be oven-cooked or
barbecued. From Albania, there's Tav Kösi (see page 82),
made of inexpensive neck lamb chops baked with
yoghurt, garlic and oregano, and our Italian-influenced
dishes include Italian Chump (see page 80) and the
showstopping Pesto Saddle of Lamb (see page 76).
Coming back to Britain, there's the old favourite of
hotpot (see page 85), but we give ours a couple of twists
to turn it into a dish with that little bit extra.

Lamb is a seasonal meat, changing as the animals grow.
Watch out for tender new-season lamb, and later enjoy
the older, larger animals that make flavoursome roasts,
and are also great in autumn and winter stews. As lamb
gets older, it becomes known first as hogget, then, after
two years, as mutton. When the sheep are kept well and
the meat handled carefully and properly hung, mutton
can have a superb flavour, and there has been a revival

of interest in this forgotten meat. Our recipe shows how
to cook it slowly in a fragrant stew (see page 91), but
well-farmed and carefully butchered mutton can even
be eaten rare. You just need to be sure of its provenance,
as the quality of older animals is more variable than
that of younger lamb.

When buying lamb, look for a nice rosy appearance
to the meat, without signs of dryness or ageing. Chops
should be cut to an even thickness so that they all cook
at the same rate if you are eating them rare. The
amount of fat on a lamb varies with the animal. Some
is needed for flavour, but you don't want too much and
a butcher will trim accordingly. A good butcher will pull
off the skin or 'bark' from rack of lamb and chops as it's
bit chewy, or you can do this yourself at home.

We're lucky in the UK to have a fine tradition of sheep
farming all over the country, from the early lambs of
Dorset to the later-maturing hillside sheep of Wales,
and those that graze on salt-marshes and even seaweed
in places such as Kent. Support our farmers by enjoying
their lamb and making it into dishes that show off this
most delicious meat.

Lamb Cuts

Best end – the most expensive and tender part of the animal, this meat is cut into little cutlets that are good for frying, or a smart barbecue if well lubricated with an oily marinade. The boned-out 'eyes' make mini-noisettes for quick frying. Left together, the cutlets become a rack of lamb (see page 264). We take off the back bone and tough 'paddywack', a ligament that runs up to the neck and helps support the animal's head, then French-trim the rack to expose the bone. Cook a long rack (6–8 bones), allowing 2–3 bones per person; alternatively, mini 3-bone racks can be served as a large single portion. Make sure you or your butcher remove the papery outer skin or 'bark' from the best end. Two racks can be tied together to make a crown roast.

Breast – a much-underrated cut, lamb breast deserves the same sort of recognition that pork belly now has. Trimmed of some of its fat, it can be stuffed, rolled and slow-cooked to make a flavoursome bargain dish (see page 94). Lamb spare ribs from young, more tender animals can be good when trimmed and not too fatty.

Chump or rump – between the loin and the leg, this is cut into a butcher's choice chop because it has plenty of meat and reasonable tenderness at a good price (Holland Park hotpot, see page 85). Leave them in one piece for a mini-roasting joint for 2–3 people (see page 80) or to skewer flat and barbecue.

Leg and shank – different countries cut the leg in different places. In Australia and the United States they often cut a long leg that includes the chump. In the UK we cut it lower and tend to use it as a tender roast (see page 207). The leg can also be cut in half to make a chump-end roast or a shank-end roast. Cut the bone out of a whole leg and open out the meat for a quicker-roasting joint that's easy to carve, or for a barbecue treat (see page 230). Steaks cut from the leg are good for quick frying. The shank is the end of the leg, with chunks of sweet meat near the bone. Fifteen years ago, we used to bone them out and use the meat for mince,

but a single one makes a good large portion and this cut has now become popular for chefs and home cooks (see page 84).

Loin and saddle – the middle part of the lamb's back, between the best end and the chump and leg, can be cut into loin chops. A boned and trimmed loin can be cut into small round noisettes for frying or searing, then quick-roasting to rare or medium-rare (take care not to overcook this pricey and lean cut). Both sides of the loin left together are cut into Barnsley chops (traditionally with kidney attached), or left as a whole saddle. This makes a spectacular roast, especially if it includes the best end. Butchers bone and roll a saddle of lamb to make an easy-carving roasting joint (see page 76). Make sure you or your butcher removes the outer skin or 'bark'.

Neck or middle neck – the lower part of the neck is less used than the top and more tender. The long 'eye' fillet, which continues to the loin, is a good and cheaper option for kebabs (see page 242) or can be roasted whole and sliced. Neck chops or fillet from young animals are tender enough for quick-stewed dishes with spring or early summer vegetables, such as navarin of lamb.

Mince – trimmings and cheaper cuts of lamb, such as breast, shoulder, middle neck and scrag, are turned into tasty mince that is good value and also versatile (see page 89, 90 or 93). Always try to get freshly made mince because the flavour fades and taints slightly after just a day or two.

Scrag end – the top part of the neck gets plenty of exercise as the sheep grazes, so is relatively tough, but has bags of flavour for good-value soups and cheap stews. Best cut into sections on the bone.

Shoulder – this is our favourite part of the animal for its sweetness, flavour and value. Can be sold cut in half as a blade or fillet-end, which has slightly more meat then the alternative foreshank or knuckle-end, which includes the tasty meat near the foreleg bone. We'd like to see a revival of the old-fashioned shoulder chop, cut across the bone on a blade-end shoulder (see page 85). Well cut, these have a nice amount of meat and excellent taste. Boned and diced shoulder is good for stews and other slow-cooked dishes (see pages 74, 91 and 215). Shoulder can also be boned, stuffed and tied for an easy-carving joint.

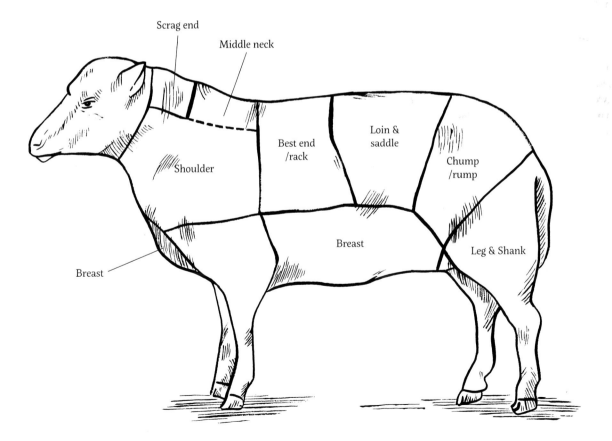

Scrag end

Middle neck

Loin & saddle

Best end /rack

Chump /rump

Shoulder

Breast

Breast

Leg & Shank

Lamb Cuts

1 Scrag end
2 Middle neck
3 Shoulder
4 Rack of lamb
5 Breast
6 Mince

7 Chump
8 Boned saddle/loin
9 Leg

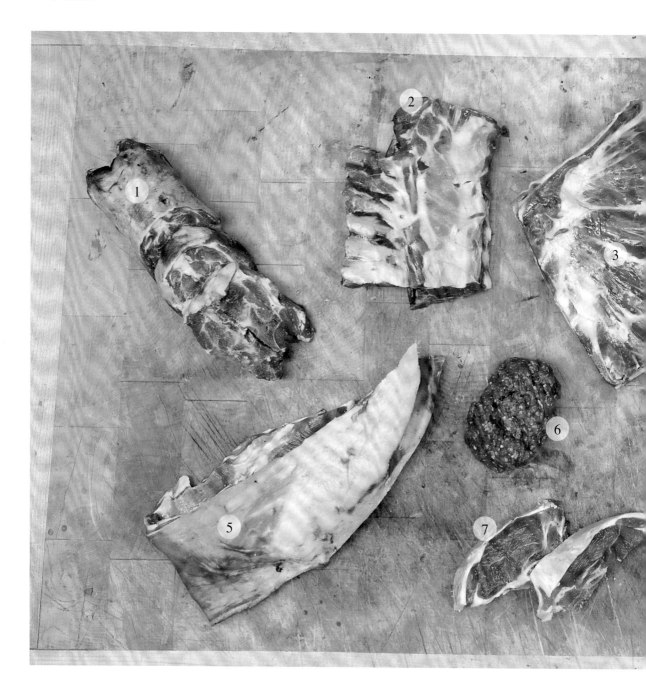

Lidgate's is famous for award-winning pies. Our 'secret' is no secret to the home cook: tasty fillings made with good ingredients. This lamb pie is a favourite with many customers and has just the right balance of sweet and savoury. Like all our pies, it has plenty of meat and will serve at least six, depending on appetite.

Lamb, leek & apricot pie

Serves 6

2 tablespoons olive oil

1.5kg (3lb) lamb shoulder, cut into 5-cm (2-in) chunks

2 large onions, finely chopped

1 tablespoon plain flour

1 tablespoon ground paprika

1 teaspoon freshly ground black pepper

1 tablespoon white wine vinegar

500ml (17fl oz) lamb stock

2 large leeks, cut into 1–1.5-cm (½–¾in) slices

2 medium carrots, cut into batons

200g (7oz) dried apricots

flour, for dusting

500g (1lb) puff pastry

1 egg beaten with 2 tablespoons milk, for glazing

salt

Place the oil in a large flameproof casserole dish over a high heat. When hot, brown the lamb in it (in 2 or 3 batches) on 2 sides. Set aside on a plate.

Add the onions to the pan, stir them around in the fat and reduce the heat to medium-low. Cook gently for 10–15 minutes, stirring occasionally, until soft.

Sprinkle over the flour and stir for 1 minute, then add the paprika and pepper. Season with salt. Pour in the vinegar and stock, stir well, then let the liquid bubble up. Return the meat to the pan and stir into the sauce. Simmer, covered, for about 1 hour.

Stir in the leeks, carrots and apricots, re-cover the pan and continue to cook for another 30–45 minutes, until the meat is tender. Taste and adjust the seasoning. The recipe can be made in advance up to this point and kept in the fridge, covered, for a day or two.

Preheat the oven to 220°C/425°F/Gas Mark 7.

Meanwhile, tip the lamb filling into a large pie dish about 30 x 20cm (12 x 8in). Lightly flour a work surface and roll out the pastry so it is about 5cm (2in) larger than the dish. Cut 2.5-cm (1-in) strips from around the edge of the pastry. Press these on to the rim of the dish and brush with the egg glaze. Cover the dish with the pastry lid and press it firmly on the pastry rim. Trim off the excess, then crimp the edges together to form a seal. If you like, reroll the pastry trimmings and cut out shapes to decorate the pie, sticking them on with the glaze.

Brush the top of the pie with the egg glaze and bake for 30 minutes, or until nice and brown. Serve with mashed potato and seasonal green vegetables.

This recipe has been a popular dinner party dish with our customers for 15 years. Making it at home is an exercise in how to prepare meat so that the end dish is easy to cook, carve and eat. It does require a little effort and patience, but if you take your time and do the work in the morning or the night before, the cooking and serving are then easy. Ask your butcher in advance for a short-cut, boneless saddle of lamb, which is the saddle minus the chumps.

Pesto saddle of lamb

Serves 4–5

1 short-cut saddle of lamb, boned and skinned
handful of pine nuts

For the pesto stuffing/topping
200g (7oz) good-quality pesto
150g (5oz) fine dry breadcrumbs

First make the stuffing. Mix together the pesto and breadcrumbs. If the pesto is very oily, you might need to add a few more breadcrumbs. What you're after is a stiff paste. Take one-third of the mixture and roll it into a 'sausage' about the length of the lamb and 2.5cm (1in) thick. Wrap in clingfilm and place in the freezer for at least 1 hour. Set the remaining pesto mixture aside.

Follow the step-by-step instructions overleaf to prepare the saddle of lamb.

When you are ready to cook the meat, preheat the oven to 180°C/350°F/Gas Mark 4. Weigh the meat and calculate the cooking time: 12 minutes per 500g (1lb), plus 15 minutes for rare; 20 minutes per 500g (1lb), plus 20 minutes for medium; 25 minutes per 500g (1lb), plus 25 for well done. Place the joint in a roasting tray and roast for the required time. About 10 minutes before the cooking time is up, you can use a meat thermometer to help get the lamb to your liking:

50–52°C (122–126°F) for medium rare

55–60°C (131–140°F) for medium

65–70°C (149–158°F) for well done

Make sure the probe goes into the thickest part of the meat, and take the lamb out of the oven when it is 5°C (40°F) under your target, as its temperature will continue to rise for a while.

Leave the meat to rest for 10 minutes, covered loosely with foil. Cut into thick slices, removing the string.

→

I   Lay the boned lamb out on a work surface, skin-side down, and cut out the two fillets. You can almost pull these out, like a chicken fillet on a breast, using a knife to cut through the attached fat.

2   Take out the oval 'eyes' of the lamb – the largest pieces of meat in the centre – by holding the lamb firmly with your free hand and sliding the knife under the thin gristle at an angle so that you cut away from you using a stroking action. Cut out the flaps – the thin pieces of meat at either end of the joint. Trim away the tough silver gristle on the surface of the eyes of the meat by sliding your knife under it at a 45-degree angle.

3   What you're left with is mostly the outer fat of the saddle. Using a sharp knife parallel to the work surface, trim away any excess fat to get a flat and even surface. Move the meat around so that you are always cutting away from yourself. Beat out the fat with a meat mallet or a rolling pin to make it into a thin, even layer. It's best do this between two pieces of clingfilm or greaseproof paper that are open at the sides so the air comes out as you beat. After doing this, you can also use the rolling pin to roll out the fat at the end to get a good finish.

4   Put the eyes across the fat in the middle of the skin, parallel to the short ends. Place the roll of frozen pesto between the eyes. Place the fillets on top of them, plus any leftover meat trimmings. Place the flaps of meat over the pesto. Lift up the short sides of the fat to cover the lamb and meet in the middle, trimming off any excess fat.

5 & 6   You want to keep the meat in a compact piece that holds in the stuffing. The easiest way to do this is to tie the rolled joint up securely in 5 or 6 regular intervals and tie a knot at each place. A butcher uses a fancier way that uses a single piece of string in a version of a blanket stitch. Either way, insert the needle about 2.5cm (1in) in from the seam.

7   Put the meat on a work surface, seam-side down. Press the reserved pesto stuffing in an even layer over the top and sides of the saddle – it is easier to do this when it isn't fridge-cold.

8   Stud the pine nuts all over the stuffing. Wrap in clingfilm and chill for at least 1 hour to firm up before roasting. For cooking instructions, see page 76.

The chump is the top of the leg, going towards the loin. It is prime meat, with the tenderness of leg, yet at a bargain price. That's why chump chops are very much a butcher's choice cut. You can get three chops from a large chump, but the last one has less meat than the rest – at Lidgate's we turn the smaller third chop into mince. Here you cook the whole boned chump in one piece, opened out slightly so that it can be stuffed and yet cooks quickly and evenly. This recipe is for two to share, but is easy to scale up for a dinner party once you've got the knack of making it. There's lots of meat on a whole chump, though the amount varies at different times of year. Late-season chump will feed two generously, but you'll have a smaller portion in the spring and early summer.

Italian chump

Serves 2

1 boned chump of lamb (ask for it in a single piece, with the 'bark' or outer skin removed)

olive oil

6–9 basil leaves, depending on size

40g (1½oz) semi-hard or firm goats' cheese

3–6 sunblush tomatoes, depending on size

salt

Preheat the oven to 180°C/350°F/Gas Mark 4.

Trim some of the fat off the lamb if you like, but leave a decent layer – you can always cut it off once cooked. Score the fat about 6–7 times on the diagonal. Turn the meat over so it is flesh-side up. Cut across the meat 3 times, going down almost to the fat (our head butcher Alan calls the cuts a 'letter rack' because they make 3 'slots' across the narrower side of the meat).

Rub the fat and meat with olive oil and season with salt. Insert 2 skewers diagonally through the opened-out piece of meat to hold it flat as it cooks.

Tuck 2 or 3 whole basil leaves into each 'slot'. Cut 3 pieces of goats' cheese about 1cm (½in) thick and half the width of the slots and put them in the centre. Put 1 or 2 sunblush tomatoes in each slot. The chump can be prepared in advance up to this point. Cover and leave in the fridge until you're ready to cook.

Pour a little oil into a frying pan and place over a medium heat. When hot, add the lamb, skin-side down, for a couple of minutes just to start browning the fat.

Transfer to a roasting tray and roast, skin-side down, for about 25 minutes, or until the meat is cooked to your liking.

→

Easy and tasty one-pot dishes are always good to have in your repertoire, and this one was suggested by one of our butchers, Olti, who comes from Albania. There it's known as Tav kösi and is somewhat similar to moussaka, with meat and rice cooked below a smooth, tangy topping of thick yoghurt set with eggs. You can use economical neck chops, which are traditional, or less boney chump chops to get more meat.

Lamb with yoghurt (Tav kösi)

Serves 4

750g (1½lb) neck or chump chops
1 onion, sliced
3 garlic cloves, finely chopped
1½ teaspoons dried oregano
300ml (½ pint) water, or lamb or chicken stock
20g (¾oz) unsalted butter, cubed
3 tablespoons long-grain rice
salt and freshly ground black pepper

For the topping
75g (3oz) unsalted butter
1 garlic clove, finely chopped (optional)
40g (1½oz) plain flour
500g (1lb) thick full-fat yoghurt
4 eggs

Put the chops, onion, garlic and 1 teaspoon of the oregano in a flameproof casserole dish. Add the water or stock and butter. Season with salt and pepper. Bring to the boil, then simmer, half-covered, for 30 minutes, or until the lamb is almost tender, turning the chops a couple of times so they cook evenly.

Preheat the oven to 180°C/350°F/Gas Mark 4.

To make the topping, melt the butter in a saucepan, add the garlic (if using) and cook for a couple of minutes. Sprinkle in the flour and mix well. Add the yoghurt and whisk until combined. Season with salt and pepper. Leave to cool for a couple of minutes, then whisk in the eggs.

Scatter the rice over and around the lamb chops, ensuring it goes into the liquid. Carefully pour the yoghurt mixture over the whole dish. Sprinkle with the remaining ½ teaspoon oregano.

Place in the oven for about 40 minutes, or until the top is patched with brown and the lamb is cooked through.

Lamb shanks come from the knuckle end of the back leg and are good as single large portions. For this reason they have become much in demand by pubs and restaurants. Apart from that, the meat is really sweet and delicious, and falls off the bone when cooked long and slow. Shanks are usually cooked in a stew, but try them instead slow-roasted with southern European flavourings. They become sauced in a rich, flavoursome goo, which isn't exactly photogenic but tastes wonderful.

Lamb shanks with feta

Serves 4

75-g (3-oz) bunch of flat leaf parsley, leaves finely chopped
75g (3oz) anchovies, finely chopped
300g (10oz) feta cheese, grated or finely crumbled
4 lamb shanks

Preheat the oven to 160°C/325°F/Gas Mark 3. Combine the parsley, anchovies and feta in a bowl, then knead lightly to make a more cohesive paste.

Score the lamb shanks all over, cutting about 5mm (¼in) into the flesh. Press the feta mixture over the fat on the shank, but not on the broad fleshy base. Smooth it down with your hands to form a firm, even layer.

Line the bottom of a roasting tray with foil. Stand the shanks of their broad end, bone upwards. Roast for 3 hours, or until the meat is tender, spooning the feta mixture over the shanks every so often after they have been in the oven for 1½ hours.

Serve with new or baked potatoes and a Greek-style salad with lettuce, red onions and tomatoes, and perhaps a sprinkle of fresh oregano.

Lancashire hotpot is a classic all-in-one dish in which meat chops and their bones flavour vegetables and gravy under a crowning layer of crisping potatoes. We've poshed it up slightly to make this 'Holland Park' version. It uses meaty chops cut from the shoulder (you get 4–5 from a block-end shoulder joint). Unlike standard chops, these are for slow-cooking, not frying. Chump chops (from the rump) are also delicious in this dish. We've included pearl spelt, which adds a certain silkiness, or you can use traditional pearl barley instead. We've also added some pickled walnuts for extra flavour, but these are not essential.

Holland Park hotpot

Serves 4–5

2½ tablespoons beef dripping, olive oil or vegetable oil

1 large onion, sliced

1½ tablespoons plain flour

4–5 lamb shoulder chops or large chump chops (about 1kg/2lb in total)

700g (1lb 6oz) potatoes, peeled and finely sliced

2 bay leaves

25g (1oz) pearl spelt or barley

2 large carrots, cut into large chunks

3 pickled walnuts, each cut into 6 pieces (optional)

500ml (17fl oz) lamb or chicken stock

1 tablespoon redcurrant jelly

1 teaspoon Worcestershire sauce

salt and freshly ground black pepper

Preheat the oven to 220°C/425°F/Gas Mark 7. Heat 1 tablespoon of the dripping or oil in a large frying pan. When hot, soften the onion in it over a medium-low heat (about 10 minutes). Meanwhile, season the flour and dust the chops with it.

Transfer the onion to a plate and set aside. Add another ½ tablespoon dripping or oil to the pan, turn up the heat and brown the chops on both sides. This is best done in batches so the pan doesn't become overcrowded and lose heat.

Put another ½ tablespoon dripping or oil into a 25-cm (10-in) flameproof casserole dish and heat briefly to spread the fat around the bottom of the dish. Cover with half the potatoes. Season with salt and pepper. Spread the onion over the surface and add the bay leaves. Arrange the browned chops on top and sprinkle with the pearl spelt or barley. Tuck the carrots and walnuts (if using) in amongst the chops. Arrange the remaining potatoes over the top.

Heat up the stock, add the redcurrant jelly and stir until melted. Add the Worcestershire sauce, then pour the gravy over the hotpot. Dot the surface with the remaining ½ tablespoon dripping or brush with the olive oil and season with salt and pepper.

Place the hotpot, uncovered, in the oven for 20 minutes, then lower the heat to 160°C/325°F/Gas Mark 3, cover and cook for 2 hours, or until the meat is tender. Serve with seasonal greens.

→

Samosas make a great lunch dish, and we sell plenty in the shop, both hot to eat straight away or for heating up at home. It's not a bad idea to make a double quantity of the filling so you can freeze half and have the makings of a delicious meal to hand for another day. We originally made our samosas with filo pastry, but it proved too fiddly for our busy kitchen, so we now use puff pastry as we discovered that it absorbs the curry sauce really well. We have also simplified the folding process here, so the samosas are rectangles rather than triangles.

Lamb samosas

Makes 6 large samosas

1 tablespoon olive or vegetable oil

250g (8oz) lean minced lamb

1 garlic clove, finely chopped

1 small carrot, diced

½ teaspoon ground turmeric

100g (3½oz) frozen petit pois or ordinary peas

1 x 150-g (5-oz) can sweetcorn, drained

15-g (½-oz) bunch of coriander, stalks finely chopped and leaves roughly chopped

½ x 400-g (14-oz) can chopped tomatoes

100g (3½oz) good-quality korma paste

½ teaspoon garam masala

½ teaspoon Worcestershire sauce

125ml (4fl oz) lamb stock

chilli powder, to taste (optional)

plain flour, for dusting

3 sheets ready-rolled puff pastry, about 215g (7 ½oz) each

For the glaze and garnish

¼ teaspoon ground turmeric

4 teaspoons vegetable oil

nigella seeds, to garnish (optional)

Place the oil in a large frying pan over a medium-high heat. When hot, spread the lamb out in the pan (you might need to do this in 2 batches) and leave it to cook for 5 minutes, or until brown. Stir it around and leave to brown for another 5 minutes.

Reduce the heat to medium-low, add the garlic, carrot and turmeric and cook for a couple of minutes, stirring occasionally. Add the peas, sweetcorn, coriander stalks, tomatoes, korma paste, garam masala, Worcestershire sauce and lamb stock. Stir well and leave to simmer for about 20 minutes, until much of the liquid has evaporated. Mix in the coriander leaves. Taste and add chilli powder if desired, and some salt if needed (the seasoning will depend upon the stock and korma paste). Set aside to cool. If making this in advance, cover and store in the fridge for up to 2 days.

Lightly dust a work surface with flour and place a sheet of pastry on it, wide side towards you. Cut it in half from top to bottom to get 2 rectangles. Place one-sixth of the lamb mixture in the centre of the right-hand rectangle and spread it out with the back of the spoon, leaving a border of about 2.5cm (1in) all round. Brush water around the border then fold the pastry over to make a rectangular parcel. Press the edges together with the back of a fork. Repeat this process with the remaining pastry so you get 6 long samosas in total. You can make these in advance and keep them in the fridge for a few hours before cooking.

Preheat the oven to 200°C/400°F/Gas Mark 6.

Combine the ingredients for the glaze and brush the mixture over the top of the samosas. Sprinkle with nigella seeds, if you wish. Place the samosas on a baking sheet and bake for 30–35 minutes, or until the pastry is golden brown. Serve hot or warm.

We named these juicy burgers after a local school that we supply with meat. Sometimes we make burgers with just mince and flavourings, such as rosemary and mint, which work especially well with lamb. Occasionally, we add a few breadcrumbs to lighten the texture and consistency, as we do here. The lamb should be reasonably fatty – shoulder is perfect – so that the burger holds together and has plenty of flavour. Kids often want food that is tasty but relatively plain, and this subtle combination fits the bill.

Fox lamburgers

Serves 4

500g (1lb) minced lamb, not too lean
4 tablespoons dry white breadcrumbs
5 tablespoons finely chopped mint
1 teaspoon finely chopped rosemary
½ teaspoon fine sea salt
1 egg white (optional)
1 tablespoon olive oil
freshly ground black pepper

To serve
4 burger buns, split open and buttered
lettuce leaves
4 tablespoons tzatziki

Put the mince in a bowl and add the breadcrumbs, mint and rosemary. Season with the salt and a generous amount of pepper. Use your hands to mix everything thoroughly. If the mince has enough fat, the mixture will hold together well when formed into burgers. If your mince is lean and the mixture seems crumbly, it's a good idea to add the egg white as a binder.

Tip the mixture on to a chopping board and divide into 4 equal pieces. Use your hands to shape each piece into a burger about 9 x 2.5cm (3½ x 2in). Transfer to a plate, cover with clingfilm and place in the fridge for at least 30 minutes to firm up. (You can do this up to a couple of hours in advance of cooking.)

Place the oil in a frying pan over a high heat. When hot, add the burgers and cook for about 3 minutes on each side, pressing down occasionally with a spatula, until well browned.

Transfer the burgers to a chopping board and leave to rest for 1 minute. Cut one open and check it is done to your liking. If not, return it to the pan and cook for a little longer.

Serve the burgers in buttered buns with lettuce and a dollop of tzatziki.

Mutton comes from sheep that are at least two years old. Although popular in the past, it acquired a bad reputation because sub-standard meat began to predominate, so it went out of fashion. That's a great pity because, provided it comes from a good supplier and is well hung, it has great depth of flavour and richness. Although mutton can be served rare, slow cooking is perhaps the best approach, especially if spices and dried fruit are included.

Mutton & prune tagine

Serves 6

1.25kg (2½lb) mutton shoulder, cut into large chunks

1–2 tablespoons vegetable oil

2 onions, sliced

3 celery sticks, cut into 5cm (2in) chunks

600ml (1 pint) chicken or lamb stock

½ teaspoon sea salt flakes

150g (5oz) pitted prunes, halved

4 tablespoons sesame seeds

3 tablespoons roughly chopped coriander leaves

For the marinade

2 teaspoons ground coriander

1½ teaspoons ground ginger

1½ teaspoons ground turmeric

1 cinnamon stick, broken in half

4 garlic cloves, finely chopped

juice of 1 orange

juice of 2 lemons

3 tablespoons olive oil

Combine the marinade ingredients in a large bowl. Add the meat, cover and place in the fridge for 2–48 hours, turning occasionally.

When you're ready to start cooking, preheat the oven to 150°C/300°F/Gas Mark 2.

Brush the marinade off the lamb, reserving the liquid, and pat the meat dry with kitchen paper. Place the oil in a large flameproof casserole dish over a high heat. When hot, brown the meat on 2 sides, doing this in batches to maintain the heat in the pan, and adding more oil if necessary.

Return all the meat to the pan and add the onions and celery. Pour in the stock, then stir in the marinade and salt. Cover and bring to the boil, then transfer to the oven for 2 hours, stirring occasionally.

Add the prunes and cook for a further hour, until the meat is tender.

Meanwhile, dry-toast the sesame seeds in a frying pan over a medium heat, stirring for a minute or so to stop them burning.

Taste the tagine and adjust the seasoning if necessary. Scatter the sesame seeds and chopped coriander over the top and serve with couscous.

As well as eating these tasty kebabs fresh, Danny has a stack of them in his freezer at home, ready to oven-cook for his kids when a quick supper is needed. They can also be cooked on a barbecue, in which case you might want to add an egg white to ensure the meat is firm enough to hold together as it's turned several times during cooking. The best mince is made by a butcher who will make it to order, ideally no longer than the day before cooking, as the cut-up meat changes in flavour over time.

Harissa & smoked paprika koftas

Makes 6 koftas

500g (1lb) fatty minced lamb, from shoulder or breast

1 small garlic clove, crushed

½ small red onion, very finely chopped

2 tablespoons dried breadcrumbs

3 tablespoons finely chopped flat leaf parsley

3 tablespoons finely chopped coriander

2 tablespoons finely chopped mint

1 teaspoon harissa

½ red chilli, deseeded and finely chopped

For the spice blend

1 teaspoon smoked paprika

1 heaped teaspoon ground coriander

1 heaped teaspoon ground cumin

¾ teaspoon fine sea salt

freshly ground black pepper

Set out 6 skewers, pre-soaking them in water for 30 minutes if wooden. Flat skewers hold the meat better than round ones.

Mix all the spice blend ingredients together in a bowl, adding a generous amount of black pepper.

Put the meat in a large bowl and add all the other ingredients, including the spice blend. Use your hands to mix everything thoroughly.

Divide the kofta mixture into 6 equal pieces. Roll each piece into a long sausage shape about 10 x 5cm (4 x 2in). Place a skewer along the centre of each sausage and press it into the meat. Roll the meat around the skewer to position it in the centre, and press the seam firmly to make it secure. You can do all this in advance and leave the koftas in the fridge, loosely covered with clingfilm, until you're ready to cook.

Preheat the oven to 180°C/350°F/Gas Mark 4. Alternatively, heat a grill to its highest setting, or light a barbecue and wait until the flames die down and you have glowing coals.

Cook the koftas in the oven on a baking tray for about 15 minutes, or cook under the grill or on the barbecue for 10–15 minutes, turning a couple of times. Check that the meat is cooked right through to the centre.

Serve with pitta bread, salad and, if you like, a trickle of natural yoghurt mixed with garlic and chopped herbs.

Breast of lamb is much underrated, rather in the way pork belly used to be. Not only is this cut relatively inexpensive, but it's really delicious when stuffed and cooked 'low and slow', and certainly good enough to serve to friends for dinner. Once you get into this particular cut, there are plenty of other stuffings to try. We also love one made of pork mince flavoured with fennel seeds, chilli, garlic and lemon juice.

When feeding a larger group, we think it's good to prepare two lamb breasts, because they do vary in size and you don't want to be short of meat – also, any leftovers are absolutely delicious. One breast is enough for 3–4 people – just halve the amount of stuffing.

Breast of lamb stuffed with almonds & apricots

Serves 6–8

2 large boneless lamb breasts, trimmed of excess fat, about 800g (1lb 12oz) each

1 tablespoon olive oil

750ml (1¼ pints) lamb stock

fine salt

For the apricot and almond stuffing (enough for 2 lamb breasts)
½ tablespoon olive oil

1 medium onion, finely chopped

2 garlic cloves, finely chopped

1 heaped teaspoon ground cumin

1 heaped teaspoon ground coriander

450g (14½oz) minced lamb, preferably from shoulder or another breast as it should be reasonably fatty

75g (3oz) dried apricots, finely chopped

75g (3oz) flaked almonds, toasted

75g (3oz) dry breadcrumbs

1 egg, whisked

2 tablespoons honey

juice of ½ lemon

40-g (1½-oz) bunch of coriander, stalks and leaves finely chopped

½ teaspoon sea salt flakes

freshly ground black pepper

Make the stuffing and roll the lamb breasts as shown in the step-by-steps instructions overleaf.

When ready to cook the meat, preheat the oven to 150°C/300°F/Gas Mark 2.

Heat the oil in a long or large ovenproof pan over a medium heat. When hot, brown the breasts in it on both sides (about 10 minutes). Add the lamb stock and bring to the boil. Cover the pan with foil or a lid and place in the oven for 3 hours, or until the meat is tender.

Transfer the meat to a warm serving plate. Whisk the juices in the pan and pour into a gravy boat. Cut the meat into thick slices (it will more or less fall apart) and serve with the gravy and a herby couscous, as shown on page 97, for a Middle Eastern slant. Alternatively, serve it with mashed potatoes and vegetables, or a salad.

→

How to stuff & roll a lamb breast

1   First make the stuffing. Heat the oil in a large
    pan and sweat the onion and garlic in it over
    a low heat, stirring occasionally, until translucent.
    Add the cumin and coriander. Cook gently for
    a further 2 minutes. Turn the heat off and allow
    to cool slightly.

2   Put the remaining stuffing ingredients into a large
    bowl, adding a generous seasoning of pepper. Add
    the onion mixture and mix well.

3   Lay the lamb breast on a work surface, fat-side
    down. Spread the stuffing about 1cm (½in) thick over
    the flesh, leaving a clear 2.5-cm (1-in) border at each
    narrow end.

4 & 5   Roll the meat up lengthways.

6   Tie the meat at 3 regular intervals, first around the
    middle and then about 5cm (2in) from each end.

7   Finally, tie the meat once lengthways, like a parcel.
    Season the outside of the rolled breast with salt and
    black pepper.

8 & 9   Cook and cut the lamb breast as described on
    page 94.

The best lamb

We're blessed in Britain to live on a long, thin island with a maritime climate that helps to produce plenty of good grazing for livestock. All over the country – from Cornwall, Devon and Dorset to the uplands of Cumbria and Yorkshire, and right up to the islands of Scotland – are sheep farmers who take pride in the fine meat they can produce. This great tradition of sheep farming has led to many classic dishes, from homely hotpot to sophisticated rack of lamb, and the much-loved British leg of lamb with mint sauce and roast potatoes.

One of the secrets to appreciating the best lamb is to notice how it changes throughout the season and varies considerably in size. When the new-season lamb arrives in April, the carcass weighs about 18kg (40lb), and its sweet meat is good for springtime stews and tender chops. By the autumn, a lamb weighs around 23kg (50lb) and the chops are extra large – perfect for a slow-cooked hotpot. At this point too, the legs are so big that they serve a large dinner party, or are sold cut into half-legs or cubed for kebabs. People often favour lamb for Easter meals, but it's particularly delicious at Christmas time, when the animals are older and the meat has even more texture and taste.

Another secret to the best lamb is to have a bit of fat. We don't like sheep to be too lean and our customers prefer lamb with a bit of fat, especially on rack of lamb and the legs. Leaner lamb is a bit floppy and doesn't best suit our British dishes, such as a roast.

Eat your way around the animal to get not just the best tastes, but also the best price. As lamb is produced and traded around the world, the competition is stronger, so its price tends to be more volatile than the meat from other animals. The cost per kilo (2lb) can go up or down by as much as 20 per cent in just a year or two. Consequently, butchers and customers are keen to explore less well-known cuts. Where once it was common to see a whole rack of lamb on restaurant menus, you're now more likely to be offered dishes that showcase a range of flavours and cuts – perhaps a cutlet or two served alongside a cheaper, slow-cooked cut, such as shoulder or breast.

Another trick to getting the most out of this meat lies in the revival of mutton. In centuries past, this was the most common form of sheep meat, largely because sheep were kept for longer in order to harvest their valuable wool. Nothing went to waste. The plentiful fat of older animals went into tallow candles, the ewes were milked for sheep's cheese, and even the dung was a useful fertilizer. Older sheep, however, are now less economically viable and tastes have swung towards younger lamb.

It has to be said that whilst mutton can be underrated, it is also less predictable than lamb, so you need to be sure it is good quality and has been hung correctly. Look for mutton from animals between two and five years old that have been fed on grass and other plants, not concentrates. The best mutton comes from mountain or downland traditional breeds, such as Hardwick and Southdown, and primitive sheep such as Soay. The meat should be hung for at least a week and ideally for two, or for as long as it can take.

Mutton can be superb, with a great texture and depth of flavour, and is often what sheep farmers themselves like to put on their plate at home. Try it in a stew or a curry, or slow-roast it and serve with a caper sauce to cut through the richness. You can also roast mutton to eat more rare, as long as you are certain of the source and quality of the meat.

Breed and feed play their part too in the best lamb. One of our most special lamb suppliers is Ronnie Eunson of Uradale farm in Shetland. His native sheep come from a breed that has been in this northerly part of Scotland for at least 3,000 years. The animals themselves know how to get the best nutrition from the land, eating not just the heather and natural herbs in the pasture, but also fresh seaweed on the foreshore when the tide is out.

The natural surroundings and unhurried farming of these sheep produces lamb that is really special. We get Ronnie's lamb in about the second week of September and it lasts until December. The carcasses are about half the size of our other lambs, and when they hang alongside each other, the difference is quite striking. The price is comparatively high, but the meat is superb and something our customers look forward to buying as a seasonal treat.

All around Britain you will find special kinds of lamb. Salt marsh lamb comes from animals that have grazed near the sea, again taking on some of the special flavour of their feed. Southdown lambs, on the other hand, were developed to feed on the sweet, herb-filled pasture of the Downs.

In the Lake District, the Herdwick sheep are 'hefted' or instinctively belong to a particular area that they roam, and the farmer gathers them in at certain times of year. Gareth Wyn Jones, sometimes known as the 'tweeting farmer' for his use of social media, is another of our suppliers, providing beautiful Welsh hillside lamb. Again, the way the sheep are adapted to the environment is what makes this meat special.

Farming, not least hill farming, can be a hard life, so we like to play our part in ensuring that fine lamb from such places reaches a wide audience who will choose it over frozen imports from the other side of the world. It's all part of the joy and value of buying from a traditional butcher.

3
Pork

As the saying goes, you really can eat every part of a pig except the squeak. At Lidgate's, we buy whole pigs and find a use for every scrap – even the trotters, which make the very best stock because of the flavour and unctuous texture they impart. Most other pork offcuts go into sausages and mince.

At a butcher's the more tender prime cuts, such as loin chops, get pride of place on the counter, but you'll also see the less well-known and good-value parts of the animal. There's a fine tradition of pork butchery in Britain, and some specialists are famous for their pork pies and regional preparations, such as Lincolnshire stuffed chine.

Pork used to be known as the 'real roast of England' because it was affordable to many more people than beef. Pigs were once commonly kept by households in the countryside and even in towns. They were housed in a sty, fed on scraps, and killed in the autumn, when some parts were eaten fresh and others were salted and preserved as hams and bacon to eat during the leaner months. This tradition has resulted in not just plenty of pork recipes, but also many dishes that use preserved pork, including the great British breakfast of bacon and eggs.

Over recent decades, and to the great detriment of flavour, pigs have been bred to be much leaner than previously. Of course, vast amounts of fat on a piece of pork are not desirable, but having some adds a great deal to a dish.

Another adverse development is that pigs have also come to be reared indoors in industrial systems, which are allowed to keep them in shamefully cramped and unnatural conditions. The result is cheap but the meat sometimes has a strange, greyish appearance when cooked, and fat that is flaccid and unappetizing. In

fact, such meat is difficult to cook well, so no wonder pork is less popular than it used to be. Intensive rearing methods go completely against the rootling and sociable nature of pigs, so we advise buying free-range, which allows the animals to lead a proper life and gives the meat a much better texture and flavour.

Buying cheaply reared meat is definitely a false economy because you lose so much in texture and flavour. Eat a bit less and of better quality and you'll really notice the difference. At Lidgate's, as at many other quality butchers, we sell pork only from females because the males can have what is called 'boar taint' – an offensive hormonal odour – and we always sell meat from animals that live a proper life rather than being shut away.

The one kind of pork that we do import from overseas is Iberico pork from the Pata Negra or black-hoofed pig, which is reared in west and southwest Spain, and also in central Portugal. The best of these animals live in oak forests, where they forage for acorns. The breed is well known for making great hams, but the fresh pork is also wonderful, and another example of a traditional animal that has come back into fashion.

Pork Cuts

Belly and spare ribs – pork belly is cut up for terrines, stews and pies, but is also one of our favourite parts of the pig to roast (see page 221). Whereas other pork cuts can become dry when cooked, the belly never does. We prefer the thick end, towards the front of the animal, and it can be roasted flat with the bone in, or boned and rolled. Spare ribs are rib bones with a decent amount of belly meat attached, and may be cooked in a sheet or individually (see page 120). Belly is also the source of streaky bacon. Butchers often have it in a whole piece, like pancetta, which you can cut into cubes to add flavour and unctuousness to a sauce or stew.

Cheek – *see* Head

Ears – *see* Head

Fat – when rendered (melted down), pork fat becomes lard, which is a traditional and tasty cooking medium, and an often overlooked ingredient for pastry (see pages 116 and 129). Lard tastes better from free-range pigs, but can be hard to find, so try our straightforward recipe for it (see page 113). Butchers who make their own sausages may well have spare fat; otherwise, ask a butcher to put some aside for you. Another good fat product is Italian lardo (cured back fat), which is ideal to wrap around lean cuts to keep them moist and well flavoured. Caul fat is a webbed, soft fat from between the pig's belly and the stomach; it's useful for holding meat together, as in faggots.

Hand and knuckle – the hand is an old-fashioned cheap roasting cut, now more often used for braising. The end of the shoulder or leg is known as the knuckle (or a hock on a pig cured for bacon and ham). A knuckle, from the front or back leg, is sometimes used as a small and inexpensive Sunday roast. The shape is slightly awkward to carve – you really pull the meat off the bone – but the taste is good. Butchers sometimes sell the hock end of a cooked ham or an uncooked gammon for delicious soup (see page 119).

Head – although we do sell the occasional pig's head, we usually remove the meat and use it for brawn, stock and soups. The tasty round cheek muscle is separated out and can be braised whole, as on page 125, or the whole cheek is made into a small ham called a Bath Chap. In Denmark the cheek is cold-smoked and thinly sliced, and in Italy it is cured as *guanciale*, the best cut of all for spaghetti carbonara. Pig's ears can be brined, sliced, coated in breadcrumbs and deep-fried for a delicious snack.

Leg, chump and knuckle – relatively tender and quick to cook, the leg can easily become dry, so take care not to overcook it. It can be roast whole, or chopped up for stir-fries, braises or quick-frying with a sauce. The top end, or chump, is sometimes cut into pork steaks, but is more often diced, sliced for stir-fries, minced or put into sausages. Leg can be cut into two roasting joints: the top fillet and the lower knuckle end. The end of the leg, near the trotter, is a small, economical and tasty roasting joint in its own right (see page 218). Ask for this unusual cut in advance.

Loin, chops and baby back ribs – loin sits inside the pig's ribcage and is the most tender and expensive part of the animal. It's the source of premium bone-in chops, and a good roasting joint with lots of crackling (the back of a pig produces better crackling than the belly). For the best crackling, we like to score the skin with lines about a finger width apart. A butcher will bone and stuff loin for an easy-carving joint for a dinner party, and a crown roast, made of two loins, is another showpiece. Loin chops are tender but can dry out, especially if from a lean breed of pig. To counteract this, you can brine the chops before cooking them (see page 124). Boned loin can be rolled up with the fattier belly to make Porchetta (see page 272). Bones removed from the loin become baby back ribs. These have less meat than spare ribs, but are inexpensive and good when slathered with sauce (see page 120).

Mince – this varies, depending on which part of the animal it comes from. Mince made from pork belly is quite fatty, and best for terrines; mince from the shoulder or leg is relatively lean, so is better for quick cooking. Many dishes, including our sausages, include both types of mince. Pork mince takes up flavours nicely and is good to use in combination with beef or lamb mince, as in the traditional beef-pork mix used for an Italian pasta sauce. In East Asia, pork mince is combined with chopped prawns for a juicy texture and good flavour (see page 112).

Shoulder – cheap and well flavoured, shoulder is one of the best cuts for smoothly textured stews, but it also makes a large, good-value joint for slow roasting. The meat softens into a spoonable texture that takes up flavours beautifully (see page 214). Shoulder can also be boned, rolled and cut into smaller pieces, such as ribeye, which is tasty but doesn't have crackling. Sliced shoulder steaks can be quickly grilled or fried, then cut across the grain to make the meat less chewy (see page

228). A pig doesn't have much of a neck, with its head continuing straight into its shoulder. At the end of the shoulder and start of the head, the round fillet muscle that runs along the back tapers down to become a mix of fat and meat. This part of the animal may be referred to as 'neck' and is good for slow cooking at a low temperature.

Tenderloin or fillet – a tender cylinder of meat, tenderloin can be cut into medallions and quick-fried, or kept whole, browned on the outside and finished off in the oven. Either way, serve with a sauce to add succulence. You can also wrap the fillet in bacon or pancetta, poach until done, then crisp up the outside in a frying pan.

Trotters – much prized by good cooks, trotters are put into stock – beef and chicken, as well as pork. We have customers who order trotters cut in half or quarters to release even more of their flavour and gelatinous texture (see page 110).

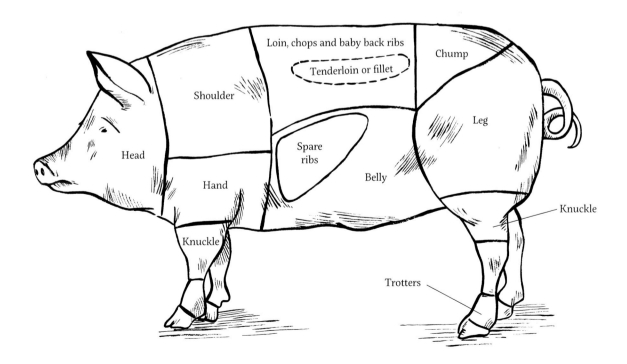

Pork Cuts

1 Trotter
2 Hand and hock
3 Belly
4 Shoulder
5 Leg and knuckle
6 Chump

7 Spare ribs
8 Mince
9 Loin chops
10 Tenderloin / Fillet
11 Loin and baby back ribs

Good butcher's sausages add lots of flavour and oomph to one-pot dishes. Here they make a tasty and inexpensive supper, suitable for family or friends. The dish was inspired by Lidgate's pork and Guinness sausages. The dark beer adds a savoury depth and here goes well, in both looks and taste, with the dark prunes and fresh leeks. Firm green lentils absorb the flavour of the other ingredients and give the dish body, making a most satisfying all-in-one meal.

Pork sausages with prunes, Guinness & lentils

Serves 4

2 tablespoons good lard, olive oil or vegetable oil

8 meaty pork sausages

2 leeks, sliced

1½ tablespoons plain flour

250ml (8fl oz) Guinness or other stout

500ml (17fl oz) chicken or pork stock

18 whole pitted prunes

100g (3½oz) firm green lentils (e.g. Puy or other small round lentils)

squeeze of lemon juice or pinch of demerara sugar (optional)

2 tablespoons roughly chopped flat leaf parsley

sea salt flakes and freshly ground black pepper

Place 1 tablespoon of the lard or oil in a flameproof casserole dish over a medium-high heat. When hot, add the sausages and brown them all over (about 8–10 minutes). You might need to do this in 2 batches, depending on the size of your dish. Set aside on a plate.

Add the remaining tablespoon of fat to the pan. When hot, add the leeks and cook over a medium-low heat until soft (about 5 minutes).

Sprinkle over the flour and stir for a minute. Pour in the stout, bring to the boil and let it bubble away for a couple of minutes. Add the stock, prunes and lentils, then return the sausages back to the dish. Add a few twists of pepper and just a touch of salt as the sausages and stock are already salted). Bring to the boil, then simmer, uncovered, for 25–30 minutes, or until the lentils are tender – they don't need to be completely soft – and the sausages are cooked. Stir a couple of times whilst cooking and check the seasoning at the end, adjusting if necessary. If the dish is too salty, a squeeze of lemon juice or a pinch of demerara can make the dish more palatable.

Scatter the parsley over the dish and serve with mashed potato.

One of Lidgate's staff, Julia, first made gyoza dumplings when she was travelling, then she told us how to make them when she came back to Britain to train as a butcher. An essential part of the recipe is a deeply flavoured pork-bone broth made with a pig's trotter, a magic ingredient that you really should try. It becomes gelatinous when cooked, and this adds great flavour and a richly smooth texture to the liquid. Given notice, a butcher will happily put one aside for you. The superb stock that results lifts any dish into a different class. Fresh or frozen dumpling skins are easy to use and can be found in Chinese or Southeast Asian shops, or ordered online.

Gyoza dumplings with pork broth

Serves 6

100g (3½oz) shiitake mushrooms, finely sliced

1 leek, finely sliced

2 medium courgettes, cut into thin semicircles (optional)

3 spring onions, finely sliced

squeeze of lime or lemon juice

2 tablespoons finely chopped chives

For the broth

1kg (2lb) pork bones

1 pig's trotter (optional, but worth including)

2 onions, unpeeled, cut into quarters

1 carrot, cut into large chunks

2 celery sticks, cut into large chunks

2 leeks, roughly chopped

100g (3½oz) shiitake mushrooms, roughly chopped

6-cm (2½-in) piece of fresh root ginger, sliced

1 bay leaf

1 star anise

1 teaspoon peppercorns

Japanese soy sauce, to taste

For the dumplings

150g (5oz) minced pork belly

½ garlic clove, crushed

3.5-cm (1½-in) piece of fresh root ginger, finely grated

1 tablespoon finely chopped chives

1 teaspoon sesame oil

½ tablespoon Japanese soy sauce

1 teaspoon rice vinegar

18 dumpling skins, 9cm (3½in) in diameter

First make the broth. Put the pork bones and pig's trotter (if using) in a large pan. Add all the remaining broth ingredients apart from the soy sauce. Pour in 2.5 litres (4 pints) water and bring just to the boil, skimming off any froth that rises to the surface. Lower the heat, cover and simmer for at least 3 hours, or up to 6 hours.

Strain the liquid, discarding the solids. Add the soy sauce to taste. (This is essential to season the broth, as well as deepening the flavour.) Set aside.

To make the dumplings, mix all the filling ingredients together in a bowl. Lay out the dumpling skins and put about 1 teaspoon of filling slightly off-centre on each one. Dip your index finger in a bowl of water and wet around the perimeter of each skin. Fold the skin over the filling, carefully pushing the air out, to make a semicircle. Pinch the edges together to make a good seal. The dumplings are best made just before cooking, but can be made up to 12 hours in advance. Keep them in a single layer covered with clingfilm in the fridge.

When you want to eat, reheat the broth and boil hard for 2 minutes. Add the dumplings, remaining mushrooms and vegetables, bring back to the boil and simmer for 5 minutes, until the filling is piping hot and the dumpling cases cooked. Taste the stock and add a little soy sauce for extra saltiness, if necessary. A squeeze of lime or lemon juice will freshen the flavour.

Set out 6 bowls and pour about 300ml (½ pint) of the broth into each one. Divide the dumplings and vegetables between the bowls, sprinkle with the chopped chives and serve hot.

Vietnamese cooking is full of fragrant herbs, and these tasty little pork and prawn meatballs are flavoured with mint, dill and coriander. The classic dipping sauce for them is *nuoc cham*, which is super-easy to make and adds more beautiful east Asian seasoning to the meat. They make smart canapés to have with drinks, but will serve 4 as a starter, or 2 as a main course with rice and vegetables. A mix of shoulder and belly pork would be the perfect combination for the mince (use the medium-small plate on your mincer, if you have one), but any ready-made mince will work well as long as it's not too lean.

Vietnamese herby pork balls

Makes 32

6-cm (2½-in) piece of lemon grass, finely chopped

1 spring onion, finely chopped

1 small garlic clove, chopped

150g (5oz) cooked, peeled tiger prawns

2 tablespoons roughly chopped mint

2 tablespoons roughly chopped dill

2 tablespoons roughly chopped coriander

250g (8oz) minced pork

1 teaspoon soft brown sugar

2 tablespoons fish sauce

1 tablespoon olive oil, for frying

For the dipping sauce

juice of 1 lime or 2 tablespoon rice vinegar

2 teaspoons fish sauce

2 tablespoons caster sugar

2 tablespoons water

½ chilli, finely chopped (deseed it first if you want less heat)

Put the lemon grass, spring onion and garlic in a food processor and whizz to a paste. Add the prawns and herbs and whizz again to blend into the paste. Add the pork, sugar and fish sauce and whizz once more.

Tip the mixture on to a chopping board and knead lightly by hand to make sure the ingredients are properly combined. Bring together into a ball. Divide this into quarters and then divide each quarter into 4, so you have 32 pieces in total. Roll each piece into a small ball and place on a plate in a single layer. Cover loosely with clingfilm and put in the fridge for at least 30 minutes to firm up. This can be done a few hours in advance of cooking.

Meanwhile, make the dipping sauce by stirring all the ingredients together. Place in 2 small serving bowls.

Heat the oil in a frying pan. When hot, fry the meatballs for about 6 minutes, until cooked through and browned all over. Serve with the dipping sauce.

It can be hard to find lard from free-range pigs, but it isn't difficult to make your own, and so delicious. Just make sure to buy your fat from a good butcher as it means you can find out how the pig was farmed. The pork fat used for lard comes from two places: the back, where the fat is relatively hard, and the belly, which has a lining of soft fat. The latter, known as flare fat, is the easiest to render at home. It comes away from the animal in one piece and a butcher, given a decent amount of notice, will put it aside and sell it to you for a good price. Butchers who make their own sausages and bacon should have plenty of spare fat. Like shop-bought lard, the homemade variety can be used for frying and making pastry (see pages 116 and 129), adding superior flavour and a glossy appearance. As a bonus, making your own lard means you also get homemade pork scratchings, a wonderful treat to indulge in now and then.

Homemade lard & pork scratchings

Makes a small bowlful

1 piece of flare fat
sea salt flakes, for the scratchings

Preheat the oven to 180°C/350°F/Gas Mark 4.

Using a small sharp knife, not a food processor, chop the fat into small pieces about 1–2.5-cm (½–1-in) square. Alternatively, if you ask a butcher nicely, he or she might put it through a mincer for you (or use your own if you have one), but then you don't get the scratchings at the end.

Spread out the chopped fat in a roasting tray and put in the oven for about 10 minutes – until the fat starts to render (melt). As it does so, carefully pour it out of the roasting tray into a heatproof jug or bowl. Return the tray to the oven and repeat this process at 5-minute intervals. Take care the fat doesn't burn or it will taint the taste of the lard. You can filter the melted fat by pouring it through muslin to catch any brown bits and end up with snow-white lard. But if you're watchful during the rendering, you can pour off the fat before the rind gets too brown, and it won't be necessary to filter it.

When most of the fat has rendered, remove the brown remnants from the pan and set aside to cool. (The 3–4 tablespoons of fat remaining in the roasting tray can be used to make a really good toad-in-the-hole because plenty of fat is the secret of getting a lovely crispy base to your batter.)

Once cooled, cover the lard (and scratchings) and store in the fridge. When you want to eat the scratchings, put them on a baking sheet in an oven preheated to 180°C/350°F/Gas Mark 4 until the outside crisps up (about 4–5 minutes). Sprinkle with sea salt flakes before serving. These are soft scratchings with a melting texture – very filling yet also very more-ish.

Making your own pork pie may take a bit of time, but the process and end result are truly satisfying. It can all be done in advance, at your own pace. The reward is a beautiful pie that is a great centrepiece for a summer party or picnic.

Layered pork & apple pie

Makes 1 large pie (about 12 slices)

75g (3oz) dried apple

90ml (3½fl oz) cider or water

700g (1lb 6oz) pork shoulder, chopped into 5-mm (¼-in) pieces

125g (4oz) smoked or unsmoked streaky bacon, finely chopped

400g (13oz) pork belly, minced

25-g (1-oz) bunch of flat leaf parsley, leaves finely chopped

1 teaspoon dried thyme

¾ teaspoon finely grated nutmeg

½ teaspoon five-spice powder

½ teaspoon fine salt

1 teaspoon coarsely ground black pepper

6 tablespoons good-quality chutney, preferably apple

1 egg beaten with 2 tablespoons milk, for eggwash

150–200ml (5–7fl oz) pork stock made with a pig's trotter (see page 110)

For the hot-water crust

125g (4oz) lard, diced

125g (4oz) unsalted butter, diced

250ml (8fl oz) water

675g (1lb 5oz) plain flour, plus extra for dusting

1 teaspoon fine sea salt

2 medium eggs

Put the dried apple in a small bowl and pour in the cider or water. Set aside to soak for at least 1 hour.

To make the hot-water crust, put the lard, butter and water in a saucepan. Heat gently so that the fat melts but the water doesn't boil and start to evaporate. Leave to cool for 5 minutes.

Put the flour in a large bowl and mix in the salt. Make a well in the middle and crack in the eggs. Mix briefly with a fork, then gradually add the fat and water,

mixing first with a table knife, and then your fingers. Bring together into a ball. Lightly flour a work surface and knead the dough: you will find it more pliable and less firm than shortcrust. Roll into a ball, wrap in greaseproof paper or clingfilm and chill for 1 hour.

To make the filling, chop the meats as directed. This takes a little time and it is best to use a sharp knife for the pork shoulder and kitchen scissors for the bacon. Place in a bowl, add the herbs, spices, salt and pepper and mix thoroughly with your hands. Drain the apples and mix with the chutney in a separate bowl.

Preheat the oven to 180°C/350°F/Gas Mark 4.

Cut off a quarter of the pastry, rewrap it and place back in the fridge. Flour a work surface and roll the rest of the pastry into a circle about 35cm (14in) in diameter and 1cm (½in) thick. Use to line a 20-cm (8-in) springform cake tin, pressing the pastry gently to the bottom. It doesn't have to come right up the sides.

Spoon half the pork filling into the pastry case. Spread the chutney and apple mixture over it. Spoon the remaining pork filling on top and press down slightly.

Roll the reserved piece of pastry into a circle slightly bigger than the tin. Brush the perimeter of it with some of the eggwash. Place the pastry lid over the pie and press the edges together firmly, crimping them as you go. Cut a 2.5-cm (1-in) hole in the centre of the lid, then brush the whole surface with eggwash.

Bake the pie for 30 minutes, then lower the heat to 160°C/325°F/Gas Mark 3 and bake for another 1¼ hours. Take the pie out of the oven and remove the springform part of the tin. Brush the sides and top of the pie with the remaining eggwash and return to the oven for another 15 minutes. Set aside until just warm.

Meanwhile, if the stock is fridge-cold, bring it to the boil, then cool it quickly in a bowl of iced water, until just warm.

Carefully and gradually pour the stock through the hole so that it fills all the cavities in the pie (the filling shrinks slightly during baking). It might leak a little from the pastry case, but do not fret. Put the pie in the fridge so that the stock solidifies into a jelly.

The flavour of the pie improves with time, so is best made at least a day in advance, but can be kept in the fridge for up to 14 days. Serve in slices with a salad.

Butchers, given notice, will sell you streaky bacon in one piece that you can then chop into nice chunky cubes. Otherwise, cut up thick rashers of streaky. You can also use Italian pancetta for this dish, which is often sold in a piece or cubed, but perhaps use 50g (2oz) less as it can be saltier and more intense than butcher's bacon. Saffron is a luxurious ingredient that is strong enough to hold its own with bacon. These delectable flavours infuse the cream to make a special pasta sauce.

Pasta with cubed bacon, saffron, basil & cream

Serves 4

500g (1lb) piece of smoked streaky bacon, or 250–300g (8–10oz) smoked streaky rashers or pancetta cubes

1 tablespoon olive oil

1 teaspoon salt

300–400g (10–13oz) tagliatelle, according to appetite

¼–½ teaspoon good-quality saffron strands

1–2 tablespoons warm water

1–2 garlic cloves, finely chopped

300ml (½ pint) double cream

juice of ½ lemon

1 tablespoon finely grated Parmesan cheese (optional)

12 basil leaves

freshly ground black pepper

If using a whole piece of bacon, take off the rind, then cut off some of the fat if you wish, being careful to leave a good amount for the flavour it imparts. Cut the flesh into small cubes or strips about 1cm (½in) wide. You should end up with about 250g–300g (8–10oz) of cubes. If using bacon rashers, cut them into strips about 1.5cm (¾in) wide.

Heat the olive oil in a frying pan and cook the bacon over a medium heat, stirring occasionally, for 15 minutes or so, until browned (rashers will take less time than cubes).

Meanwhile, bring a large pan of water to the boil, add the salt (no more than 1 teaspoon, as the sauce will be salty) and then the pasta. Cook, stirring now and then, for 10–12 minutes, until al dente.

Meanwhile, crush or snip the saffron strands and soak them in the warm water for 10 minutes. This dissolves the waxy coating on the stamens and allows them to give a richer colour and flavour to the dish.

When the bacon is cooked, add the garlic to the pan and continue to fry for another minute or so. Pour in the cream plus the saffron and its water. Stir and allow to bubble for about 2 minutes or so to thicken slightly. Add the lemon juice and season with plenty of black pepper. If you want a richer sauce, add the Parmesan. Roughly tear the basil leaves into the sauce and stir until they have wilted. Turn off the heat.

Drain the pasta, reserving a little of the cooking water in the pan. Return the pasta to the pan, add the sauce and mix well. Taste and add a little more pepper or lemon juice if necessary.

A ham hock is very good value and makes delicious soup. This is the cured end of the leg and provides the dream team of sweet meat and tasty bone. In this case, the meat is smoked as well, adding yet more flavour. We make honey-roast smoked ham in the shop, and often have a hock or knuckle, as we call it, that can be used in the soup – hence the name of this recipe – but any kind of smoked ham hock will be great. The hock flavours the stock as it cooks, and then you can then use half the meat for sandwiches and other dishes, and half of it goes back into the soup.

Honey-roast ham hock & lentil soup

Serves 6–8

1 tablespoon olive oil

2 medium onions, finely chopped

3 medium carrots, finely chopped

2 celery sticks, finely chopped

4 garlic cloves, finely chopped

1 tablespoon ground cumin

250g (8oz) red lentils

2 bay leaves

½ teaspoon chilli flakes (optional)

500ml (17fl oz) dry cider

2 litres (3½ pints) water

1 smoked ham hock (about 1.25kg/3½lb)

lemon juice, if necessary

freshly ground black pepper

To serve

2 tablespoons roughly chopped flat leaf parsley

olive oil or thick yoghurt

toasted cumin seeds (optional)

Place the oil in a large pan over a medium-low heat. Add the onions, carrots and celery and fry for about 10 minutes, stirring occasionally, until soft.

Stir in the garlic, cumin, lentils and bay leaves. Add the chilli flakes, if using. Pour in the cider and water, stir to combine, then nestle the ham hock in the middle of the pan. If you haven't used chilli flakes, season with plenty of black pepper. Cover with a lid, bring just to the boil, then lower the heat and skim off the froth that rises to the surface. Cover and simmer for about 1½ hours, turning the hock over halfway through the cooking time. It's ready when the lentils have turned to mush and the hock is tender.

Transfer the meat to a plate and set aside to cool for 10 minutes. Tip the juices it releases back into the pan, then use a stick blender to purée the mixture. Taste for seasoning and add a squeeze of lemon juice if too salty.

Take the meat off the bone, chopping about half of it (250–275g/8–9oz) to stir back into the soup. Cut the rest into slices and store it in the fridge, ready to be used for sandwiches and other dishes.

Serve the soup with a sprinkling of parsley, a slick of olive oil or a dollop of yoghurt, and a sprinkle of toasted cumin seeds if you want to dress it up a bit.

There are two types of ribs. Baby-back ribs are taken off the loin and sold as small racks. These are tasty but don't have much meat. Spare ribs come from closer to the belly and can be magnificently meaty. Cut into single ribs with plenty of meat attached, they make a fantastic main course or part of a barbecue feast. Butchers and supermarkets can buy frozen spare ribs that are a by-product of pork production, but it's always best to go for fresh (and not previously frozen) if possible. The method below offers three different ways of finishing off the ribs. To ensure soft flesh and a crisp outside, first cook the ribs slowly, then marinate and cook them so that the marinade reduces down to a glaze towards the end of the cooking time.

Sticky spare ribs with a honey-pineapple glaze

Serves 4

4 single meaty pork spare ribs (about 750g/1½lb in total)

300ml (½ pint) pineapple juice

1 tablespoon sea salt flakes

½ tablespoon five-spice powder

For the honey-pineapple marinade/glaze

200ml (7fl oz) pineapple juice

3 tablespoons Japanese soy sauce

2 garlic cloves, crushed

½ teaspoon five-spice powder

1½ tablespoons soft brown sugar

3 tablespoons honey

2 tablespoons olive oil

Place the ribs in a large pan, then add the pineapple juice and enough water to cover them (about 300ml/½ pint). Add the salt and five-spice powder. Bring to the boil, then cover and simmer for about 1 hour, or until tender.

Meanwhile, put all the marinade ingredients into a pan. Bring to the boil and bubble away for 3–4 minutes, until slightly thickened.

When the ribs are cooked, drain off the liquid. Pour the marinade into a shallow, non-metallic dish or a Ziplock plastic food bag and add the ribs, turning them over until thoroughly coated. Once cold, leave to marinate in the fridge for at least 1 hour, but overnight if you have time, turning them occasionally.

To grill the ribs

Heat a grill to its highest setting. Line a baking tray with foil, arrange the ribs on it and place under the grill about 7cm (3in) below the heat source. Cook for 3 minutes on each side, basting now and then with the marinade, until browned and heated through; the marinade will thicken into a glaze. When done, roll the ribs around to give them a final coating of the glaze and serve straight away.

To fry the ribs

Place an empty heavy-based frying pan over the heat. Once good and hot, add the ribs, reserving the marinade. Cook on one side until starting to brown, then turn and cook the other side. Once the meat is hot all the way through, pour in the marinade and heat until it has reduced to a glaze and the meat is coated and sticky.

To barbecue the ribs

Light a barbecue and wait until the flames have died down to a hot grey ash. Place the ribs on the rack, reserving the marinade. Cook on both sides, turning occasionally and brushing with the marinade, until charred, glazed and cooked through.

At its simplest, a sausage roll can just be a sausage wrapped in pastry, but it's really easy to posh it up a bit by adding extra flavourings. The possibilities are endless – or at least as broad as the contents of your fridge and store cupboard – but here are a few ideas. Try adding chopped bacon, Stilton or caramelized onion chutney to a good pork or venison sausage; apricot or mango chutney to a spicy merguez or pork and chilli sausage; or Thai chilli sauce to a chicken sausage. To make elegant cocktail rolls, cut the sausages into small pieces before wrapping them in pastry. To make a posh monster sausage roll, encase all the meat in puff pastry and cut the sausage roll into four large pieces once cooked.

Posh sausage rolls

Serves 4

4 meaty sausages (about 100g/3½oz each)

plain flour, for dusting

500g (1lb) puff pastry

1 egg whisked with 2 tablespoons milk

1 teaspoon nigella or poppy seeds, or 2 teaspoons sesame seeds, to garnish

For the extra flavourings (choose one kind according to your sausagemeat)

75g (3oz) smoked back bacon (about 3 rashers), finely chopped

65g (2½oz) Stilton cheese, finely crumbled

3 tablespoons chutney

Slit the sausage casings open and ease the meat into a bowl, discarding the skin. Add the extra flavouring of your choice and mix it in with your hands.

Lightly wet your hands and shape the meat back into 4 sausage shapes about 11cm (4½in) long.

Lightly flour a work surface and roll out the pastry to the thickness of a £1 coin. Cut into 4 rectangles measuring 20 x 15cm (8 x 6in). Brush around the edge of each with the eggwash or water. Place a sausage off-centre on each rectangle and fold the pastry over the top to enclose it. Press to seal tightly. Transfer to a plate, cover with clingfilm and place in the fridge for at least 15 minutes to set firm. The rolls can be chilled for up to 5 hours.

Preheat the oven to 220°C/425°F/Gas Mark 7 and insert a baking tray to heat up. Brush the rolls with the eggwash. Sprinkle with the seeds, if using, and lightly pat down. (If using various meats and fillings, you can top the rolls with different seeds to show which is which, e.g. sesame seeds on lamb and chutney rolls, or poppy seeds on pork and Stilton rolls.) Transfer the sausage rolls to the hot baking tray and bake for 25 minutes, or until the pastry has browned and the meat within is cooked through.

Pork chops can often be a touch dry when cooked, but immersing them in brine for 10–12 hours beforehand will keep them moist and add flavour during cooking. This simple trick is used by chefs and is a great one to adopt at home. The brine or cure contains sugar, so it is best to brown the chops briefly in a pan, and then put them in the oven; this is because they can over-caramelize if cooked over direct heat. The honey and lemon in the sauce enhances the sweet-salty-sour combination that is so delicious when it comes to pork.

Juicy pork chops with sweet-and-sour red peppers

Serves 4

4 pork loin chops
1 tablespoon olive oil

For the brine
1 litre (1¾ pints) water
4 tablespoons sea salt flakes
3 tablespoons demerara sugar
2 star anise
2 bay leaves
3–4 bushy sprigs of thyme

For the sauce
1 large garlic clove, finely chopped
160g (5½oz) piquillo peppers from a jar, drained and roughly chopped
leaves from 4 sprigs of thyme
50ml (2fl oz) dry sherry
2 tablespoons lemon juice
2–3 teaspoons honey, or to taste

First make the brine by combining all the ingredients for it in a shallow non-metallic container. Stir well to help dissolve the salt and sugar. Put the pork chops in the brine, cover and place in the fridge for 10–12 hours.

Remove the chops from the brine and pat dry with kitchen paper. Cut off all the rind, and some of the fat if you wish, but leave a decent amount on to help the chops to cook well; you can always cut it off on the plate if you don't want to eat it. Use kitchen scissors or a sharp knife to cut about 1cm (½in) into the fat at 5-cm (2-in) intervals. This stops the chops from curling up when cooking.

Preheat the oven to 180°C/350°F/Gas Mark 4. Pour the oil into an ovenproof frying pan and place over a medium heat. When hot, use tongs to hold the chops fat-edge down in the pan for 1 minute or so, until lightly browned, allowing the fat to run slightly. Then briefly brown the meat for about 1½–2 minutes on each side (the sugar in the cure means it will brown more quickly than usual).

Place the pan in the oven, or transfer the chops to a roasting tray, and cook for 5–10 minutes, or until cooked through and the juices run clear. The exact timing will depend upon the thickness of your chops. When done, keep them warm on a serving plate.

To make the sauce, place the pan over the heat and sizzle the garlic in it for a few seconds, then add the peppers and thyme. Cook for a minute or so, to soften slightly. Pour in the sherry and lemon juice. Bubble up so it thickens slightly, then add the honey. Pour the sauce over the chops and serve hot.

The chunky round muscle of a pork cheek used to be widely appreciated, but fell from favour as people turned to more expensive cuts. This 'forgotten' food has now been rediscovered by chefs, who have put them back on the menu in flavourful, well-priced dishes. Everyone who tries pork cheeks loves them for their tender yet toothsome texture and superb flavour. Here they are slow-cooked, with black pudding standing in for the morcilla that the Spanish would use. You can also replace the fresh or canned chickpeas with the excellent Spanish bottled ones.

Order cheeks in advance so that the butcher can put them aside or order them in. Make sure you ask for the single round cheek muscles with the jowl and rind trimmed away.

Spanish pork cheeks with chickpeas & black pudding

Serves 6

1 tablespoon good-quality lard or olive oil

2 onions, sliced

3 celery sticks, 1 finely sliced and 2 cut into large batons about 7 x 1.5cm (3 x 1½in)

2 garlic cloves, finely chopped

¼ teaspoon sea salt

2 teaspoons Spanish smoked paprika

2 regular red peppers or 3 long romano peppers, deseeded and cut into 5-cm (2-in) strips

1 green pepper, deseeded and cut into large squares

100g (3½oz) dried chickpeas, soaked in water overnight, or use 400g (14oz) canned or jarred chickpeas, drained and rinsed

4 pork cheeks (about 475g/15oz in total), cut into 6 pieces each

1 x 400-g (14-oz) can chopped tomatoes

200ml (7fl oz) apple juice

500ml (17fl oz) pork or chicken stock

150g (5oz) black pudding, casing removed and filling cut into 2.5-cm (1-in) chunks

3 tablespoons roughly chopped flat leaf parsley

freshly ground black pepper

Preheat the oven to 160°C/325°F/Gas Mark 3.

Heat the lard or oil in a flameproof casserole dish over a medium-low heat. Add the onions, the finely sliced celery and the garlic, then season with the salt and a few good twists of pepper. Cook gently for 15 minutes, until soft.

Sprinkle the smoked paprika over the onion mixture and stir well. Add the peppers and cook gently for a couple of minutes to soften slightly. If using chickpeas you've soaked yourself, drain them and add to the pan now, along with the pork cheeks, celery batons, tomatoes, apple juice and stock. Bring to the boil, then cover and place in the oven for 1 hour.

If using canned or jarred chickpeas, add them to the pan now and cook for another 30 minutes. Gently stir in the black pudding and cook for another 30 minutes, or until the pork is tender.

Before serving, scatter the chopped parsley over the dish. Serve with mashed potato and a green vegetable, such as Savoy cabbage or green beans.

High-quality butcher's bacon is good enough to showcase, as in this Brit version of a quiche lorraine. Lard makes great pastry, pliable and strong, so it's easy to form and roll, and delicious to eat.

Bacon & egg tart
with a lard crust

Serves 4–6

knob of good lard or unsalted butter

150g (5oz) banana shallots, finely sliced

200g (7oz) smoked back bacon, cut into strips 2.5cm (1in) thick

4 whole eggs, plus 2 yolks (and an optional 3 eggs for decoration)

300ml (½ pint) double cream

200ml (7fl oz) milk

freshly grated nutmeg

25g (1oz) Parmesan cheese, freshly grated

salt and freshly ground black pepper

For the pastry

150g (5oz) plain flour, plus extra for dusting

75g (3oz) good-quality cold lard or unsalted butter, cut into small cubes

1 large egg, or 1 medium egg and a dash of water, beaten

fine sea salt

First make the pastry. Put the flour and a pinch of salt into a mixing bowl. Add the fat and rub it in using the tips of your fingers. When the mixture resembles breadcrumbs, add the egg, stirring it in with the blade of a table knife. Then, using your fingertips, gradually form the mixture into a dough. Knead lightly and form into a ball. Wrap in greaseproof paper or clingfilm and place in the fridge for 30 minutes.

Dust a work surface with flour and roll the pastry into a circle about 35cm (14in) in diameter. Drape the pastry over your rolling pin and unroll it over a 25-cm (10-in) loose-bottomed tart tin about 3.5cm (1½in) deep. Push the pastry carefully but firmly into the tin and trim off the excess. Place in the fridge for at least 15 minutes, or up to 1 day if doing this well in advance, in which case cover it with clingfilm.

To make the filling, melt the lard or butter in a large frying pan. Add the shallots and bacon plus a pinch of salt and a few twists of pepper. Cook over a medium-low heat for about 30 minutes, or until the shallots are soft and sweet but still pale, stirring quite often towards the end. You're not looking to get much colour on the bacon, just to cook it through.

Put the eggs, yolks, cream, milk and nutmeg in a bowl and whisk together. Season lightly with salt and pepper and set aside.

Preheat the oven to 190°C/375°F/Gas Mark 5 and insert a baking sheet to heat through – this will help the base of the tart to cook properly. Line the pastry case with greaseproof paper and baking beans or uncooked rice, place on the hot tray and blind-bake for 10 minutes. Remove the paper and beans and cook the pastry for another 5 minutes to colour slightly.

Lower the oven to 160°C/325°F/Gas Mark 3.

Spread the bacon and onion inside the pastry case. Whisk up the reserved egg mixture to redistribute the seasoning, then carefully pour it over the filling. If you want to give the tart a trio of sun-like yolks for decoration, carefully crack the 3 extra eggs over the top so that the yolks sit in the middle. Scatter over half the Parmesan and add a final twist of pepper.

Bake the tart for about 40 minutes, turning it around after 20 minutes, and scattering the rest of the Parmesan over it to get a two-tone effect. The tart is ready when the filling is set and browned in patches. Eat hot, warm or cold with a green salad.

In the shop we sometimes have leftover cooked sausages, so we developed this pie to make good use of them, and included the caramelized onions to give it the flavour of an onion gravy. Our customers liked this dish so much that we now cook sausages specifically to make it. Many of our pies sell best during the colder months, but this is a year-round favourite, perhaps because people associate sausages with summer barbecues, and perhaps because the sweetness of the onions feels light and right for summer as well as colder days.

Sausage & mash pie with caramelized onions

Serves 6

25g (1oz) unsalted butter

2 tablespoons olive oil

500g (1lb) red onions, sliced

2 tablespoons caster sugar

2 tablespoons sherry vinegar

1 tablespoon plain flour

500ml (17fl oz) beef stock

8 cooked sausages, cut into chunks

small pinch of ground cloves (optional)

¼ teaspoon ground nutmeg (optional)

knob of unsalted butter, cut into small pieces

50g (2oz) Cheddar cheese, grated

sea salt and freshly ground black pepper

For the mash topping

1kg (2lb) baking or floury potatoes (e.g. King Edward), peeled and chopped into medium chunks

1 teaspoon sea salt flakes

25g (1oz) unsalted butter

250ml (8fl oz) milk

Place the butter and oil in a large frying pan over a medium heat. When hot, add the onions and a good pinch of salt and cook for 10 minutes, stirring occasionally. Lower the heat and soften gently for another 20 minutes.

Meanwhile, make the mash. Put the potatoes and salt in a large pan, cover with water and bring to the boil. Lower the heat and simmer until tender. Drain thoroughly. Add the butter and milk and mash well so there are no lumps.

Preheat the oven to 190°C/375°F/Gas Mark 5.

Add the sugar and vinegar to the softened onions and simmer for about 5 minutes. Sprinkle in the flour and cook, stirring, for 1 minute. Add the stock and stir well to combine, then simmer for another 10 minutes, or until the sauce has thickened. Add the chopped sausages to the onion mixture. Season with salt and pepper, and the spices, if using. (Cloves and nutmeg go well with traditional pork sausages, but vary the spices according to your banger.)

Put the filling into a 30 x 20-cm (12 x 8-in) pie dish and top with the mash. Use a fork to make a criss-cross pattern over the top. Dot the pieces of butter over the surface, scatter the cheese on top and add a few twists of pepper.

Put the pie in the oven for 25 minutes, until golden brown. Serve with seasonal greens or traditional baked beans.

The best sausages

Lidgate's hand-makes around 26 kinds of sausage, always in small batches, so they are eaten fresh. There's often a tasting selection on the counter, which promotes delicious new creations, such as venison with crushed juniper, or pork and wild garlic, and we also like to show off several old favourites.

When Lidgate's started making sausages about 30 years ago, it had become an unusual craft for a city butcher. Country butchers, with more space at the back of their premises, still made their own, but the status of the sausage wasn't all that high, and many butchers bought them in. Danny's father, David Lidgate, decided to make the best sausages possible, and we've never looked back.

Sausages are now considered good grub, and have moved from breakfast to an all-day food that is served in gastropubs and restaurants. Everyone loves a sausage. For our summer street party we barbecue about 30kg (66lb) in three hours, and demand is such that we can never get them cut up and on to toothpicks fast enough.

What sets a good sausage apart? First of all, you need good-quality meat: that really does make a big difference. Then you need natural casings as opposed to synthetic ones. For standard-size sausages we use pig intestines, and smaller lamb ones for the chipolatas. Most mass-market sausages use synthetic casings, but we think these lack flavour and don't crisp up well. Compared to the real deal, it's like eating sausagemeat wrapped in plastic.

The texture of the mince, which is determined by the size of the mincer plates it passes through, give the meat the right level of coarseness – something to get your teeth into, rather than a textureless pulp. You also need the right mixture of meat and fat. For pork sausages, we use mostly shoulder and belly, plus the odd chop and offcuts of pork rump and leg.

Then come the flavourings, some of which have been developed over a long time. For example, our

Victoria and Albert sausage, flavoured with horseradish and mustard, is made from an old family recipe that we've tweaked a little bit. The original Victorian version was considered too strong for present-day palates, so we made some adjustments to make it more subtle and delicious. Some recipes, however, never change. We believe our Old English Sausage has just the right amount of ground cloves and a hint of nutmeg. As with the meat, it's important to use good-quality ingredients and to pay attention to texture, such as getting the right size chunks of nut in our chicken, asparagus and pistachio sausages.

The style of a British banger, as opposed to the all-meat and cured Continental sausages, means that, in general, we add bit of rusk and water to the mix. The sausage-maker uses his skill and judgement to get exactly the right amount into each batch to get the right kind of juicy texture. Customer tastes and dietary needs also play a part in what Lidgate's sell. We make sausages from different kinds of meat, not just pork, and have developed a low-salt chipolata for children, and a number of gluten-free bangers, such as our wild boar sausage, that are 100 per cent meat.

The shelf-life of our fresh butcher's bangers is shorter than those bought from supermarkets, but we don't consider that a problem. Our sausages are intended to be enjoyed soon after getting them home, not left in the fridge for days and regarded as convenience food when there's nothing else to eat. A sausage, too, can be special.

4
Chicken

Chicken is now Britain's most popular meat, and available in several different forms: whole birds, chicken pieces, chopped fillet and occasionally mince.

'Poultry is to the cook what canvas is for the painter' wrote the eighteenth-century gastronome Jean Anthelme Brillat-Savarin. As this chapter shows, chicken is a meat that can take every sort of flavour, from aromatic spices and intense herbs to sharp citrus, the mineral edge of asparagus and subtle sauces. But a proper chicken is also magnificent just plain roasted.

Versatile chicken also suits a wide range of cooking styles. It can be poached, roasted, grilled, fried, casseroled, curried ... you name it! On page 160 is a recipe for escalopes that take just minutes to cook, and we also explain how to make escalopes yourself, both from breasts and inexpensive thighs.

As with all meat, it's good to cook chicken on the bone to get the very best flavour and juiciness, but boneless meat is certainly convenient. Chicken fillet, for example, is perfect for baking in a pie, and we have recipes for two great ones. Our popular Chicken & Asparagus Pie is on page 141, and we've also included Jerk Chicken Pie (see page 138), a recipe we tailor-made for a customer who wanted it for a church fête.

A high-quality, slow-grown bird makes a magnificent roast, and for this we tend to sell large birds at least 70 days old and weighing about 2kg (4lb 8oz) when oven-ready. These birds are more expensive than faster-grown ones, but ultimately good value. If they have been well reared outside, the skin will be thicker – ideal for crisping up – and they will have more meat with a better structure and richer flavour. The bones too will be stronger, and therefore good for combining with the giblets to make stock and gravy. (When you don't have bones to hand, it's worth seeking out butchers who supply restaurants with ready-jointed birds because, on particular days, they will have piles of spare bones, wings and chicken backs that can be used to make excellent stock.)

When buying a bird, look out for unblemished skin and clean leg joints. Intensively or poorly farmed can have what's known as 'hock burn', a dark mark on their leg joints that indicates they have sat immobile on their litter. Remember, it's much better value to buy a whole bird than pieces – just follow the step-by-step instructions on page 136 to joint it yourself.

As an alternative to chicken, you might like to buy a poussin – a small young bird that is ideal for one person. We usually sell them spatchcocked (opened out and flattened) in a marinade, which makes them quicker to cook. The recipe for our delicious Peri-peri Poussin is on page 150, and the hot and sharp sauce also lends itself to many other uses.

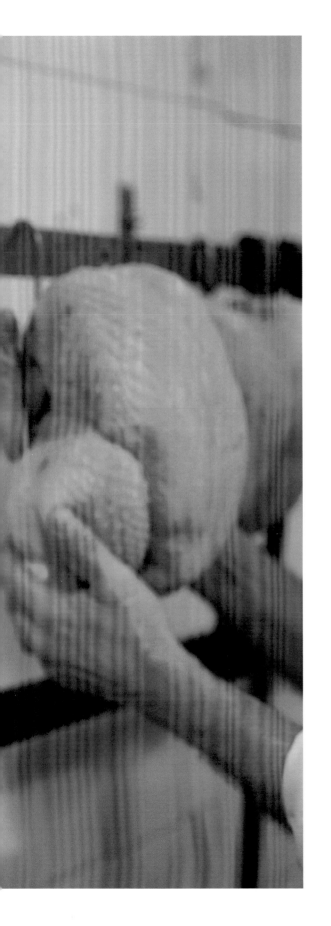

How to joint a chicken

This butcher's method of jointing a chicken into eight pieces keeps as much of the bird on the bone as possible. (Cooking meat on the bone improves its taste and juiciness.) Use the rest of the bones for stock.

I If necessary, untruss the chicken so that the legs are not tied together. Pull the legs forward and spread them out slightly. Cut the skin between the legs and the body.

2 Use a sharp, large knife to cut diagonally under the breasts until you get to the backbone at the end of the leg bones. To help break the backbone, hook your thumb into the cavity and pull the breast half-back, holding on to the legs. Use the knife to cut through the backbone and separate the chicken into two halves.

3 Pull one drumstick downwards and away from the thigh so it comes out of its socket. Repeat on the other side. On one leg, cut around the round 'oyster', then hold the leg up so you can more easily cut down to remove the leg and thigh from the backbone. Repeat for the other leg.

4 Cut the spur off the end of each leg and discard or use for stock. Trim off and discard any excess skin.

5 To separate the drumstick from the thigh, look for the diagonal seam of fat that runs between the drumstick and the thigh, and use your thumb to feel where the joint is.

6 Cut diagonally through the seam of fat and through the joint, pressing down on the back of the knife if necessary. Repeat for the other leg, so you have two drumsticks and two thighs.

7 Turn the breast half of the chicken so it is skin-side down. Trim away the loose skin at the neck and, if you like, cut out the wish bone so you can cut the bird in half more easily. Position your knife along the middle of the breastbone at the neck end and cut through it using a chopping or sawing motion. You will need to press on the heel of your knife to get through the tougher first bit of the bone, then use your free hand to press on the back of the knife to give the blade enough force to cut through the cartilage (alternatively, you can cut to one side of the cartilage, which is easier but less neat).

8 Separate the two pieces of breast and trim off any loose flaps of skin.

9 Put one breast skin-side down on the work surface. Trace the breastbone to find where cartilage turns to bone about a third of the way from the tip of the breast. You cut here to get two equal portions in terms of flesh (one piece has more bone, the other more breast). Place the tip of your knife here, then cut down hard, pressing down on the back of the knife with your other hand, and cutting through the ribs at a slight angle (alternatively, you can trim off some of the ribs before cutting). Finally, cut off the wing tips. Repeat for the other breast.

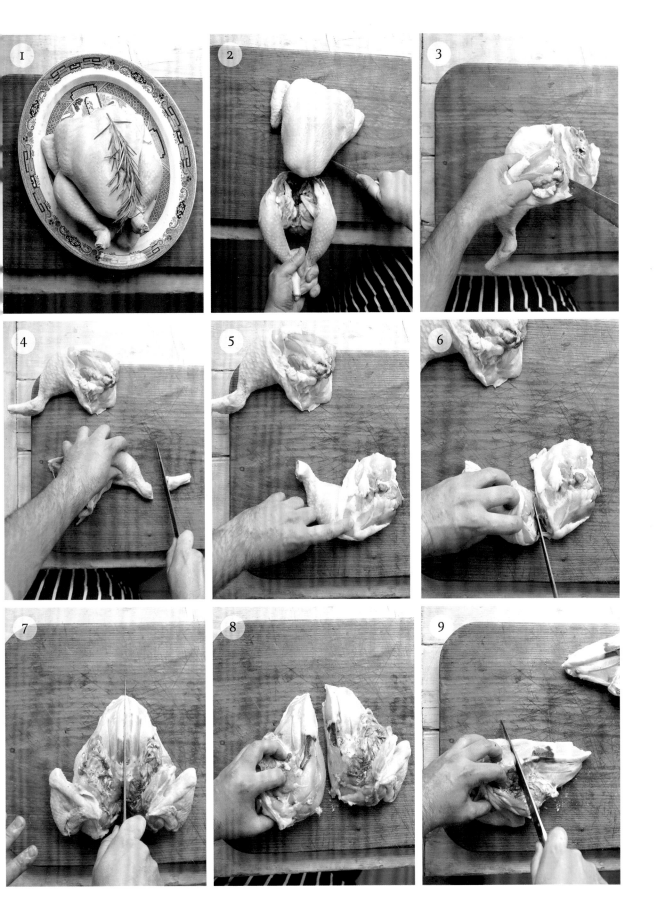

Jamaican jerk seasoning, heady with allspice, thyme and chilli, is a tasty addition to a Caribbean-style chicken pie, the meat mixed with a light and creamy coconut sauce, and topped with golden sweet potato mash. Colourful and packed with flavour, this is a pie for summer and winter alike. Spice it hot or not: the pie is delicious either way.

Jerk chicken pie

Serves 6

1 tablespoon olive or vegetable oil

2 red onions, finely sliced

3 peppers, ideally red, yellow, green, deseeded and finely sliced

625g (1¼lb) chicken thigh fillets, cut into 5-cm (2-in) chunks

¾ tablespoon jerk seasoning

finely grated zest of 1 lime

100g (3½oz) fresh coriander, leaves roughly chopped

½ teaspoon dried thyme leaves, or slightly more if fresh

knob of butter, chopped into small pieces

chilli flakes (optional)

6 lime wedges, to serve

For the mash

750g (1½lb) sweet potatoes, peeled and cut into medium chunks

500g (1lb) floury potatoes, peeled and cut into medium chunks

75g (3oz) unsalted butter

½ teaspoon grated nutmeg

50–75ml (2–3fl oz) milk

salt and freshly ground black pepper

For the sauce

400ml (14fl oz) milk

250ml (8fl oz) coconut cream (not milk)

50g (2oz) butter, cut into small pieces

2 tablespoons plain flour

Preheat the oven to 190°C/375°F/Gas Mark 5.

First make the mash. Put the sweet potatoes and potatoes in a saucepan, cover with water and season well with salt. Bring to the boil, then simmer until tender. Drain and mash well with the butter, nutmeg and just enough milk to make a firm mash (not sloppy). Season to taste, then set aside.

While the potatoes are cooking, make the sauce by putting the milk, coconut cream, butter and flour in a large saucepan. Bring slowly to the boil, whisking constantly. Simmer for 2 minutes to thicken slightly, stirring or whisking, and taking care the mixture doesn't boil over.

Heat the oil in a large ovenproof frying pan. When hot, add the onions and peppers and fry over a medium heat, stirring occasionally, until soft (about 10 minutes). Add the chicken, jerk seasoning and lime zest and cook for 5 minutes, stirring quite often to prevent the chicken sticking. Pour in the coconut sauce and stir well, scraping up any tasty bits on the bottom of the pan. Simmer over a medium-low heat for 10 minutes, stirring occasionally, then mix in the coriander leaves.

Carefully dollop the mash all over the chicken mixture and spread it out with a table knife. Use a fork to make a criss-cross on top. Sprinkle with the thyme, then dot with the chopped butter. You can also scatter a few chilli flakes on top if you like things spicy – the amount depends on the spiciness of the jerk seasoning and your own taste.

Bake the pie for 40 minutes, or until the top is lightly browned and the meat inside is tender. Serve with lime wedges.

Lidgate's kitchen fills with the tempting aroma of wine when this pie is cooking. Our secret ingredient is a touch of apricot jam, which isn't authentic, but somehow boosts the savoury ingredients. You can also use the filling to make a casserole, using browned whole legs and thighs or a whole chicken cut into 8 portions instead of fillets, and cooking the meat for about 1 hour in total, or until tender.

Coq au vin pie

Serves 6

1 tablespoon olive or vegetable oil

150g (5oz) smoked streaky bacon, roughly chopped

2 onions, finely chopped

2 garlic cloves, finely chopped

300g (10oz) button mushrooms, trimmed and cut in half if large

1kg (2lb) boneless, skinless chicken thighs, cut into 5-cm (2-in) pieces

2 tablespoons plain flour, plus extra for dusting

500ml (17fl oz) red wine

300ml (½ pint) chicken stock

2 tablespoons apricot jam

500g (1lb) puff pastry

1 egg beaten with 2 tablespoons milk, for eggwash

sea salt and freshly ground black pepper

Pour the oil into a sauté pan over a medium heat. When hot, add the bacon. Cook for 5 minutes, stirring occasionally. Add the onions and garlic and cook over a medium-low heat for 10 minutes, or until soft, stirring occasionally.

Add the mushrooms, turn up the heat slightly and cook until they start to release their juices (about 5–10 minutes). Add the chicken to the pan and cook, stirring occasionally, until the outside of the meat is opaque. Sprinkle over the flour and cook for a minute or so, stirring to combine.

Pour in the wine, bring to the boil and bubble for 2 minutes to burn off the alcohol. Add the stock and jam, bring back to the boil, then simmer, uncovered, for 30 minutes, or until the chicken is tender and the liquid has slightly thickened. Taste and season with salt and pepper as required.

Preheat the oven to 220°C/425°F/Gas Mark 7. Tip the coq au vin into a large pie dish, about 30 x 20cm (12 x 8in).

Dust a work surface with flour and roll out the pastry so it is about 5cm (2in) larger all round than the pie dish. Cut 2.5-cm (1-in) strips from each edge of the pastry. Press these on to the lip of the pie dish, trim off any excess and brush with the eggwash. Press the pastry lid firmly on top of the pastry rim, then crimp the edges together to seal. Reroll the pastry trimmings and cut out shapes to decorate the pie, sticking them on with the eggwash.

Brush eggwash all over the pastry lid, then bake for 30 minutes, or until nice and brown. Serve with seasonal greens or a salad.

We always look forward to the English asparagus season. In this pie, the spears form a great partnership with chicken – a real treat for a family supper or an informal dinner party. The woody ends, often discarded, are used here to make a tasty stock for the sauce.

Chicken & asparagus pie

Serves 4

20g (¾oz) unsalted butter

1 banana shallot, finely chopped

1 celery stick, finely chopped

½ tablespoon plain flour

150ml (¼ pint) full-fat crème fraîche

freshly grated nutmeg

450g (14½oz) asparagus, woody ends broken off and reserved

squeeze of lemon juice

sea salt and freshly ground black pepper

For the pastry

200g (7oz) plain flour, plus extra for dusting

pinch of fine sea salt

100g (3½oz) cold unsalted butter, cut into small dice

1 egg beaten with 2 tablespoons milk, for eggwash

For the stock and chicken

1 tablespoon olive oil

1 celery stick, roughly chopped

1 onion, roughly chopped

1 carrot, roughly chopped

1 bay leaf

125ml (4fl oz) white wine (optional)

6 meaty chicken drumsticks

500ml (17fl oz) water

First make the pastry. Combine the flour and salt in a bowl. Add the butter and rub into the flour using your fingertips, until the mixture resembles breadcrumbs. Add half the eggwash and mix roughly with a table knife. Use your hands to form it into a dough, then knead briefly. Shape it into a ball, wrap in clingfilm or greaseproof paper and chill for at least 30 minutes.

Meanwhile, make the stock. Pour the oil into a saucepan, add the celery, onion, carrot, bay leaf and woody asparagus bits and sweat over a medium-low heat for 10 minutes, stirring occasionally. Add the wine (if using), bring to the boil and bubble for a minute to burn off the alcohol.

Add the drumsticks and water to the pan, return to the boil, then cover and simmer for 45 minutes.

Preheat the oven to 200°C/400°F/Gas Mark 6.

Strain the stock and measure out 400ml (14fl oz). Save any left over for use in another dish. Discard the vegetables and bay leaf. Allow the chicken to cool slightly, then take the meat off the bones, discarding the skin. Cut into large chunks.

Melt the butter in a sauté pan on a medium-low heat, add the shallot and celery, season well and cook until soft (about 10 minutes), stirring occasionally. Sprinkle in the flour, add the measured stock and crème fraîche, stir to combine and bring to the boil. Allow to bubble away to thicken slightly. Add the chicken chunks and asparagus tips and simmer for 3 minutes. Add a squeeze of lemon juice, then taste and adjust the seasoning if necessary.

Tip the chicken mixture into a pie dish, about 25 x 20 x 7cm (10 x 8 x 3in). Put a pie funnel or an upturned eggcup in the centre.

Dust a work surface with flour and roll out the pastry so it is about 5cm (2in) larger all round than the pie dish. Cut 2.5-cm (1-in) strips from each edge of the pastry. Press these on to the lip of the pie dish, trim off any excess and brush with the remaining eggwash. Press the pastry lid firmly on top of the pastry rim, then crimp the edges together to seal. Reroll the pastry trimmings and cut out shapes to decorate the pie, sticking them on with the eggwash.

Bake for 30–40 minutes, until golden and the pastry is cooked through.

→

Some people use only chicken breasts in this traditional Italian dish – hunter's chicken – but a whole bird, cut into portions, gives the dish extra flavour and juiciness because the meat is cooked on the bone.

Chicken cacciatore

Serves 4

25g (1oz) dried wild mushrooms

2 tablespoons plain flour

1.5–1.75kg (3–3½lb) chicken, jointed into 8 pieces (ask your butcher or see steps on page 136)

1 tablespoon olive oil

25g (1oz) unsalted butter

1 onion, chopped

2 garlic cloves, finely chopped

250g (8 oz) fresh button or chestnut mushrooms, chopped

2 tablespoons tomato purée

2 sprigs of thyme

300ml (½ pint) hot chicken stock

splash of brandy (optional)

200ml (7fl oz) red wine

fine sea salt and freshly ground black pepper

For the garnish (optional)

15g (½oz) butter

1 teaspoon olive oil

½ garlic clove, finely chopped

100g (3½oz) fresh wild mushrooms (e.g. chanterelles), halved if large

2 tablespoons finely chopped flat leaf parsley

Put the dried mushrooms in a bowl, add enough hot water to cover and set aside to soak.

Meanwhile, put the flour on a plate and season with salt and pepper. Roll the chicken pieces in it to coat lightly.

Place the oil and half the butter in a large flameproof casserole dish and melt together over a medium-high heat. Don't make it too hot or the meat will scorch rather than brown. Add the chicken pieces and fry until browned on both sides. Set aside on a plate.

Melt the remaining butter in the pan. Add the onion, season with a little salt and fry over a low heat until soft (about 10 minutes). Add the garlic and fresh mushrooms and cook for 10 minutes, until the juices are released and the flesh has softened.

Add the tomato purée and cook for a couple of minutes, stirring occasionally, then stir in the thyme. Add the dried mushrooms plus their soaking water and the hot stock. Add the brandy (if using), then turn up the heat for 1 minute to let the alcohol evaporate. Add the wine and stir again.

Return the chicken pieces to the pan, bring to the boil, then simmer, half-covered, for about 1 hour, turning them over halfway through, until the meat is cooked through and tender.

Meanwhile, if you want to make the garnish, melt the butter with the olive oil in a frying pan over a medium heat. Add the garlic and cook for 30 seconds, then add the mushrooms and cook for about 10 minutes, until the juices are released and the flesh is soft. Set aside until the chicken is cooked. Reheat the mushrooms, then turn off the heat and stir in the parsley. Spoon some over the mixture over each portion of chicken. Serve with potato dauphinoise or baked potatoes, or with rice/wild rice.

One of our former butchers, James, picked up tips on how to make an authentic curry when working alongside Indian chefs in restaurant kitchens. There are quite a few ingredients in this curry and several stages of cooking, but the result is very much worth the effort.

Aromatic chicken curry

Serves 8

1.5kg (3lb) boneless, skinless chicken thighs, each cut into 4 pieces

3 onions, finely chopped

¼–½ teaspoon fine sea salt, or to taste

90ml (3½fl oz) water

1 tablespoon tomato purée

1 x 400-g (14-oz) can chopped tomatoes

finely chopped leaves from 1 bunch of fresh coriander

50g (2oz) butter, diced

juice of ½ lemon

For the marinade

1 tablespoon finely chopped garlic

1 tablespoon finely grated ginger

1 tablespoon deseeded and finely chopped chilli

200g (7oz) full-fat natural yoghurt

1 tablespoon garam masala

1 teaspoon ground turmeric

1 teaspoon salt

juice of 1 lemon

finely chopped stems from 1 bunch of fresh coriander

For the spice mixture

5–6 tablespoons sunflower or other vegetable oil

5 green cardamom pods

5 cloves

2 star anise

2 bay leaves

1 cinnamon stick

10 black peppercorns

1 teaspoon mustard seeds

1 tablespoon cumin seeds

2 tablespoons coriander seeds

1 dried chilli (optional)

1 teaspoon ground cumin

2 teaspoons ground coriander

2 teaspoons garam masala

1 teaspoon ground turmeric

First make the marinade. Combine the garlic, ginger and chilli in a small bowl and mix to a paste. Place the remaining marinade ingredients in a shallow non-metallic container. Add half the garlic paste and mix well.

Add the chicken pieces to the marinade and mix well. Cover and chill for up to 24 hours, but at least 1 hour.

To make the spice mixture, place the oil in a large pan over a medium heat. Add the whole spices, including the chilli if you like your curry hot. When the mustard seeds start to pop, after about a minute, add the ground spices and stir briefly.

Stir the onions into the spice mixture, then mix in the salt to help prevent the onions burning. Cook on a low heat for about 15–20 minutes, stirring occasionally, until they are soft and translucent.

Meanwhile, preheat the oven to 220°C/425°F/Gas Mark 7.

Add the remaining garlic paste to the softened onions and cook for 2 minutes more, stirring occasionally. Add the water and cook for 3 minutes, stirring occasionally. Stir in the tomato purée and tomatoes, adding a canful of water to the pan, which helps swill out any tomato left behind in the can. Bring the mixture to a simmer and cook, uncovered, for 10 minutes.

Meanwhile, lift the chicken out of the marinade and arrange the pieces in a large roasting tray. Roast for 10 minutes.

Remove the cinnamon stick from the marinade, then blend what's left until smooth. Return the liquid to the pan, add the roasted chicken pieces and simmer for a further 20–30 minutes, until cooked through completely and the sauce has thickened slightly.

Just before serving, stir in the coriander leaves, butter and lemon juice.

North African flavours brighten up a simple stew that you can make in summer or winter as a mid-week supper for family and friends. Chicken thighs are good value, their firm texture and great taste making them one of the best parts of the bird for home cooking.

Moroccan chicken with green olives & preserved lemons

Serves 5–6

2 tablespoons olive oil

1kg (2lb) boneless, skinless chicken thighs, cut into 5-cm (2-in) chunks

1 large leek, roughly chopped

2 preserved lemons

½ tablespoon plain flour

1 ½ tablespoons ground cumin

300ml (½ pint) chicken stock

25g (1oz) pitted green olives, roughly chopped

3 tablespoons finely chopped flat leaf parsley

2 tablespoon finely chopped coriander

juice of ½ lemon, or to taste

salt and freshly ground black pepper

Pour 1 tablespoon of the oil into a flameproof casserole dish over a high heat. When hot, add the chicken and fry for 5 minutes, stirring occasionally, until the meat is opaque. Transfer to a plate and set aside.

Place the remaining tablespoon oil in the casserole over a medium heat and fry the leek until soft (about 8 minutes), stirring occasionally.

Meanwhile, remove and discard the pithy centres, flesh and pips from the preserved lemons. Cut the peel into small pieces.

Sprinkle the flour and cumin over the leek, stir to combine, and cook for another 2 minutes. Season with salt and pepper. Return the meat to the pan and pour in the stock. Let the mixture bubble up, then lower the heat and add the olives and preserved lemons. Cover and simmer for 25–30 minutes, until the meat is tender, stirring occasionally.

Before serving, stir in the parsley and coriander, then add lemon juice to taste. Adjust the seasoning as necessary. Serve with couscous and a Moroccan-style salad and/or a green salad.

→

This recipe is based on a Portuguese–African sauce that originally used peri peri, or piri piri, a type of chilli grown in Africa (the name means 'chilli chilli' in Swahili). It has both heat and a refreshing tartness that soon becomes addictive. We use it to marinate spatchcocked poussin, both for the oven and the barbecue, and it also goes brilliantly with other meats. It's worth making at least a double quantity and keeping the extra in a bottle or jar so you have a homemade chilli sauce to put on the table. We make up a big tubful for the shop, and some of the staff use it to add 'pow' to their lunch, be it pizza, chicken, pork or salad.

Peri peri poussin

Serves 4

4 spatchcocked poussins (ask your butcher in advance, or see steps overleaf)

2 tablespoons roughly chopped coriander leaves, to garnish

For the peri peri sauce

50g (2oz) roasted piquillo pepper (about 2), roughly chopped

2 red chillies, deseeded and finely sliced

2 green chillies, deseeded and finely sliced

3 fat garlic cloves, roughly chopped

2 tablespoons red wine vinegar

juice of 1 lemon

50ml (2fl oz) olive oil

1 teaspoon dried oregano

1 teaspoon ground paprika

1 teaspoon caster sugar

1 teaspoon sea salt flakes

¼–½ teaspoon chilli powder, or to taste (optional)

First make the sauce. Put the chopped pepper and chillies in a blender. Add the garlic, vinegar, lemon juice and olive oil and whizz to smoothish paste. Add the oregano, paprika, sugar and salt, then your preferred amount of chilli powder (if using). The mixture can be divided into batches if you like, and various amounts of heat added to some or none. Whizz again and pour into a screwtop jar. The sauce keeps well in the fridge for a few weeks.

Place the spatchcocked poussins skin-side up in a large, foil-lined roasting tray. Coat all over with the peri peri sauce, then cover and leave to marinate in the fridge, ideally overnight, but for at least a couple of hours. Take them out of the fridge and allow to come to room temperature whilst you are heating the oven or barbecue for the next step.

→

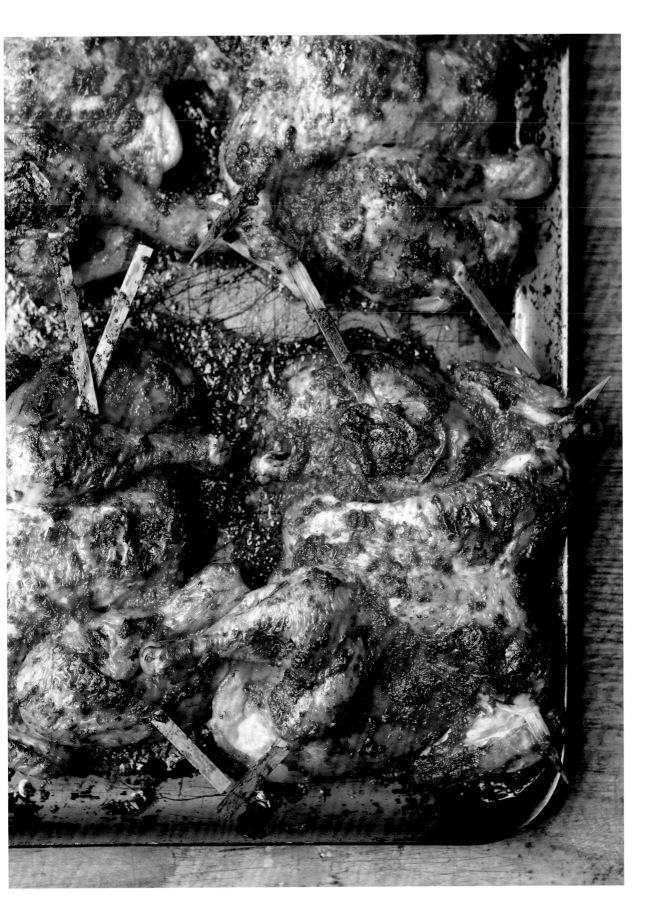

To oven-cook the poussins

Preheat the oven to 190°C/375°F/Gas Mark 5. Roast for 30–40 minutes, basting frequently. The birds are done if the juices run clear when the flesh is pierced with a skewer, and the leg joint comes away easily from the body.

To barbecue the poussins

Heat a barbecue until it is pulsing hot. Place the birds on the rack, breast-side down, for 10 minutes, basting frequently. Turn and cook for 10 minutes on the other side, continuing to baste. After that, cook for another 2–3 minutes on each side until the juices run clear when the flesh is pierced with a skewer, and the leg joint comes away easily from the body.

Sprinkle the chopped coriander over the birds and serve with salad and rice or potatoes.

How to spatchcock a poussin or chicken

Spatchcocking a bird means to take out the backbone (or sometimes the breastbone) so you can flatten it, which allows it to cook more quickly and evenly, especially on a barbecue or a grill. This technique can also be used for large chickens and other birds.

To spatchcock a poussin

1 & 2 Place the bird on a board and cut off the string that ties the legs together. Cut off the wing tips and the flap of skin at the neck end. These bits can either be discarded or used to make stock.

3 With the bird breast-side down, and the cavity and drumstick ends pointing towards you, use poultry shears, good kitchen scissors or a small, sharp knife to cut either side of the parson's nose.

4 Cut all the way along either side of the backbone. Discard the bone or save it to make stock.

5 It's helpful but not essential to score the breastbone slightly. This helps you to flatten the bird.

6 Place the bird skin-side up. Tuck the thighs of the drumsticks inwards so the bird is 'knock-kneed', with the end of the legs pointing outwards. If you want a neater appearance, cut the 'spur' or end off each drumstick. Press down gently but firmly on the breastbone to flatten the bird slightly. You want the bird to be as flat as possible to cook as quickly and evenly as possible.

7 & 8 Use two skewers to help to keep the bird flat. Push the first one diagonally through the thick part of the thigh, under the breastbone and up through the other side. Repeat this on the other side so that the skewers cross.

9 Your poussin is now ready to marinate and cook.

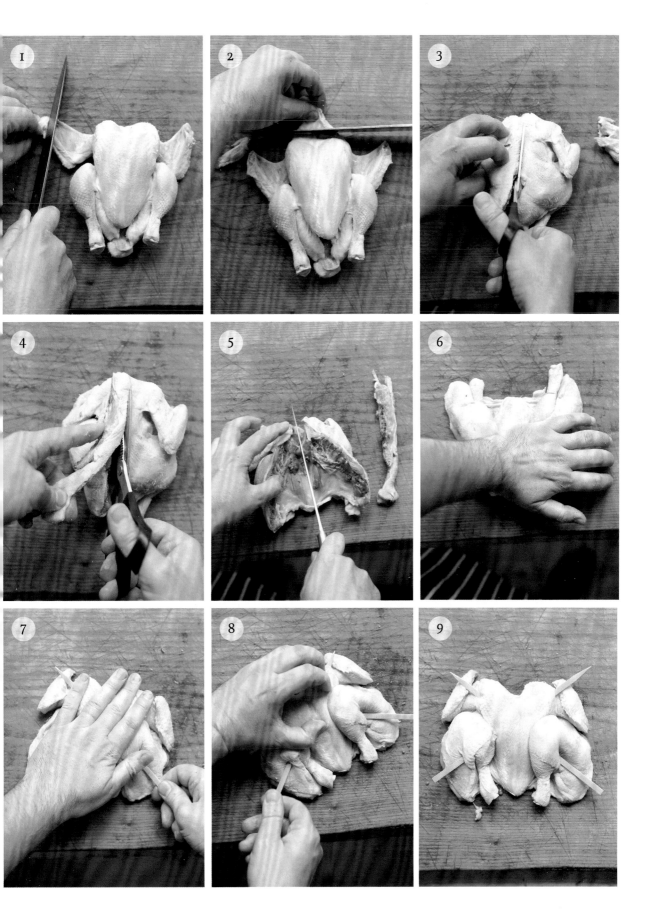

White meat, black mushrooms and green pistachios make for an attractive and well-textured terrine. The soft and creamy sweetbreads (thymus glands) combine well with the firmer chicken, adding a delicate flavour. They can be omitted if you wish, but are well worth trying. You'll need to order them in advance so the butcher can prepare them. Thomas Maieli, a chef who now runs a company called Mr Duck Delicacies, supplies Lidgate's with his delicious products and came up with the recipe below.

Chicken & sweetbreads terrine

Serves 6

250g (9oz) skinless boneless chicken thighs, cut into 2.5-cm (1-in) chunks

250g (9oz) lamb sweetbreads, trimmed (or replace with the same weight of chopped chicken thighs)

milk, for soaking (optional)

50g (1¾oz) pied de mouton or other dried mushrooms

250g (8oz) minced chicken

1 heaped tablespoon fresh marjoram leaves, finely chopped

1 scant tablespoon dried savory herb (or use more chopped marjoram)

½ teaspoon dried sage, or ¾ teaspoon finely chopped fresh sage

50g (1¾oz) shelled pistachios

50ml (2fl oz) white wine

½ small garlic clove, finely chopped

1 teaspoon fine sea salt

½ teaspoon ground white pepper

For the best visual effect in the finished dish, soak the chicken and sweetbreads in milk overnight in the fridge. This will make them whiter. Drain and pat dry with kitchen paper. Transfer to a large bowl.

Rehydrate the mushrooms by soaking them in warm water for 30 minutes. Drain and pat dry with kitchen paper. Chop into small pieces.

Add the minced chicken and mushrooms to the sweetbread bowl, along with the herbs, pistachios, wine, garlic, salt and pepper. Mix well.

Spoon the mixture into a 750-g (1½-lb) nonstick loaf tin, slightly doming the top. If your tin isn't nonstick, grease it first with butter or oil, and line the bottom with baking parchment.

Preheat the oven to 160°C/325°F/Gas Mark 3 and boil a kettle. Put the terrine in a roasting tray and place it on the middle shelf of the oven. Pour the just-boiled water into the tray so it comes about halfway up the side of the tin. This will help the terrine to cook more gently and evenly. Bake for about 1–1½ hours, or until the temperature in the centre of the terrine reaches 75°C/165°F and the chicken is cooked through.

Using the base of another loaf tin, press down gently but firmly on the terrine so that the juices come out, then pour them away. Transfer the terrine to a tray of cold water to cool it down as quickly as possible. Sit the tin on a plate or in a shallow dish and place a double layer of clingfilm directly on the surface of the terrine. Cover with a board or plate, put a heavy weight on top – a bag of sugar is ideal – and place in the fridge overnight to firm up.

Remove the weight and clingfilm, then (if necessary) gently slide a knife around the terrine to loosen it. Place a plate over the tin and quickly invert both to turn out. The terrine will keep for 2–3 days if wrapped in clingfilm and stored in the fridge. Alternatively, freeze for up to 1 month and defrost when required.

To serve, cut the terrine into slices and offer it with bread or toast, butter, cornichons and salad.

Fresh chicken livers have so much flavour that they can hold their own with a devilled (spicy) sauce, a traditional English way of adding heat to a dish. The livers are best served on toast for a starter, or with salad for a light and good-value lunch or supper dish.

Devilled chicken livers

Serves 4

500g (1lb) chicken livers

200ml (7fl oz) dry cider

2 tablespoons tomato purée

2½ tablespoons plain flour

1 teaspoon English mustard powder

1½ teaspoons smoked paprika

1–2 large pinches of cayenne pepper

¼ teaspoon fine sea salt

1 tablespoon olive or vegetable oil

1 garlic clove, finely chopped

1½ tablespoons Worcestershire sauce, or to taste

squeeze of lemon juice or a pinch of caster sugar

2–3 tablespoons finely chopped chives or parsley

To prepare the livers, cut off any tubes or discoloured parts. Pour the cider into a bowl or jug. Stir in the tomato purée and set aside.

Combine the flour, mustard powder, paprika, cayenne pepper and salt in a bowl. Toss the livers in the flour so they are lightly coated, shaking off any excess.

Pour the oil into a large frying pan over a high heat. Add the garlic and cook for 30 seconds. Add the floured livers, in two batches if necessary to avoid overcrowding the pan, and cook for 2 minutes, then turn and cook the other side for 1 minute.

Pour in the cider mixture and let it bubble and thicken for around 30 seconds, or until the livers are done to your liking – they are best when pink in the middle.

Turn off the heat. Add the Worcestershire sauce, then taste to check the seasoning: add a squeeze of lemon juice if you want to sharpen the flavour, or a pinch of sugar if you want it more mellow. Sprinkle with the chopped herbs.

Serve with a salad and hot buttered toast or crusty bread, or with plain boiled rice.

This is a special version of a British classic that was created to celebrate the Coronation of Queen Elizabeth II. We use apricots to give both colour and another layer of flavour, and toast the almonds to add extra crunch. Using a whole chicken is better value than buying lots of breasts, and poaching the bird provides tender meat plus the bonus of stock for other dishes. Use the best mayo you can, with homemade best of all. The dish can be made in advance, which is another reason it's so popular for entertaining.

Coronation chicken

Serves 6

1.5–1.75kg (3–3½lb) chicken

1 onion, quartered

1 celery stick, roughly chopped

1 carrot, roughly chopped

2 bay leaves

1 tablespoon sea salt flakes

For the sauce

100g (3½oz) flaked almonds

1 tablespoon olive oil

1 onion, finely chopped

2 tablespoons korma paste

100g (3½oz) canned apricots (drained weight), roughly chopped

1 tablespoon apricot or mango chutney

100g (3½oz) best-quality or homemade mayonnaise

90ml (3½fl oz) thick Greek yoghurt

3 tablespoons roughly chopped flat leaf parsley leaves

4 fresh apricots, cut in half and stones discarded (if unavailable, use 6 dried apricots soaked in water for 1 hour, then drained)

4 spring onions, finely sliced

sea salt

First poach the chicken, which can be done a day in advance. Put the bird into a snug-fitting saucepan. Add the onion, celery, carrot, bay leaf and salt. Add enough water to cover, place over a high heat and bring just to the boil. Lower the heat and skim off any froth on the surface. Cover with a lid and simmer for about 1¼ hours, or until the chicken is cooked. Use a knife and fork to gently pull apart the meat on a drumstick to check it is tender and that there are no pink juices. Transfer the chicken to a plate and set aside to cool slightly. Meanwhile, strain the stock, cool it as quickly as possible and store in the fridge or freezer for future use.

Once the meat is cool enough to handle, remove it from the bones and cut into 5-cm (2-in) chunks. Transfer to a bowl, cover with clingfilm and put in the fridge.

Now start the sauce. Toast the almonds in a dry frying pan, or place in an oven preheated to 160°C/325°F/Gas Mark 3 for about 10 minutes, turning them over about halfway through and taking care they don't burn. Set aside to cool.

Pour the oil into a frying pan over a medium-low heat. When hot, add the onion seasoned with a large pinch of salt, and fry until soft (about 10 minutes). Stir in the korma paste and cook for 2 minutes. Add the canned apricots and cook for another 2 minutes, adding a splash of water or chicken stock if the mixture becomes too dry. Tip into a food processor or blender, add the chutney and whizz to a thick purée. Pour into a dish and set aside to cool.

To assemble the dish, mix the mayonnaise and yoghurt with the curry purée. Stir in the chicken, toasted almonds and parsley. Taste and adjust the seasoning if necessary. Cover and store in the fridge until needed.

Just before serving, cut the fresh apricots into 6–8 strips. If using reconstituted apricots, cut the flesh into small chunks. Stir the fruit into the chicken mixture, along with the spring onions.

Chicken thighs, especially large meaty ones, make a great supper dish. Here they are cooked with a tangy sauce based on the classic pairing of chicken and tarragon. It is best to cook the thighs skinned so that they get a nice crust from the sauce. But if you love crispy chicken skin, place it in a separate roasting tray, sprinkle with salt and cook it in the hot oven for the last 10–15 minutes or so of the chicken cooking time, making sure it doesn't burn.

Tangy tarragon chicken thighs

Serves 6–8

8 large skinless chicken thighs, on the bone
1 lime, quartered
1 teaspoon finely chopped tarragon

For the marinade

2 ½ tablespoons Dijon mustard
3 teaspoons red wine vinegar
1 tablespoon olive oil
2 teaspoons ground paprika
1 tablespoon soft brown sugar
½ teaspoon freshly ground black pepper
2 tablespoons roughly chopped tarragon
¼ teaspoon sea salt flakes

Put the marinade ingredients in a bowl and whisk them together.

Using a sharp knife, score each of the chicken thighs 3 times, nearly down to the bone. Massage the marinade into the chicken and, if you have time, cover and leave in the fridge for up to 24 hours.

Preheat the oven to 190°C/375°F/Gas Mark 5.

Put the chicken in a roasting tray lined with baking parchment and cook for about 40 minutes, or until the marinade is brown and the meat cooked through. Squeeze the lime juice over the chicken and sprinkle with the tarragon.

Serve with rice or potatoes (mash, wedges or salad), plus a green salad or vegetables.

An escalope, a thin piece of flattened meat, gets its name from an Old French word for 'shell'. Not only does it cook quickly and evenly, but it has a large surface area that turns crisp and golden when breadcrumbed and fried. Escalopes are a useful way of making two chicken breasts feed four people for a light lunch, or four children for supper. Alternatively, they can serve two people as a main course.

Chicken escalopes with lemon breadcrumbs

Serves 2–4

2 skinless boneless chicken breasts, or 4 skinless boneless thighs, made into escalopes (ask your butcher in advance, or see steps on page 162)

50g (2oz) dry breadcrumbs, preferably Japanese panko as they are fine and light

1 egg

finely grated zest of 1 small lemon

20g (¾oz) unsalted butter

1 tablespoon olive oil

salt and freshly ground black pepper

Cut each breast escalope into 2 pieces (leave thighs whole). Put the breadcrumbs on a large flat plate. Whisk the egg in a large, shallow bowl. Add the lemon zest and season with salt and pepper. Whisk to combine.

Dip each escalope into the egg mixture, coating both sides, then dip them in the breadcrumbs. Scatter more breadcrumbs over the top and gently press them into the flesh. This step can be done up to a couple of hours in advance. Transfer the escalopes to a plate, cover with clingfilm and store in the fridge until required.

Melt half the butter with half the oil in a large frying pan over a high heat. When hot, fry the escalopes 2 at a time, turning after 1½ minutes, or when the breadcrumbs are brown. The second side will need only another minute or so. You can cut into the escalope to to check if it is cooked through. Transfer to a plate and keep warm. Add the rest of the butter and oil to the pan and cook the remaining 2 escalopes in the same way.

Serve with a green salad and potatoes, and perhaps a blob of mayonnaise.

→

How to make a chicken escalope

Chicken breasts are traditionally used for escalopes, but we also use thighs because they are flavoursome and good value.

Using a chicken breast

1 Place a skinless boneless chicken breast on a chopping board, top-side down.

2 Flip the small fillet of meat from the centre over to the thinner side of the breast.

3 & 4 Turn the breast around so that the thin end is nearest to you. Place one hand on top of the meat to keep it steady and use the tip of a sharp knife to cut into the thick part of the breast at a 45-degree angle. This means you cut diagonally into the meat, almost stroking the flesh open with the knife, and going three-quarters of the way down.

5 Carefully open out the breast like a book so that the 2 halves lie flat, joined at the centre.

6 Cut a little further into the other side of the top, thick part of the breast to open it out slightly more.

7 Place the breast skin-side up between 2 sheets of greaseproof paper or clingfilm.

8 Use a meat mallet, rolling pin or heavy-based pan to hit and flatten it to a thickness of about 5mm (¼in).

9 Cut each half of the escalope in half to make 4 pieces altogether, trying to make them as even as possible (they don't have to be perfect).

Using a chicken thigh

1 Place a skinless boneless chicken thigh on a chopping board and open it out to ensure that any small bones, especially the kneecap, are removed. The meat has almost a u-shape, with the thickest parts on either side.

2 Using a sharp knife and working from the middle to the outer edge, cut through the thick part on one side at a 45-degree angle. Repeat this with the other thick side.

3 Open out the cut pieces like a book. If your thighs are thick ones, place the meat between 2 sheets of greaseproof paper or clingfilm, and give it a light tap with a meat mallet, rolling pin or heavy-based pan to flatten it out a bit.

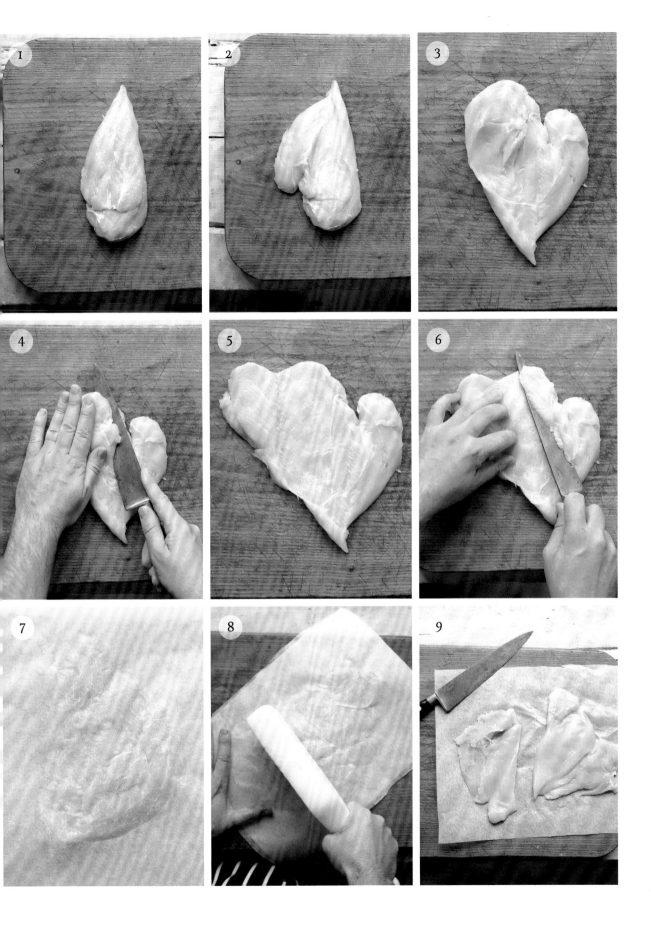

The best chicken

At a butcher's, you still find birds that have been raised in relatively small flocks and led a natural life with a natural diet. These chickens live for at least twice as long as intensively farmed birds (broilers), which are fast-farmed indoors and never see the light of day. The organic chickens sold at Lidgate's come from Otter Valley Poultry in Devon. They are a slow-growing breed that live for at least 70 days, and are kept in flocks of 500, as opposed to the tens of thousands reared in intensive broiler sheds.

As with all animals, what the chickens eat is extremely important. Intensively reared birds may be fed a diet that includes undesirables, such as antibiotics and genetically modified soya. An Otter Valley free-range bird, on the other hand, goes outside once it has passed the 'small chick' stage and can therefore supplement the cereal diet it is given with grass, clover, worms and other plants and insects. The exercise and varied diet mean the bird is healthier than an intensively reared chicken and ultimately we benefit too as the meat is more flavoursome and nutritious.

The land on which the chickens are reared is geared to suit their natural instincts. It has lots of trees, plus shelters made of potato boxes placed upside-down on logs. These satisfy their need for shelter in order to protect themselves from buzzards, seagulls and other large birds that will swoop down to attack. At night, they readily return to the farm's large, purpose-built shelters, which keep them warm and safe from foxes.

When ready for the table, the birds are carefully gathered up by the farmer and his team and killed at the company's on-farm processing plant, which minimizes any stress on the birds and also gives the best-quality meat.

The very best chickens are dry-plucked, which improves their keeping quality, as they can be hung for longer. You more often find this sort of plucking with turkeys than chickens, as it is an expensive process, but

it is worth paying the extra if you see a bird that is produced in this way.

At one time it was common at Christmas for butchers to sell capons – castrated male birds that fattened quickly. This practice is now basically illegal, so the extra-large birds we sell during the festive season are simply ones that live longer – about 15 weeks or more – and therefore grow bigger. Male birds grow faster and bigger than females, so the cockerels are oven-ready at about 4kg (9lb), and the hens at 3–3.5kg (7–8lb).

This type of large chicken is an excellent option for a small household that doesn't have the appetite for a turkey. The meat is special and succulent, and there is plenty of delicious fat from the bird, which makes great roast potatoes, both on the day and for other meals to come (keep it in a pot in the fridge).

Given that chicken is so easily available these days, it seems strange to think that just 50 years ago it was regarded as a treat to be eaten on high days and holidays. Going even further back, it was a big deal to kill a bird for the pot, as chickens were traditionally raised by the farmer's wife, who sold their eggs for extra income. The season for selling the birds themselves started at Easter and went on until the birds stopped laying in the darker months.

The relative scarcity of chicken explains why it was carefully cooked wherever in the world it was raised, and why so many dishes have been created to make use of every part of the bird. Some of these are in this book, including Chicken & Asparagus Pie, Chicken Cacciatore and Coq au Vin Pie (see pages 141, 145 and 140). The Gallic rooster is a national symbol in France, and great pride is taken in chicken farming. Consequently, free-range birds are much more common in France than Britain, but the renowned Poulet de Bresse can be found in some specialist UK shops. The French note that there are many subtly different types of meat on one bird, not just 'white' and 'dark'. Take your time eating a good chicken and you will notice this for yourself – from the succulent oyster muscle to the three parts of a wing. Even the skin is different on various parts of the bird.

Given the superiority of free-range birds, why on earth did Britain turn to intensive chicken farming in

the 1950s? The answer is 'efficiency'. The first broilers were produced here using technology and breeding techniques developed in the United States. Farmers soon learnt how to grow birds faster so they could be killed sooner, which made a quicker profit and pleased a nation weary of rationing and deprivation. Since then, the genetics have been pushed to the max to produce birds that are the most 'efficient' to rear. Most intensively reared birds are now owned by two large companies, and the running of their chicken sheds is contracted out to what you might call 'shed operators' rather than farmers.

It must be noted, though, that the same sort of intensive system also produces many so-called 'free-range' birds. They are given access to the outdoors and their numbers are smaller, but the way they are raised is still a long way from the free-range ideal that genuinely encourages the birds to roam and feed outside. Next time you eat chicken, have a look at the leg bone: it will be long, strong and straight if the bird has lived long enough and exercised properly.

When well farmed and allowed to grow and mature, chicken is full of flavour and nutrition – a bird to be proud of, not a bland commodity. We feel it's time to return chicken to the centre of the table and really appreciate its magnificent taste and toothsome texture. Whether you like crunching on the wing, gnawing on a drumstick or savouring smooth slices of breast, a proper chicken offers something for everyone.

5

Duck & Game

At one time, game was regarded by many as a slightly mysterious food, sold so high and whiffy that, in the case of game birds, the feathers were virtually dropping out. Then restaurants and TV chefs starting using it more, rightly praising its excellent flavour and wild provenance. It also became better known that game need not be expensive. Rabbit and wood pigeons in particular can provide high-quality protein at a very good price.

In the last ten years or so, game sales at Lidgate's have gone up by more than 20 per cent. You could almost say that game, particularly venison (which is now sold on most high streets) has gone mainstream. That, however, is not true of all game. Some types are still slightly elusive because it is wild food and the supply is not just seasonal, but dependant on all sorts of uncontrollable factors, such as the condition of the moors, marshes and woodlands where the animals live and breed. As a result, game still has a certain glamour, even if it is no longer exclusive. It's certainly easier to eat as we don't sell it rotting-high.

As a city butcher selling relatively small quantities of meat, we're in a good position to gather and sell the best-quality game. A country butcher with direct connections to local shoots is another good place to go for such specialities. They will also sell the likes of wild rabbits from nearby farms.

Some of what is regarded as game, such as venison, rabbit and duck, is farmed and sold pretty much all year round. We tend to buy farmed duck to get a consistent product, but it is also worth looking out for wild duck, which we sometimes sell in season during the autumn and winter months.

The lean quality of game meat means that it suits careful roasting and other quick-cooking techniques. It can also be casseroled in stock to keep the meat moist. Butchers and game dealers sometimes sell a well-priced game mixture for using in stews and pies. Partner it with good smoked bacon, especially streaky rashers or lardons, as these add succulence and extra flavour.

Game bones make excellent stock, tasty enough to serve as an easy starter or light lunch. You can ask a butcher to save a few bird carcasses for you, or take the breasts off the birds yourself and keep the rest for stock.

The opening of the game season is still regarded as special, and we decorate our display with food-grade feathers to celebrate its arrival. Game is a treat that is all the more enjoyable for being so fleeting and hard to predict.

Here's a great-looking dish for a dinner party, straightforward to make and easy to eat. If possible, ask your butcher for a hen rather than a cock pheasant because although the females are smaller, they are plumper. If buying a whole bird, you can easily tell the cock because it has spurs on its legs. Otherwise, the cock's breastbone sticks out more. But don't worry, as both male and female are good for this dish. Not all butchers can supply a boneless crown, in which case see the steps on page 173.

Pheasant breast stuffed with bacon & basil

Serves 4

4 boneless pheasant crowns or double breasts (you may be able to order in advance from your butcher), or buy 4 whole pheasants and follow steps on page 173

2 thick rindless smoked streaky bacon rashers (about 75g/3oz in total), cut in half

For the stuffing

50-g (2-oz) bunch of basil

3–4 garlic cloves

1/4 teaspoon sea salt flakes

1/4 teaspoon cracked black peppercorns

3 thick rindless smoked streaky bacon rashers (about 100g/3½oz in total), finely chopped

2 tablespoons olive oil

First make the stuffing: put the basil leaves in a small blender with the garlic, salt and peppercorns and whizz until finely chopped. (This can be done by hand if you prefer.) Transfer to a bowl, add the bacon and olive oil and mix well.

The breast meat must now be taken off each pheasant carcass in one piece before being stuffed. To do this, follow the step-by-step instructions overleaf.

When you are ready to roast the stuffed pheasant breasts, preheat the oven to 180°C/350°F/Gas Mark 4.

Place the parcels in a roasting tray and roast for 30–40 miutes until the meat juices run clear when a knife is inserted into the thickest part. Set aside to rest in a warm place for 10 minutes.

Serve with the traditional roast pheasant accompaniments – game chips, bread sauce (see page 286) and gravy – plus steamed vegetables, such as carrots and green veg. Alternatively, serve dauphinoise or roast potatoes instead of the game chips.

→

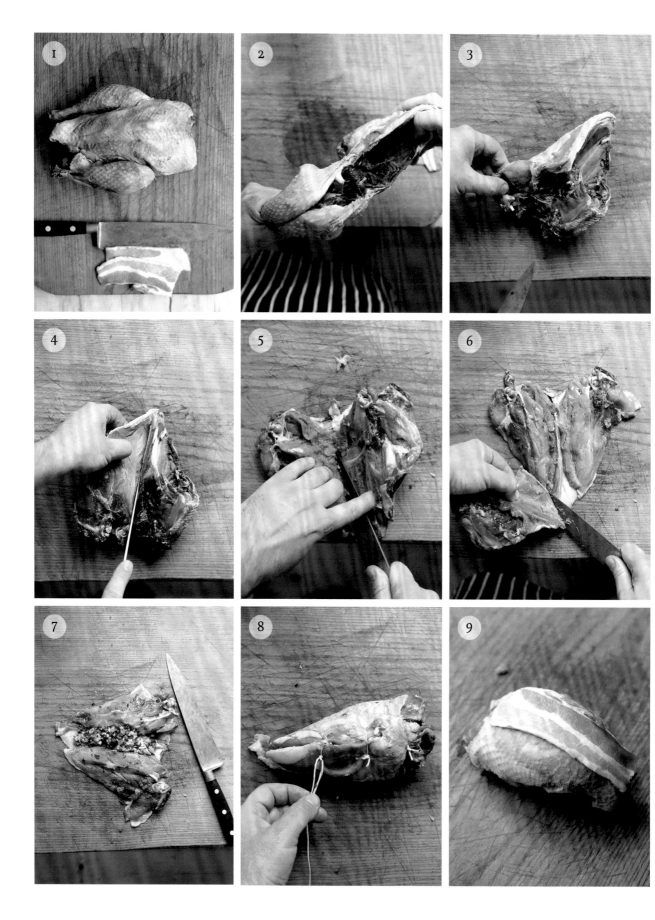

How to bone & stuff pheasant breasts

I Place the bird on a chopping board, legs pointing towards you. Push the legs outwards and use a sharp knife to cut between the right-hand thigh and the breast. Repeat on the left-hand side.

2 Hook your thumbs into the cavity of the bird. Pull the breast in one direction and the legs in the other so that the top half of the bird snaps away from the lower half. Cut the two parts in half at the base. Reserve the legs to use in another dish (you can poach the meat and use it in a curry or game pie, while the bones and other remnants can be used to make a delicious stock), or roast them with the pheasant crowns, with slices of bacon on top.

3 & 4 Place the breast half of the bird on a chopping board, wing-end nearest to you, skin-side down. Using a sharp knife, cut out the breastbone, taking care not to break through the skin. To do this, ease the flesh gently away from the breastbone. Use short strokes to run the tip of a knife between the flesh and the ribs on one side of the bird. Ease the flesh away from the ribs.

5 Repeat on the other side, ideally cutting away the meat from the bone so that you include the little wing joints.

6 Remove the breastbone, trying not to break the skin. (But if you do, don't worry: bacon will cover up any holes.) Repeat this process for the other pheasant crowns.

7 Lay the boned breasts out on the chopping board and check that there are no little splinters of bone left in the meat. Place a quarter of the stuffing mixture in a strip along the centre of each one. Fold the sides of the meat over the stuffing to enclose it.

8 Using a butcher's needle and string, sew the meat together in front of the wings, then tie with a knot. Repeat behind the wings, and then at the neck end. Alternatively, use roasting bands to do the same job.

9 When you have made 4 parcels as described above, turn them over so they are breast-side up. Plump them up so they look like little roasting birds. Lay half a rasher of streaky bacon on each one and transfer to a plate. Cover and place in the fridge until ready to cook, taking them out 30 minutes before roasting so they aren't fridge-cold.

Britain now has numerous wild boar, many farmed, but others escapees that are now breeding in the woods of East Sussex, Kent and Gloucestershire. The meat is much prized and makes great sausages, which you can enjoy in this version of a classic British dish. Substitute good pork sausages if wild boar aren't roaming your neighbourhood shops. One of the tricks of producing a good toad-in-the-hole is to use plenty of fat: good dripping or lard if you have either, or else olive oil.

Wild-boar-in-the-hole with grainy mustard gravy

Serves 4

3 tablespoons beef dripping, lard or olive oil, plus 1 tablespoon extra for the sausages

8 wild boar sausages

4 tablespoons finely chopped chives (optional)

For the batter

200g (7oz) plain flour

250ml (8fl oz) water

250ml (8fl oz) milk

2 large eggs, plus 1 yolk, whisked together

sea salt and freshly ground black pepper

For the gravy

½ tablespoon dripping, lard or butter

½ tablespoon plain flour

400ml (14fl oz) hot chicken, beef or pork stock

25ml (1fl oz) port or sherry, or 50ml (2fl oz) red wine (optional)

1 tablespoon wholegrain mustard

First make the batter: put the flour in a large bowl and make a well in the centre. Pour in the water, milk and whisked eggs and stir gradually into the flour, giving the mixture a good hard beating at the end to get rid of any lumps. Season with a pinch of salt and plenty of black pepper. If you have time, cover the batter and leave for at least 30 minutes, or up to a couple of hours.

Preheat the oven to 220°C/425°F/Gas Mark 7.

Meanwhile, heat 1 tablespoon of the fat or oil in a large frying pan. When hot, brown the sausages on top and bottom. Put the remaining fat or oil in a roasting tray and place in the oven for a couple of minutes, until smoking hot. Quickly whisk up the batter with the chives (if using), and pour it into the hot fat. Arrange the sausages in the batter so they are easy to divide into 4 portions. Return the tray to the oven for 30 minutes, or until the batter is nicely browned.

Whilst the toad is cooking, make the gravy. Melt the fat in a saucepan, stir in the flour and cook for 1 minute, stirring constantly. Gradually add the hot stock, whisking as you do so to prevent lumps from forming. Pour in the alcohol (if using), bring to the boil and allow to bubble for a couple of minutes. Stir in the mustard, taste and add salt if necessary. Set aside and reheat just before serving the wild-boar-in-the-hole.

Serve with a salad or your favourite greens.

Here is a good method for cooking perfectly pink duck breasts, every time. The flavours of this dish make it a delectable dinner for two. The sophisticated dryness of Madeira complements the other ingredients especially well, but dry sherry or dry white wine would also work.

Duck with petit pois, tarragon & Madeira

Serves 2

2 duck breasts, about 200g (7oz) each

50ml (2fl oz) Madeira

200ml (7fl oz) chicken stock

150ml (¼ pint) double cream

150g (5oz) frozen petit pois

2 sprigs of tarragon, plus 1 teaspoon finely chopped leaves

squeeze of lemon juice

sea salt flakes and freshly ground black pepper

Take the duck breasts out of the fridge 30 minutes before cooking so they aren't fridge-cold when they go into the pan. Season the meat on both sides, then place it skin-side down in a cold frying pan. (There's no need for fat, as it renders out of the duck while it cooks.) Turn the heat to medium-high and cook until the skin is crisp and browned (about 10 minutes).

Transfer the duck breasts to a plate, then pour the fat from the pan into a small bowl. Cool and keep covered in the fridge for making roast potatoes. Return the duck to the pan, skin-side up, and place over a medium-high heat. Add the Madeira and let it bubble for a minute or so to evaporate the alcohol. Pour in the stock and cream, then stir in the petits pois and tarragon sprigs. Season with a little salt and pepper.

Continue to cook the duck on a medium-high heat, giving it 5 more minutes for medium rare, or 7 minutes for well done. (If using a digital thermometer, the temperature should be 55–60°C [130–140°F] for medium rare to medium, and 70°C [160°F] for well done, remembering that the temperature will rise by 5°C [40°F] or so after you take the duck off the heat.) Transfer the duck to a plate, cover with foil and leave to rest for 5 minutes.

Increase the heat under the pan and reduce the liquid to a sauce. Remove the tarragon sprigs, then add a little lemon juice to balance out the sweetness of the peas. Taste and adjust the seasoning if necessary.

Cut into one breast to check it is done to your liking; if not, return it to the pan with the sauce and cook for a little longer.

Cut the duck into thin diagonal slices. Spoon some of the sauce and peas on to plates and sit the duck slices on top. Sprinkle with the chopped tarragon and serve with seasonal greens and potatoes.

Les Landes is a coastal region of southwest France that is renowned for its ducks and walnuts – and this salad, with its sharp dressing, showcases them extremely well. Use whatever pieces of prepared duck you can find. Like many butchers, we sell confit duck that can be kept at home ready for quick and delicious meals. Ours come from our friend Thomas Maieli, aka Mr Duck (see page 154), who also makes confit gizzards. These firm little morsels are really interesting to eat and well worth trying.

Salade landaise

Serves 4

prepared duck, such as 2 confit duck legs, or 1 confit duck leg and 65g (2½oz) sliced smoked duck breast, and/or 150g (5oz) confit duck gizzards

100g (3½oz) crustless white bread, cut into 2.5-cm (1-in) cubes

50g (2oz) walnuts

150g (5oz) tasty lettuce (frisée is traditional), leaves separated

8 flavoursome cherry tomatoes, halved

For the dressing
1 banana shallot, very finely diced

1 teaspoon Dijon mustard

3 teaspoons sherry or white wine vinegar

1 teaspoon honey

5 tablespoons olive oil

1 tablespoon finely chopped chives

Preheat the oven to 220°C/425°F/Gas Mark 7.

Put the confit duck in a roasting tray and cook for about 20 minutes, or until the skin is crisp and the meat hot all the way through.

Meanwhile, if using confit gizzards, fry them in their own fat until crisp and cooked through.

To make the dressing, combine all the ingredients in a bowl and whisk together.

Remove the cooked duck from the roasting tray but leave the fat. Turn the oven down to 160°C/325°F/Gas Mark 3. If you've cooked gizzards instead of 2 confit duck legs, pour some of the fat into a roasting tray. Turn the bread cubes over in the fat and put the walnuts on the other side of the tray.

Once the oven has reached the lower temperature – it must not be too hot – put the bread and walnuts in the oven and toast for 10 minutes, turning the cubes over after 5 minutes. Take care that the walnuts do not overbrown or they will become bitter.

Cut the confit duck, including the skin, into medium shreds. Slice the gizzards (if using) into medium-sized pieces.

Put the lettuce, tomatoes, walnuts and croûtons in a large bowl and toss with the dressing. Divide between 4 plates. Arrange your pieces of duck over the salad. Serve immediately.

Partridge takes well to a tandoori treatment, and the marinade also counteracts the risk of dryness in such lean meat. This isn't a beautiful dish but it tastes great. It's also good served cold for a decadently messy picnic on a mild autumn or winter day: simply pull the meat off the bird with your fingers and stuff inside naan bread with rocket leaves, yogurt and mango chutney.

Tandoori partridge

Serves 4

4 partridge, spatchcocked (ask your butcher in advance, or see poussin steps, page 152)

1 lime, cut into quarters

3 tablespoons roughly chopped coriander leaves

4 naan bread, to serve

sea salt flakes

For the tandoori marinade

200g (7oz) natural full-fat yogurt (not Greek)

1½ tablespoons tandoori powder

2 garlic cloves, crushed

6-cm (2½-in) piece of fresh root ginger, grated

juice of 1 lemon

1 teaspoon sea salt flakes

Mix the marinade ingredients in a bowl.

Put the birds in a shallow non-metallic container large enough hold them almost in a single layer. Dollop over the marinade and massage it into the meat. Cover with clingfilm and put in the fridge to marinate for anything from 20 minutes to 24 hours.

Take the birds out of the fridge about 30 minutes before cooking. Season the flesh with salt and squeeze a lime quarter over each bird.

Preheat the oven to 180°C/350°F/Gas Mark 4.

Line a baking tray with foil, place the meat in it and spoon the marinade on top. Cook for 30 minutes or so, until the meat is cooked through to the bone. Set aside to rest in a warm place for 10 minutes; the meat will relax a little and the juices redistribute evenly throughout the meat. Before serving, scatter the coriander over the meat.

Serve with warmed naan bread (place in the oven for 5 minutes or so), or with plain boiled rice. Offer dressed rocket leaves, thick yogurt and chutney alongside.

The most tender (and expensive) cut of venison is the loin, but this recipe also works with less pricey alternatives, such as steaks cut from the haunch. If you are able to state a preference, go for steaks cut from the rump end or topside for tenderness. Otherwise, use silverside, which is more of a working muscle but still good and tasty. The photo overleaf shows the loin fillet coated in lardo (cured and thinly sliced Italian pork fat) to keep the lean meat nice and moist. You can cut this fat off on your plate, or eat some or all of it. The rich flavour of venison is complemented here by a deliciously piquant sweet-and-sharp sauce.

Venison with pink peppercorns & redcurrants

Serves 4

3 tablespoons pink peppercorns in vinegar, rinsed and roughly crushed

1 teaspoon fresh thyme leaves

2 tablespoons olive oil

¼ teaspoon sea salt flakes

4 venison steaks, each about 2.5cm (1in) thick and 125–150g (4–5oz), or 4 larded loin fillet steaks, about 5cm (2in) thick and 7cm (3in) in diameter (fillet can be up to 5cm [2in] thick, depending on the season and what type of deer it comes from. A butcher can join 2 loins together to make a bigger portion)

For the Sauce

200ml (7fl oz) chicken or game stock

50ml (2fl oz) red wine

juice of 1 orange

50ml (2fl oz) double cream

1 bay leaf

1 tablespoon redcurrant jelly

8 sprigs of fresh redcurrants (optional)

1 teaspoon Worcestershire sauce

Combine the peppercorns, thyme leaves, oil and salt in a small bowl. Lay the venison steaks or fillets on a chopping board and spread about half the peppercorn mixture over just the top of them. If using loin, pat about a quarter of the mixture on both sides of the meat.

If using steaks

Place a large, heavy-based frying pan over a high heat. When hot, add 2 of the steaks and cook, peppered-side down, for about 2 minutes, or until brown. (Don't cook more than 2 at a time as it will lower the temperature of the pan too much and make it harder to brown the meat.) Brush more of the peppercorn mixture on the steaks, then turn and cook for another 2 minutes, or until brown, and the meat is medium-pink inside. (If using a digital thermometer, the temperature should be 55–60°C [130–140°F] for medium rare to medium, and 70°C [160°F] for well done, remembering that the temperature will rise by 5°C [40°F] or so after you take the meat off the heat.) Transfer to a plate, cover and keep warm, then cook and rest the other steaks in the same way.

If using fillets

Preheat the oven 190°C/375°F/Gas Mark 5. Meanwhile, place a large ovenproof frying pan over a high heat. When hot, cook the fillets 2 at a time for about 1½ minutes on each side. Transfer to the oven for 10 minutes, until done to your liking. This timing will give you meat that is pink in the middle. If using a digital thermometer, the temperature should be the same as specified above. Transfer the fillets to a plate, cover and keep warm, then cook and rest the other fillets in the same way.

To make the sauce, put the pan back on the hob, pour in the stock and stir to scrape up any tasty bits stuck to the bottom. Add the wine, orange juice, cream and bay leaf (and any remaining peppercorn mixture if cooking loin), bring to the boil and let it bubble away until reduced by about half. Stir in the redcurrant jelly and redcurrants (if using). Once the jelly has dissolved, stir in the Worcestershire sauce. Return the steaks to the pan to warm briefly in the sauce. Serve immediately.

→

Rabbit has always been popular in France and Italy, but only recently has it been starting to reappear on British tables. We tend to sell the more tender farmed rabbit for roasting in dishes such as this. Wild rabbit can be tougher and benefits from longer stewing, but is also a meat that's worth rediscovering. Rabbit offal is famously delicious, so get this with the rabbit if possible in order to use it in the sauce.

Roast rabbit with pancetta

Serves 4

1 farmed rabbit, jointed into 2 pieces of saddle and 4 legs (ask your butcher in advance)

6 small sprigs of tarragon

100g (3½oz) thin-cut smoked pancetta or smoked streaky bacon

2 banana shallots, cut in half lengthways

2 celery sticks, each cut into 3 long pieces

sea salt and freshly ground black pepper

For the sauce
knob of butter

1 teaspoon plain flour

200ml (7fl oz) hot chicken stock

rabbit offal (optional but good)

150ml (¼ pint) full-fat crème fraîche

1 teaspoon Dijon mustard

1 tablespoon finely chopped tarragon

Preheat the oven to 190°C/375°F/Gas Mark 5.

Season the rabbit joints with a little salt and a fair amount of pepper. Lay a sprig of tarragon on top of each piece. Wrap a slice of the pancetta around each piece of saddle and lay slices over the legs so that they fit snugly, tucking the ends underneath.

Put the shallots and celery in a roasting tray and place the rabbit on top. Roast in the oven for 45 minutes, or until the pancetta is crisp and the rabbit cooked through but still juicy. Transfer to a plate, cover with foil and a couple of tea towels, and leave in a warm place.

To make the sauce, put the roasting tray on the hob over a medium-low heat. Melt the butter in it, then sprinkle with the flour and stir well. Gradually add the hot stock, stirring hard as you do so to mix it with the flour and scraping up any tasty bits in the bottom of the pan. If using rabbit offal, add it now as it will give extra flavour to the stock. Stir in the crème fraîche and mustard and leave to simmer for a couple of minutes. Bring to the boil and bubble away to thicken slightly. Strain the liquid into a jug and stir in the chopped tarragon.

Put the rabbit pieces on warm plates, one leg on each plate and adding the saddle pieces to the forelegs, which are less meaty than the hind legs (or giving them to the people with the biggest appetites). Pour some sauce on to each plate and serve with potatoes and a crisp green salad or green beans.

Butchers and game dealers often sell chunks of mixed game for casseroling. Adding the right flavours – smoked bacon, bay, juniper and thyme – will give you a special and tasty supper dish (which can also be used as a pie filling), and generally at a good price compared to other game. We like to use dark meat, such as venison leg or shoulder, mallard duck and wild boar, along with paler game (pheasant, rabbit and suchlike). The other trick is to use the best smoked bacon you can buy – the stronger the smoke, the better. As it cooks, it combines with the other ingredients to release a magical wintry aroma.

Game casserole

Serves 6

1 tablespoon olive oil

2 onions, chopped

100g (3½oz) smoked streaky bacon, chopped

2 garlic cloves, finely chopped

1 tablespoon plain flour

400ml (14fl oz) hot chicken or game stock

200ml (7fl oz) red wine

1.25kg (2½lb) game, ideally 50:50 dark and white meat, cut into 3.5–5-cm (1½–2-in) chunks

100g (3½oz) cranberry or redcurrant sauce

2 bay leaves

2 teaspoons fresh thyme leaves, or 1 teaspoon dried

½ tablespoon juniper berries, crushed

225g (7½oz) carrots, cut into matchsticks

225g (7½oz) button mushrooms, trimmed

sea salt and freshly ground black pepper

Pour the olive oil into a large flameproof casserole dish over a medium-low heat. When hot, add the onions and bacon with a little sea salt and plenty of black pepper, and fry until soft (about 10–15 minutes), stirring occasionally. Add the garlic and cook for another minute or so, then sprinkle in the flour. Pour in the hot stock and mix well. Add the wine, bring to the boil and bubble for a couple of minutes to thicken slightly.

Add the game, cranberry or redcurrant sauce, bay leaves, thyme and juniper berries. Bring to the boil, then cover and simmer for 45 minutes. Add the carrots and mushrooms and cook for another 45 minutes, until the meat is tender. Taste and adjust the seasoning as necessary.

Serve with dauphinoise, baked or sauté potatoes and seasonal vegetables.

Some cooks consider that the bones of game birds make the ultimate stock. In fact, it's almost worth cooking a pigeon or pheasant just to get the delicious broth. You don't need to use the bones of cooked birds. Wild birds have most of their meat on the breast, so you can take this off to cook separately (see Pigeon & Port Pie, page 190) and use the rest of the body to make stock for soup. Venison bones (shin and knuckle) are also good – the best ones of all come from the saddle, because of the tasty meat between the ribs. A butcher may have these after taking off the fillets, so ask in advance if they might be kept aside for you.

To turn your soup into a more substantial dish, use the Italian trick of adding tiny pasta shapes, such as stelline (little stars) or orzo (like rice grains). Alternatively, use pearl barley instead of pasta, but don't add more than specified as it swells up a lot. Just simmer it in the stock for about 30 minutes, then add the vegetables and cook until tender.

Game broth with small pasta

Serves 4

1 litre (1¾ pints) well-flavoured game stock (see page 286)

2 tablespoons Madeira, dry sherry or port

juice of ½ orange

40g (1½ oz) tiny pasta shapes, or 20–25g (¾–1oz) pearl barley

1 carrot, cut into thin matchsticks

1 leek, white part only, cut into thin slices

finely chopped flat leaf parsley, to garnish

sea salt and freshly ground black pepper

Pour the stock into a saucepan and bring to the boil. Stir in the Madeira, then add orange juice to taste.

Add the pasta, carrot and leek. Season with salt. Bring to the boil, then simmer, covered, for about 8 minutes, or until the pasta is cooked and the vegetables are tender.

Taste the soup and adjust the seasoning if necessary. Sprinkle with the parsley before serving.

We sell a lot of these kebabs in the shop, mostly for dinner parties and suppers, though they are good for a smart barbecue as well. The aniseed flavour of fennel is a great partner for duck, and this rich combination of flavours goes well with a Chinese-style dressing of plum sauce and orange zest.

Duck & fennel kebabs

Serves 4

4 duck breasts

2 medium fennel bulbs, trimmed

4 large plums

2–3 tablespoons Chinese plum sauce

finely grated zest of 1 orange

Remove the skin from the duck breasts by firmly gripping the end and pulling it away. Cut each breast widthways into 4 chunky pieces.

Cut the fennel bulbs in half lengthways. Pull off the outer leaves, trim off any discoloured parts and discard the woody core. Cut each half into 3 large pieces; you want 12 pieces of fennel in all. Cut 3 large pieces off each plum.

Push one piece of fennel, curved-side down, on to a wooden skewer. Bend a piece of the duck breast around it to form a squat c-shape and push the skewer through both sides of the meat. Push a piece of plum on to the skewer. Repeat with the rest of the fennel, meat and plums.

Lay the kebabs in a dish and brush about $\frac{1}{2}$ tablespoon of the plum sauce over each one. Cover and place in the fridge to marinate for up to 24 hours, until you're ready to cook.

Heat a barbecue or grill until very hot. Place the kebabs on a rack about 7cm (3in) from the heat source and cook for about 4 minutes on each side, or until the duck is cooked through but still pink. Sprinkle over the orange zest.

Serve as part of a barbecue, or as a supper dish with stir-fried vegetables and rice.

Dark, dense and delicious, pigeon is a fantastic meat. Squab pigeon is especially tender, though this dish is also delicious made with wood pigeon. Most of the flesh is in the breasts, so get your butcher to take these off, and give you the carcasses to make a stock for the sauce.

Pigeon & port pie

Serves 6

1 tablespoon olive oil

large knob of butter

2 onions, finely chopped

3 smoked streaky bacon rashers, finely chopped

1 teaspoon fresh thyme leaves

200g (7oz) large mushrooms, cut into 1–2.5-cm (½–1-in) slices

2 tablespoons plain flour

75ml (3fl oz) port

400ml (14fl oz) hot stock made from the pigeon carcasses, or use chicken stock

5 tablespoons finely chopped flat leaf parsley

12 squab pigeon breast fillets, cut into 3 pieces

1½ tablespoons sesame seeds (optional)

salt and freshly ground black pepper

For the stock

6 squab pigeon carcasses, breasts removed

2 onions, cut into quarters

2 celery sticks, cut into large chunks

1 carrot, cut into large chunks

2 star anise

2 bay leaves

small bunch of thyme

6 peppercorns

For the pastry

200g (7oz) plain flour, plus extra for dusting

pinch of fine sea salt

100g (3½oz) cold unsalted butter, cut into small dice

1 egg whisked with 2 tablespoons milk, for eggwash

First make the stock. Put all the ingredients into a large pan, cover with cold water and bring just to the boil, skimming off any froth that rises to the surface. Lower the heat and simmer, uncovered, for 2 hours. Strain, discarding the solids, then return the stock to the pan. Bring back to the boil and bubble hard until reduced by about one-third. You'll need 400ml (14fl oz) for the pie, but save the rest for making soup.

To make the pastry, put the flour in a bowl and mix with the salt. Add the butter and rub it into the flour using the tips of your fingers. When the texture resembles breadcrumbs, stir in half the eggwash using a table knife. Bring the mixture together with your hands to form a dough. Knead briefly, then wrap in clingfilm or greaseproof paper and chill for at least 30 minutes.

Preheat the oven to 200°C/400°F/Gas Mark 6.

To prepare the pie filling, put the oil and butter in a large sauté pan over a medium heat. When hot, add the onions and bacon, season with a little salt, plenty of pepper and the thyme, and fry until soft (about 10–15 minutes), stirring occasionally. Add the mushrooms, turn up the heat slightly and cook until they release their juices (about 10 minutes), stirring occasionally.

Sprinkle over the flour and stir into the fat. Add the port and hot stock and mix well. Bring to the boil and cook for about 5 minutes, until the sauce has thickened. Stir in the parsley. Add the pigeon breasts, then tip the mixture into a pie dish, about 25cm (10in) in diameter.

Dust a work surface with flour and roll out the pastry until it is about 5cm (2in) larger all round than the pie dish. Cut 2.5-cm (1-in) strips from around each edge of the pastry. Press these on to the lip of the pie dish and brush with the remaining eggwash. Cover the pie with the pastry lid, sticking it firmly to the pastry rim. Trim off the excess, then crimp the edges together to form a seal. If you like, reroll the pastry trimmings and cut out shapes to stick on top of the pie. Brush with the eggwash, then sprinkle with the sesame seeds, if using.

Bake for 30–40 minutes, until the pastry is golden and cooked through.

Grouse is a superb British treat, and we have customers who eagerly await the 'Glorious 12th' of August when the season starts, tailing off in December. The price of grouse varies, depending on the availability of the birds and the butcher you buy from. They're often cheaper if you live near a shoot. Grouse is best roasted simply, so we've done that, but added an optional extra to the gravy. Bilberries grow on the moorland where the grouse roam, but they are not widely available. If you can't gather them yourself, use blueberries instead.

Roast grouse with bilberry gravy

Serves 2

2 oven-ready grouse

knob of unsalted butter, plus 25g (1oz) extra, for frying

2 smoked streaky bacon rashers, cut in half

olive oil

2 round pieces of crustless white bread, about 12cm (5in) diameter

sea salt flakes and freshly ground black pepper

For the gravy
1 tablespoon plain flour

2 tablespoonss red wine

200ml (7fl oz) game stock (see page 286)

large handful of fresh bilberries or blueberries

Preheat the oven to 230°C/450°F/Gas Mark 8.

Put the birds in a roasting tray. Smear a little butter over the top of each bird and season with salt and pepper. Drape a half-rasher of bacon over the breast of each bird (to protect the delicate and fatless meat from fierce heat). Trickle over a little of the olive oil.

Put the birds in the oven for 10 minutes. If the bacon is browned, remove and set it aside. Return the birds to the oven for another 10 minutes. Transfer them to a warm plate, cover with foil and a tea towel, and set aside to rest.

Put the extra butter and a little more olive oil in a clean pan over a medium-high heat. When hot, add the bread and fry until brown on both sides.

Meanwhile, make the gravy. Put the roasting pan over a medium-low heat and melt the butter. Sprinkle in the flour and stir it around to cook a little. Add the wine and let it bubble, stirring as it does so, and scraping up any tasty bits stuck in the bottom of the pan. Add the stock and bilberries and cook for a couple of minutes, squashing the berries slightly to release their juices. Let the sauce bubble away until slightly thickened. Taste and season with salt and pepper.

Serve the grouse sitting on top of its fried round croûton, with watercress and good potato crisps, or some other form of potato.

The best game

Game is British, seasonal, natural, healthy and delicious. In other words, it suits the way that many people like to eat these days. The meat comes from wild animals – birds, deer, rabbit, hare and suchlike – which are gathered from moors, fields and forests and brought to butchers by game dealers. Their skill is to preserve the essential naturalness of this wild food so that it arrives on the table with all its beautiful flavours intact.

Our dealer is Yorkshire Game, a company that supplies many of the top London restaurants and has helped transform game dealing from a 'sling-the-birds-in-the-back-of-the-van' operation to a bespoke service that brings the truly wild to the sophisticated city plate in the best possible way.

Grouse is a good example of a game bird that Yorkshire Game supplies to us from the start of the season, 12 August. The company has contacts with 30-odd heather moorland shoots, from Angus in east Scotland down to Derbyshire. Refrigerated vans collect the freshly shot game and take it straight to a holding chiller in north Yorkshire. All the time, they are checking temperatures, handling the birds as little as possible and putting them neatly on trays. Chefs and good butchers (like Lidgate's) prefer to get birds 'oven-ready naked' – in other words, not wrapped in clingfilm but hung to the right degree and gutted. We just put some bacon on top to keep the flesh moist and they are ready to roast.

Venison exemplifies the variables of game. The saddle of a hind (female deer) generally weighs 3–5kg (7–11lb), while that from a mighty Galloway stag can weigh as much as 14kg (30lb). Some of the best times to eat venison are in the summer, before the stag's meat gets spoilt by testosterone in the build-up to the autumn rut (mating period). However, summer is when the animals go up to the high ground to get away from the midges, so they are harder to stalk and kill.

Game dealers, such as Ben Weatherall of Yorkshire Game, know what is best in any particular week, and can advise butchers and chefs accordingly. They select the best-quality animals, preferably those shot in the head so there are no small pieces of metal to remove from the meat.

Now that game is more available and better than ever, chefs are developing ideas for using it and people are becoming more adventurous in buying it. That's good news because there's a great deal to explore. Some game birds, such as pheasant, originated in Asia, and its lean, flavoursome meat takes well to curry spices. Other good partners for meat of this type include fruit, smoked bacon, cream, juniper and tarragon.

A word of warning, though: don't expect game to be predictable. Big hotels or restaurants sometimes ask Lidgate's for, say, 250 woodcock, but there's just no way we can meet that sort of order. Game is wild, so the numbers cannot be guaranteed – everyone must take what comes. That is part of the charm of game: it's the polar opposite of a mass-produced commodity. You have to be patient and enjoy what turns up.

Game Seasons*
Below are listed the shooting seasons for the main types of game. What we have available in the shop won't tally exactly with these dates – certain birds, such as mallard, teal and snipe, can be sold only between 1 September and 28 February – but the list

is a good guide to what you might see and when. Rabbit, wild boar and wood pigeon can be sold all through the year.

 * Information courtesy of the British Association for Shooting and Conservation (www.basc.org.uk)

Game birds

Red grouse	12 August – 10 December
Duck and goose (inland)	1 September – 31 January
Duck and goose (below high-water mark)	1 September – 20 February 1 September – 20 February
Hare	1 September – 31 March
Red-legged Partridge	1 September – 1 February
Pheasant	1 October – 1 February
Woodcock	1 October – 31 January

Deer

Venison seasons vary according to species and different parts of the country. Those listed below are relevant to a most butcher's counters. Out of season, you can often buy frozen venison.

Red Deer:	
Stags (England & Wales)	1 August – 30 April
(Scotland)	1 July – 20 October
Hinds (England & Wales)	1 November – 31 March
(Scotland)	21 October – 15 February
Roe Deer:	
Bucks (England & Wales)	1 April – 31 October
(Scotland)	1 April – 20 October
Does (England & Wales)	1 November – 31 March
(Scotland)	21 October – 31 March

6

Roasts

Behind the main counter in the shop we display a row of carefully butchered joints for roasting. Part of our craft is to make a joint easier and more economical for the cook, and we do this by cutting it for minimal wastage and tying it up so that it cooks evenly.

Roasts are often more tender cuts, such as leg and loin, that cook relatively quickly. While we trim away excess fat, we believe that even lean cuts should have some fat in order to baste the meat as it cooks. Accordingly, the meat we favour carries some fat, on the outside and as internal marbling, or else we tie some fat – carefully chosen and flattened to an even thickness – around the meat to add extra flavour and keep it juicy. When tying up a joint, we also aim for neat knots all lined up in a row.

Our customers are often after prime cuts for roasting, and we include recipes for some of these in this chapter. The many other, less expensive parts of the animal can be roasted more slowly in order to melt their tough connective tissues and produce a succulent joint at a more economical price. Pork belly, lamb and pork shoulder, for example, all roast beautifully, and recipes for them are given here too.

Bone is a good conductor of heat, so roasting on the bone is the best way to get heat into the centre of a joint. Once cooked, the bones retain heat, so the meat stays hot for longer as it rests and redistributes its juices.

There are various theories about how best to roast meat. Some cook a joint for many hours at a very low temperature. Others go high and fast. In this book we tend to recommend starting the meat off at a high temperature to brown the outside, then lowering it to around 160°C/325°F/Gas Mark 3 so that the meat cooks more gently and there's less risk of it drying out. Then rest the meat for at least 10 minutes to let the juices redistribute.

Oven temperatures do vary a great deal, and are also affected by the amount of food in the oven and the size of the joint you are cooking. It's a good idea to check for readiness about 20 minutes or so before the end of the calculated cooking time. You can always cover the meat and set it aside to rest until you are ready to eat.

A growing number of our customers these days are using a digital probe thermometer to measure when meat is cooked to their liking. Make sure the probe is inserted in the coolest place – the thickest part of the meat – and leave it there until the reading settles. Don't take the temperature nearer the surface, or go through the centre and near the other side, as this means the temperature can be as much as 10 degrees out.

Another tip is to take the meat out of the oven when the temperature is 5°C (40°F) under your target, as the temperature continues to rise for a while once the meat has been removed. Danny also touches the metal probe to notice how hot the meat is at a certain temperature. This is like the traditional 'metal-skewer method' of assessing the temperature and 'done-ness' of meat. Leave the skewer in the centre of the meat and count to three. Put the tip of the skewer on your lips. Cold means not cooked, warm means rare and hot means well done.

FIRST
FROM
RIGHT

Rib of beef is the ultimate roast, magnificent to set on the table and fantastic to eat. This one has three ribs and will feed a family for Sunday lunch, leaving some juicy cold meat to eat during the week. A four-rib joint will feed a dinner or lunch party, and at Christmas, for a real showstopper, we sell huge seven-rib joints that include part of the sirloin. We always cut off the back bone and some of the other muscles to leave just the round central rib-eye. This means that the meat cooks evenly and is easy to carve. However, we leave in the fingerbones and also plenty of luscious fat in order to add flavour to the meat.

Roast rib of beef with Yorkshire pudding & red wine gravy

Serves 6–8

3-rib joint of beef, back bone removed and fingerbones trimmed (about 3–3.5kg/7–8lb trimmed weight)

2 onions, halved

2 carrots, cut into large chunks

2 celery sticks, halved

salt and freshly ground black pepper

For the Yorkshire batter

300g (10oz) plain flour

pinch of fine sea salt

3 large eggs plus 1 large egg yolk

350ml (12fl oz) milk

350ml (12fl oz) water

3 tablespoons dripping or olive oil

For the gravy

400ml (14fl oz) beef stock and/or vegetable cooking water

1 tablespoon plain flour

about 150ml (¼ pint) red wine

Preheat the oven to 220°C/425°F/Gas Mark 7. Take the meat out of the fridge 1 hour before roasting so it doesn't go into the oven stone-cold.

Meanwhile, make the batter. Combine the flour and salt in a large bowl and make a well in the centre. Crack in the eggs and extra yolk and pour in a little of the milk. Start mixing the flour into the liquid, and continue mixing as you add the remaining liquid bit by bit, stirring hard to get a smooth batter. Cover with clingfilm and place in the fridge.

Put the onions, carrots and celery in a roasting tray. Place the meat on top, fat-side up. Season well all over with salt and pepper. Roast for 15 minutes, then lower the temperature to 160°C/325°F/Gas Mark 3 and continue cooking for one of the following times per 500g (1lb), depending on how you like your meat:

15 minutes for rare

20 minutes for medium

25 minutes for well done

About 15 minutes before the end of the cooking time, you can use a meat thermometer to help get the beef to your liking:

45–47°C (113–117°F) for rare

50–52°C (122–126°F) for medium rare

55–60°C (131–140°F) for medium

65–70°C (149–158°F) for well done

Make sure the probe goes into the thickest part of the meat, and take the joint out of the oven when it is 5°C (40°F) under your target, as its temperature will continue to rise for a while.

Put the joint on a carving board, cover with foil and a couple of clean tea towels and set aside to rest while you cook the Yorkshire pudding. Alternatively, if you have a double oven, warm it to 110°C/225°F/Gas Mark ¼ and pop the meat inside.

Turn the main oven back up to 220°C/425°F/Gas Mark 7. Put the dripping or oil in a baking tin and place it in the oven. When the fat is smoking hot, pour in the batter and bake for 30 minutes.

Meanwhile, make the gravy. Place the roasting tray still containing the veg over a medium-low heat. Pour in the stock and stir well, scraping up the tasty bits stuck in the bottom of the pan. Strain the liquid into a jug, discarding the vegetables. When the fat has risen to the top, spoon or pour it off into a bowl.

Return 1½ tablespoons of the fat to the roasting tray, place over a medium heat and sprinkle in the flour (you can add a teaspoon or so more if you like thickish gravy). Stir well for 1 minute. Add about 90ml (3½fl oz) of the hot stock and/or vegetable water and stir well to combine. Now add the wine and let it bubble up. Gradually add the rest of the liquid and let the gravy simmer until it has thickened slightly. Season to taste with salt and pepper. Keep the gravy warm until needed, pouring in the juices from the rested meat just before serving.

To carve the joint, hold it firmly with a carving fork and cut off slices, starting at the end of the lowest bone, as this will come away the most easily. Cut away the bones and string as you go, not all at once, because they hold the joint together and make carving easier.

Serve the meat on warm plates with the Yorkshire pudding and gravy, along with potatoes and vegetables of your choice, such as steamed leeks and carrots.

→

The French method of roasting chicken is to add wine and stock to the roasting pan and it turns into a delicious *jus* as the bird cooks. The flavour of this liquid can be intensified by reducing it right down. Always buy the best-quality bird you can find: it will generally come with giblets, which make excellent gravy, and the flesh itself will be beautifully moist and flavoursome. The best way to carve a chicken is to remove the whole breasts and cut them into slices across the grain. Then take the leg and thigh off the carcass and cut them in half to share out the brown meat amongst those who like it.

French roast chicken with roast potatoes

Serves 6

1 large free-range chicken (1.75–2kg/3½–4lb)
50g (2oz) unsalted butter
a few bushy sprigs of thyme or tarragon
1 onion, halved
1 celery stick, cut into chunks
1 carrot, cut into chunks
200ml (7fl oz) white wine
400ml (14fl oz) chicken stock
salt and freshly ground black pepper

For the roast potatoes
1.25kg (2½lb) floury potatoes, e.g. King Edward
75g (3oz) duck or goose fat
6 garlic cloves, unpeeled
2 sprigs of thyme

After buying the bird, remove the giblets from their bag and put them in a small bowl. Cover and place both bird and giblets in the fridge. Take the bird out of the fridge 1 hour before cooking so it isn't fridge-cold.

Preheat the oven to 200°C/400°F/Gas Mark 6.

Prepare the potatoes: if they are large, cut them into quarters; if not, cut them in half. Simmer them for 5 minutes or so in boiling salted water, then drain and rough up the outside with a fork. Sprinkle with the flour if you wish and toss to roughly coat.

Smear the breasts of the bird with butter and season well with salt and pepper. Put the thyme or tarragon in the cavity, where it subtly flavours the meat as it cooks.

Put the onion, celery and carrot in a roasting tray. Sit the chicken on top and place in the oven for 20 minutes to brown. To get a richly coloured gravy, pour in half the wine and 100ml (4fl oz) of the stock. Allow the liquid to evaporate almost to nothing and start to caramelize, but take care it doesn't burn.

→

When the chicken has been cooking for almost
20 minutes, start the roast potatoes. Put the duck or
goose fat in a separate roasting tray and place in the
oven for a couple of minutes, until melted and smoking.
Add the potatoes and seasoning, then roll them around
in the fat. Scatter in the garlic and thyme. Put the
potatoes in the oven below the chicken and lower the
temperature to 160°C/325°F/Gas Mark 3. Baste the bird
with any juices in the tray, then pour in the remaining
wine and stock. Continue cooking for 20 minutes per
500g (1lb). Test for readiness by sticking a small sharp
knife into the thickest part of the thigh. If the juices
run clear rather than pink, the bird is ready.

Transfer the chicken to a carving board or platter.
Cover with foil and a couple of clean tea towels and set
aside to rest for about 10 minutes. If the potatoes need
further crisping, increase the heat to 220°C/425°F/Gas
Mark 7 and blast them for another 10 minutes or so.

Meanwhile, strain the roast vegetables and discard.
Return the liquid to the roasting tray, place on the hob
and bring to the boil, using a wooden spoon to scrape
up any bits stuck in the bottom of the pan. Boil hard to
reduce slightly if you wish.

Serve the chicken with the roast potatoes and plenty
of freshly steamed vegetables.

Butchers are increasingly taking off the top of the rump to sell it separately as a cut called a 'picanha' (see page 58). The rest of the rump can then be separated into two muscles that can be rolled together, covered with a thin layer of fat and tied into a superb small roasting joint. Any leftovers are great in salads or sandwiches. To be properly tender, rump must be well hung by the butcher as it is tougher than sirloin. A good butcher will have dry-aged the beef on the bone for a minimum of 21 days.

Rolled roast rump with thyme-baked shallots

Serves 6 (or 4, with delicious leftovers)

1–1.25kg (2–2½lb) beef rump, rolled (ask your butcher)

¼ teaspoon mustard powder

400ml (14fl oz) hot beef stock

1 teaspoon plain flour

50ml (2fl oz) red wine

sea salt flakes and freshly ground black pepper

For the thyme-baked shallots

400g (13oz) small shallots

2 tablespoons beef dripping or butter

about 8 sprigs of fresh thyme

Take the meat out of the fridge 1 hour before cooking. Preheat the oven to 220°C/425°F/Gas Mark 7.

Meanwhile, peel the shallots and place them in a snug-fitting baking dish. Dot the dripping or butter over them and scatter with the thyme sprigs. Season with salt and pepper.

Put the beef in a roasting tray and season all over with salt and pepper. Place in the oven and put the shallots on a lower shelf. Roast for 15 minutes, then lower the heat to 160°C/325°F/Gas Mark 3. Take out the shallots, stir them around, and return to the oven. Depending how well done you like your beef, continue roasting it for the following times per 500g (1lb):

15 minutes for rare

20 minutes for medium rare

30 minutes for well done

About 15 minutes before the end of the cooking time, you can use a meat thermometer to help get the beef to your liking:

45–47°C (113–117°F) for rare

50–52°C (122–126°F) for medium rare

55–60°C (131–140°F) for medium

65–70°C (149–158°F) for well done

Make sure the probe goes into the thickest part of the meat, and take the joint out of the oven when it is 5°C (40°F) under your target, as its temperature will continue to rise for a while.

Transfer the meat to a warm plate, cover with foil and a couple of clean tea towels and leave to rest for 15 minutes. Continue cooking the shallots, covering them with foil if they are getting too brown.

Meanwhile, make the gravy. Place the mustard powder in a small bowl, add a small ladleful of the hot stock and stir to combine. Put the beef roasting tray on the hob over a medium heat. Sprinkle in the flour and stir so it absorbs the fat and cooks slightly. Pour in the stock gradually, stirring as you do so to avoid lumps forming. Stir in the wine and then the mustard mixture. Bring to the boil and bubble away until the gravy is as thick as you like – add a bit more stock or water if it gets too thick. Taste and adjust the seasoning if necessary.

Serve the meat with the gravy and shallots, plus mashed or new potatoes and seasonal greens.

A leg of lamb is a handsome joint to put on the table either at a dinner party or for Sunday lunch. Here vegetables are roasted around the meat, absorbing the delicious juices to make an improvised ratatouille that acts as a saucy accompaniment. If necessary, ask your butcher to remove the aitch-bone at the thick end of the leg in order to make carving easier. We've named this dish after the speciality seasonal lamb from the Pyrenees we sell in the shop, because the recipe is a French version of the traditional roast.

Pyrenees leg of lamb with roasted vegetables

Serves 8

2.25–2.75kg (5–6lb) leg of lamb

8 tomatoes, quartered

2 red peppers, deseeded and each cut into 8 long strips

2 orange or yellow peppers, deseeded and each cut into 8 long strips

3 red onions, quartered

2 medium aubergines, cut into 2.5-cm (1-in) cubes

6 garlic cloves, finely chopped

6 tablespoons olive oil

5 sprigs of thyme

5 sprigs of rosemary

1.5kg (3lb) small potatoes

1 tablespoon balsamic vinegar

about 20 basil leaves, roughly torn

1–2 teaspoons honey, or to taste

salt and freshly ground black pepper

Take the meat out of the fridge 1 hour before cooking so it isn't fridge-cold.

Preheat the oven to 220°C/425°F/Gas Mark 7.

Combine the tomatoes and all the vegetables, apart from the potatoes, in a large bowl. Add the garlic, half the oil, a good seasoning of salt and pepper and 3 sprigs each of thyme and rosemary.

Put the potatoes in a roasting tray. Drizzle over 2 tablespoons of the remaining oil, season with salt and pepper, and sprinkle with the remaining sprigs of thyme and rosemary.

Place the lamb in a separate large roasting tray. Drizzle the remaining tablespoon of oil over the meat and season well with salt and pepper. Roast for 20 minutes, then lower the heat to 160°C/325°F/Gas Mark 3. Put the potatoes on a shelf below the meat. Tip the bowl of vegetables into the lamb roasting tray, lift the meat up with a spatula and push some of the veg underneath it.

→

Roast the mixture for 15 minutes per 500g (1lb) of meat
if you like it medium (pink), or 20 minutes for well
done, stirring the vegetables every 20 minutes so that
they cook evenly. About 30 minutes before the cooking
time is up, you can use a meat thermometer to help get
the lamb to your liking:

60°C (140°F) for medium

70°C (158°F) for well done

Make sure the probe goes into the thickest part of
the meat, and take the joint out of the oven when it
is 5°C (40°F) under your target, as its temperature will
continue to rise for a while.

Place the meat on a carving board, cover with foil
and a couple of clean tea towels, and set aside to rest
for 15 minutes.

Pour the vinegar into the roasting tray still containing
the vegetables. Add the basil leaves and stir well. Taste
and add enough honey to give a balanced, mellow
flavour. Season if necessary with more salt and pepper.

A leg of lamb can be carved in different places to
provide meat that is either pink or more well done,
thus keeping everyone happy. Start by cutting slices
at a 45-degree angle through the thickest part, going
right down to the bone. This means you are cutting
across the grain of the meat, which makes it more
tender to eat. Serve with the roast vegetable mixture
and the potatoes.

Ducks come in slightly different shapes and sizes according to breed, but all of them have quite a high percentage of fat and bone to flesh. This means that the actual amount of meat you get is much less than with a chicken. In general, you could say that one bird feeds four people.

Roast duck with blackcurrants & cassis

Serves 4

1 oven-ready duck (1.75–2.25kg/3½–5lb)

½ an orange

50g (2oz) blackcurrants, defrosted if frozen

a few sprigs of thyme

1 onion, halved

1 celery stick, cut into large pieces

1 carrot, cut into chunks

sea salt and freshly ground black pepper

For the stock

duck giblets

a few sprigs of thyme

1 onion, roughly chopped

1 celery stick, roughly chopped

1 carrot, roughly chopped

For the blackcurrant sauce

1 teaspoon plain flour

50ml (2fl oz) crème de cassis

150g (5oz) blackcurrants, defrosted if frozen

juice of ½ orange

1½–2 tablespoons honey, or to taste

After buying the bird, remove the giblets from their bag and put them in a small bowl. Cover and store in the fridge. Wipe the duck skin dry and place, uncovered, in the fridge. Take it out of the fridge 1 hour before cooking so it isn't fridge-cold.

Preheat the oven to 220°C/425°F/Gas Mark 7. Cut the wing tips off the duck and place them in a medium saucepan with the giblets and other stock ingredients. Add 400ml (14fl oz) water, bring to the boil, then simmer gently whilst the duck cooks.

Prick the duck all over, especially the fatty parts. Rub the orange half over the skin. Cut the orange into large pieces and push them into the duck cavity, followed by the blackcurrants, a few sprigs of thyme and a seasoning of salt and pepper. Sprinkle the duck skin generously with salt, and add a few twists of pepper.

Put the onion, celery and carrot in a roasting tray and sit the duck on top. Roast for 20 minutes, then lower the heat to 180°C/350°F/Gas Mark 4 and cook for another 1–1¼ hours, basting every so often with the fat that renders out of the bird. At that point start testing the bird to see if it is done by sticking a skewer into the thickest part of the leg: if the juices run clear, the duck is ready. If not, return to the oven, roast for another 15 minutes, then test again. The bird may need up to 1½ hours in total. When ready, transfer to a plate, cover and keep warm.

Now make the sauce. Strain the stock, discarding the solids. Pour most of the fat out of the roasting tray (you can keep this to make wonderful roast potatoes). Sprinkle in the flour and mix it into the remaining fat. Gradually add 300ml (½ pint) of the stock and stir well to get rid of any lumps. Add the cassis and blackcurrants, bring to the boil and let it bubble for 2 minutes. Lower the heat and simmer hard for 5 minutes, until slightly reduced, occasionally squashing the currants with the back of a wooden spoon so that they release their juice and flavour.

Strain the sauce into a saucepan, discarding the solids, and bubble for a few more minutes if you want to reduce it further. Add the orange juice and just enough honey to balance out the tartness. Season with salt and pepper. Pour any juices from the rested duck back into the sauce and heat through again.

There are different ways of carving a duck, depending on breed. Gressingham (a cross between a small wild duck, a mallard and a big peking duck), is mostly breast, so you can carve that in long slices, then cut and pick away the rest of the meat. Otherwise, the neatest way is to cut the whole breasts off the bone (leaving the wing bone in place if you like) and slice the breast meat at an angle. Then cut the whole legs off the carcass and cut them between the thigh and leg.

Give each person both breast and leg meat, pouring the blackcurrant sauce partly over and around it. Serve with greens or peas and potatoes or rice.

This is a great joint for a relaxed Sunday lunch. You leave the meat in the oven for five hours, then razz up the heat at the end to crisp the crackling. Pork shoulder is a cut we favour over leg or even loin because of its flavour and succulence. Rolled, boned meat is easy to carve, but even on-the-bone is easy to pull apart when slow-cooked, although less neat on the plate. This joint feeds about eight people (or more if they are moderate meat eaters and you serve plenty of vegetables). The rub used here is based on flavours you get in barbecue pulled pork: fennel – a natural partner for pork – and smoked paprika, to give that barbecue buzz.

Fennel & smoked paprika slow-roast pork shoulder

Serves 8–10

2kg (4lb) pork shoulder off the bone, rolled, or 2.5g (5lb 8oz) on the bone, skin scored at 1-cm (½-in) intervals

For the rub
1 tablespoon smoked paprika

1 tablespoon fennel seeds, lightly crushed

1 tablespoon prepared English mustard

2 tablespoons olive oil

1 teaspoon sea salt flakes

Preheat the oven to 140°C/275°F/Gas Mark 1. If your butcher hasn't scored the meat – or hasn't scored it enough – sharpen a knife, or use a Stanley knife, and make sure you have incisions at 1-cm (½-in) intervals.

Combine all the rub ingredients in a bowl and mix to a smooth paste. Put the meat in a roasting tray, skin-side down. Spread the rub over the flesh (not the fat). Cover tightly with foil and place in the oven for 5 hours.

Remove the meat from the oven and turn up the heat to 220°C/425°F/Gas Mark 7. The shoulder should be tender, the fat soft and the meat surrounded by delicious juices. Pour the juices off into a saucepan. This is your saucy 'gravy'.

Turn the meat over so it is fat-side up and return to the oven for 20 minutes or so, until the crackling is nice and crisp. Set the meat aside to rest in a warm place for 10–15 minutes, but do not cover it or the crackling will be less crisp.

Just before serving, heat up the gravy, pouring off some of the fat first if you like. Carve the meat and serve on hot plates to compensate for it not being piping hot. Offer spuds, greens and the hot gravy alongside.

We often refer to shoulder of lamb as 'the thinking man's roast'. It has fantastic succulence, texture and flavour, and provides plenty of meat – all for a comparatively reasonable price. The flavourings used below go particularly well with lamb, and this is a great dish on a cold winter weekend. As it's slow-cooked, the timing is not too critical, so you'll have a free morning to read the Sunday papers.

Slow-roast shoulder of lamb with rosemary, anchovies & orange

Serves 6–8

1 orange (organic or scrubbed to remove wax)

3 bushy sprigs of rosemary

1 x 50-g (2-oz) can anchovies in oil, drained

2.25kg (5lb) shoulder of lamb, on the bone

2 garlic cloves, thickly sliced

1 litre (1¾ pints) lamb stock

sea salt and freshly ground black pepper

Preheat the oven to 220°C/425°F/Gas Mark 7.

Using a vegetable peeler, pare the zest off the orange, avoiding the white pith if possible. Cut 14 thin strips from this zest, making them about 2.5cm (1in) long and 3mm (⅛in) wide. Reserve the leftover zest.

Pick off about 14 spriglets of rosemary, reserving the rest. Cut the anchovy fillets in half widthways.

Using the tip of a small sharp knife, poke holes 2.5cm (1in) deep in 5 places on the base of the joint, mostly around the edges, where the bone doesn't get in the way. As you do so, push a piece of garlic into each hole, then a piece of orange zest, half an anchovy and finally a spriglet of rosemary, which can stick out a little bit. Turn the meat over and make another 9 holes on the top, filling them in the same way as before. Season lightly with salt (as the anchovies are salty) and more generously with pepper.

Place the lamb in the oven for 30 minutes, then lower the temperature to 160°C/325°F/Gas Mark 3. Pour in the stock and add the remaining orange zest and rosemary. Cover the lamb with foil and continue to cook for 3–4 hours, until the meat is completely tender.

Transfer the lamb to a plate, cover and leave in a warm place. Strain the stock from the roasting tray, discarding the solids and skimming off the fat. Pour what's left into a saucepan and boil for a minute or so to emulsify, and longer if you want a slightly thicker gravy. Taste and season as necessary.

The meat is easy to 'carve' because it falls off the bone. Serve with mashed or roast potatoes, a green vegetable such as steamed Savoy cabbage, and the gravy.

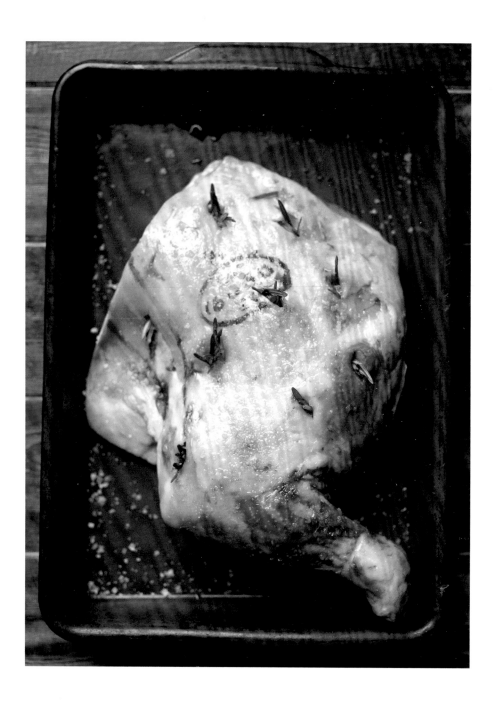

Danny's mother, Jo, favours the end of the leg to serve at home for Sunday lunch. Known as the fore-knuckle on the forelegs, and the knuckle on the rear legs, it is a butcher's choice cut, and not just because it is economical: 'the sweetest meat is nearest to the bone and closest to the ground', as the saying goes. The knuckle doesn't provide big slices of meat, or masses of it, but the taste is delicious. You'll need to order it in advance as it's a slightly unusual cut. David Lidgate, fourth-generation butcher and Danny's father, especially likes this joint served with sauté potatoes, a good alternative to roast spuds. Incidentally, the back knuckle has a small bone that was traditionally cleaned and used as a mustard spoon.

Mrs Lidgate's roast pork knuckle with sauté potatoes

Serves 4

2 fore or back knuckles of pork, or 1 of each (about 1–1.5kg/2–3lb in total), skin scored at 1-cm (½-in) intervals

salt and freshly ground black pepper

For the saute potatoes
750g (1½lb) firm-textured or salad potatoes (e.g. Charlotte or Ratte), unpeeled

2 unpeeled garlic cloves

2–3 tablespoons goose fat, or 2 tablespoons butter and 1 tablespoon olive oil

3 sprigs of rosemary

For the gravy
½ tablespoon plain flour

400ml (14fl oz) hot chicken or pork stock, or water

1 teaspoon apple, quince or medlar jelly (optional)

a squeeze of lemon juice (optional)

Preheat the oven to 220°C/425°F/Gas Mark 7.

Put the pork in a roasting tray. Season well with salt and pepper. Roast for 20 minutes, then lower the heat to 160°C/325°F/Gas Mark 3 and cook for 1 hour or more, until the juices run clear when a skewer is inserted into the thickest part. (At this temperature there's no rush to take the meat out, so if it's convenient to leave it in for 1½ hours, that's fine.) Turn the heat up to 220°C/425°F/Gas Mark 7 and cook for another 10 minutes to crisp up the crackling. (Alternatively, you can cook the joint from start to finish at the higher temperature for 45–60 minutes in total, or until the juices run clear when the meat is pierced with a skewer in the thickest part. Jo cooks hers in the hot top oven of an Aga, moving the roasting tray into a lower oven if the crackling shows signs of overbrowning.)

While the meat is roasting, cut the potatoes into large, equal chunks. Put in a saucepan, cover with salted water and bring to the boil, then simmer until nearly tender (about 7–10 minutes). Drain well and set aside. When cool enough to handle, remove the skin and cut the flesh into pieces about 2.5cm (1in) thick.

Bash the garlic cloves with the side of a heavy knife to squish them slightly. Melt the fat in a large sauté or frying pan. Add the potatoes, garlic and rosemary, plus a pinch of salt and plenty of pepper. Cook on a low heat, turning the potatoes after 10–15 minutes, until golden and crisp (about 45 minutes).

Transfer the meat to a carving board and leave to rest uncovered in a warm place. If necessary, you can cut off the less crisp crackling from the underside of the pork and put it back in a hot oven (220°C/425°F/Gas Mark 7) to crisp up.

To make the gravy, place the roasting tray over a medium heat, pouring off some of the fat to leave about 1–2 tablespoons. Sprinkle over the flour and stir it around on the heat. Pour in the hot stock or water gradually, stirring as you go. If you have some apple, quince or medlar jelly, stir it in now, adding more if you like. Adjust the seasoning if necessary and add a squeeze of lemon if you want to brighten the flavour.

Cut chunks of meat off the bone, then cut them into slices. Serve with the crackling and sauté potatoes, plus seasonal vegetables and the gravy.

This is an easy-timing roast because the meat is layered with fat and lies flat in one piece, so it cooks evenly and with no fear of drying out. Pork belly used to be a real bargain until more and more chefs and cooks cottoned on, but it is still good value. Danny sometimes uses a Gordon Ramsay trick of roasting the pork belly in advance, removing the bones, then wrapping the cooled meat in foil and leaving it in the fridge with a board and weights on top to compress it slightly. When he wants to eat, he cuts the meat into large one-portion squares to roast in a hot oven until thoroughly reheated and the crackling is crisp.

Roast belly of pork with cider gravy

Serves 6

2kg (4lb) belly of pork, ideally from the thick end, skin scored at 1-cm (½-in) intervals

½ tablespoon sea salt flakes

small handful of thyme sprigs

fine salt and freshly ground black pepper

For the gravy

½ tablespoon plain flour

300ml (½ pint) hot chicken or pork stock, or vegetable cooking water

200ml (7fl oz) dry cider

1 teaspoon thyme leaves

After buying the meat, store it in the fridge, uncovered, for at least a couple of hours and ideally overnight to help it dry out. This will give it better crackling.

Remove the meat from the fridge 1 hour before cooking. Preheat the oven to 190°C/375°F/Gas Mark 5.

Place the joint in a roasting tray and rub the skin with the salt flakes. When the oven reaches the correct temperature, use kitchen paper to wipe the excess salt and any moisture off the skin. Sprinkle with a little more fresh salt and the thyme, and season well with black pepper.

Roast the meat in the oven for 2 hours. Lower the heat to 150°C/300°F/Gas Mark 2 and roast for another hour, or until the meat is tender. Transfer to a serving plate and keep warm. If the crackling isn't as crisp as you'd like, put the belly back in a hot oven (220°C/425°F/Gas Mark 7) for 5 minutes or so.

Pour off all but 1 tablespoon or so of the fat from the roasting tray. Put the tray on a medium heat, sprinkle in the flour and stir to cook slightly and get rid of any lumps. Gradually stir in the hot stock or vegetable water and then the cider. Add the thyme leaves. Bring to the boil, then lower the heat slightly and cook until reduced to a nice gravy. Taste and adjust the seasoning as necessary.

To carve the meat, stand the belly on its side and cut off the bones in a sheet. (Keep these ribs to eat at another time, perhaps coated in barbecue sauce and grilled until hot.) Cut the belly meat into thick slices. Serve with seasonal vegetables, potatoes and the cider gravy.

7
Grills & Barbecues

All the recipes in this chapter are suitable for cooking outside on a barbecue or inside on a griddle pan. The charred outside of the meat contrasts beautifully with the juicy centre, and the aroma is one of the most tempting and evocative scents of summer. In fact, some people now cook this way all through the year, when weather permits.

Outdoors or in, we recommend certain cuts for this quick type of cooking. They range from tender lamb cutlets to tasty but tougher meat, such as slices of pork shoulder, which can be marinated, cooked and sliced across the grain to serve. Plenty of meat is already 'good to go': just whack it on the heat and you've got supper. (It's no surprise that our sausage sales soar during the summer.)

Over the years, we have developed ready-to-cook dishes that add a touch of glamour to informal outdoors eating. In particular, we've come up with ideas for a number of kebabs involving unusual skewers. Our Veal Kebabs (see page 240), for example, are threaded on to asparagus stalks, our Lamb Kebabs (see page 242) on to rosemary twigs, and our Chicken Kebabs (see page 236) on lemon grass stalks. These natural skewers look great and add fragrance and flavour to the meat from the inside out.

People are more sophisticated about outdoor eating these days, and some now want bigger pieces of meat to slow-smoke. Ideas for this come from all over the world, where the barbecue is a standard way of cooking. Richard, the Brazilian butcher who makes our sausages, says in his country a barbecue can be an all-day affair. The men might hang out by the meat, throwing the remains of their warm beer on to a big piece of brisket as it cooks, which flavours the meat and frees up their glass for a fresh cold beer from the fridge.

In this chapter, we give a recipe for a Butterflied Leg of Lamb (see page 230), an easy large piece of meat to barbecue or grill. This doesn't take very long to cook and will feed a good number of people. We show you how to bone the meat, or you can ask your butcher to do this for you in advance. As with many barbecue classics, you can get plenty of marinade into this flattened-out meat to add yet more flavour before it is chargrilled.

The beauty of barbecuing or griddling is that you can do almost all the preparation, especially the marinating of meat, well in advance. It's amazing what a difference a marinade makes to the texture and taste of meat, especially if you include ingredients such as yoghurt, vinegar and citrus juices.

A few hours before you're ready to start cooking, you can chill the drinks in the fridge, make the salads, gather up your sauces and make sure you've bought some good bread. Then all you have to do is stand by the barbecue with friends and family, cooking and turning the meat as necessary. This really is the ultimate sociable and easy-going way to eat and entertain.

A baby back of ribs is the sheet of ribs trimmed off the loin. As a by-product of a more expensive cut, it can often be found at a good price. While baby racks may not have as much on them as chunkier spare ribs, when they are cut to be meaty, they make a tasty barbecue or supper dish as bones always add flavour to meat. This recipe has a classic fingerlickin' barbecue sauce, smoky and sweet. Add some chilli if you'd also like some heat.

Barbecue baby back of ribs

Serves 4–6 as a main course, or more as part of a barbecue

3 baby backs of ribs (about 400–450g/13–14½oz each)

3 celery sticks, cut in half

1 tablespoon smoked paprika

1 teaspoon crushed coriander seeds

salt

For the barbecue sauce
2 tablespoons olive oil

90ml (3½fl oz) maple syrup

60ml (2¼fl oz) cider vinegar

90ml (3½fl oz) tomato ketchup

2 tablespoons Worcestershire sauce

1 tablespoon soy sauce

1 teaspoon crushed coriander seeds

1 teaspoon smoked paprika

Put the racks of ribs in a large pan. Cover with water and add the celery, paprika, coriander seeds and salt. Bring to the boil, then simmer, covered, for 45–60 minutes, or until the meat is tender.

Meanwhile, put all the ingredients for the sauce in a saucepan. Stir well and bring to the boil, then simmer, uncovered, for 15 minutes, stirring occasionally until slightly thickened.

Drain the ribs and place them in a shallow ceramic dish or large plastic food bag. Slather with the barbecue sauce, leave until cool and then cover the dish or seal the bag and leave in the fridge for up to 24 hours, but no less than 1 hour, turning occasionally, or (if using a bag) massaging the sauce into the meat.

Take the meat out of the fridge 30 minutes before cooking so it isn't stone-cold. Heat a barbecue until the coals are glowing hot, or preheat a grill to its highest setting. Alternatively, preheat the oven to 200°C/400°F/Gas Mark 6.

Barbecue or grill the racks for about 5 minutes on each side, basting with the sauce, until nice and brown. If using an oven, cook them for around 30–40 minutes, or until browned on top.

To serve 4 people as a main course, cut each rack in half. To serve as a starter or part of a barbecue, cut the racks into individual ribs.

Greek cuisine has some dishes particularly associated with outdoor eating, not least this one – herby barbecue pork stuffed into pitta breads along with salad and a tangy yoghurt dressing. The relish used here is quick to make, pretty and also excellent with other grilled meats. Pork shoulder is a good-value cut with lots of flavour, and enough fat to keep it nice and juicy on a barbecue.

Pork souvlaki with honeyed red onion relish

Serves 4 as a main course, or more as part of a barbecue

4 pork shoulder steaks (about 175g/6oz each), cut 1.5–2.5cm (¾–1in) thick

olive oil, for brushing

4–8 pitta breads

100g (3½oz) rocket leaves

sea salt flakes

For the marinade
juice and finely grated zest of 1 lemon

2 tablespoons olive oil

1 tablespoon roughly chopped marjoram

freshly ground black pepper

For the relish
1 tablespoon honey

2½ tablespoons cider vinegar

5 tablespoons olive oil

large pinch of sea salt flakes

2 red onions, finely sliced

For the dressing
4 tablespoons full-fat Greek yogurt

2 tablespoons mayonnaise

1 small garlic clove, crushed

First combine the marinade ingredients in a non-metallic bowl or dish, or a large sealable plastic bag. Add the pork and toss or massage the marinade into the meat. Cover the dish or seal the bag and place in the fridge, ideally for 3 hours, but for at least 1 and up to 24, turning occasionally. Take out of the fridge 30 minutes before cooking.

Meanwhile, make the relish. Put the honey, vinegar, oil and salt in a non-metallic bowl. When the honey has dissolved – stir it around from time to time until it does – add the onions and stir well. Cover and leave to marinate in the fridge, ideally for 3 hours, but for at least 1 hour and up to 24. The mixture will turn a beautiful pink colour.

Heat a barbecue until the coals are glowing hot. Alternatively, heat a griddle pan or heavy-based frying pan on the hob until really hot.

Brush the marinade off the pork, then brush the meat with some oil and sprinkle with sea salt flakes. Cook for 2 minutes on each side, then turn and cook for a further 1½–2 minutes on each side, until browned outside and cooked within.

Transfer the meat to a board and leave to rest for 5 minutes. Meanwhile, combine the dressing ingredients in a bowl and mix well. When that's done, quickly heat up the pitta breads.

Cut the meat into thickish diagonal slices (cutting it like this, across the grain, makes it more tender to eat). Split open the pitta bread and stuff each one with some rocket, a good amount of the relish and some of the meat (the amount depends on whether you want to give each person 1 or 2 pitta breads). Top with dollops of the yoghurt dressing and serve with the rest of the rocket alongside.

Whether cooking outdoors or indoors, this is a brilliant way to cook a whole leg of lamb in 25 minutes, rather than roasting it whole for 1½ hours or so. Basically, you remove the two leg bones and spread the meat out into a long, flat piece that is shaped like a butterfly, hence the name. This way, you can also get a marinade right into the meat and have plenty of delicious roasted surface for everyone to eat, plus it is easy to carve. Butterflying a leg isn't difficult once you get the hang of the bones and muscles; the cuts become more intuitive with practice. It's one of the pieces of home-butchery that people always want to be shown when they come to spend half a day in the shop as a raffle prize.

Moroccan butterflied leg of lamb

Serves 8

1 boned and butterflied leg of lamb – about 1.9–2.5kg (4¼–5½lb) on the bone (aitch bone removed), or 1.5kg (3lb) off the bone (ask your butcher in advance, or follow the step-by-step instructions overleaf)

For the Moroccan marinade

1½ teaspoons ground ginger

1½ teaspoons ground turmeric

2 teaspoons ground coriander

2 teaspoons smoked paprika

½ teaspoon freshly ground black pepper

2 teaspoons sea salt flakes

4 garlic cloves, crushed

4 tablespoons olive oil

2 unwaxed lemons (finely grated zest of 1 and juice of 2)

First make the marinade. Combine all the ingredients for it in a shallow, non-metallic container. Place the lamb in it and spoon the marinade all over. Cover and place in the fridge for 12–48 hours, depending how much time you have, turning the meat occasionally.

Take the meat out of the fridge 1 hour before cooking so it isn't stone-cold.

To barbecue

Heat a barbecue until the coals are glowing hot. Place the lamb fat-side down on an oiled rack and cook for 15–20 minutes, until nicely brown. Turn it over and cook for another 10 minutes or so, or until done to your liking. Set aside, covered with foil and a couple of clean tea towels, and leave to rest for 10 minutes, then carve. Pour the juices over the meat.

To griddle and roast

Preheat the oven to 190°C/375°F/Gas Mark 5. Heat a griddle pan on the hob until very hot. Cut the marinated meat into 3 large pieces and put them, skin-side down, in the hot pan to brown, then turn them over to brown the other sides. Transfer to a roasting tray, skin-side up, and cook in the oven for 20–30 minutes, until done to your liking. Leave to rest for 10 minutes, then cut into slices and pour over the juices.

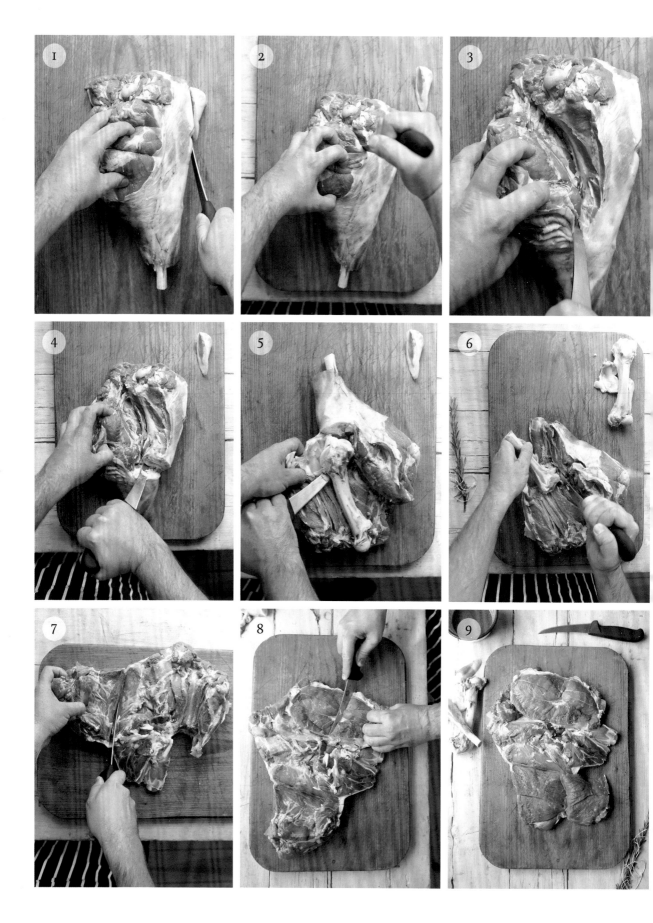

How to butterfly a leg of lamb

If possible use a boning knife for this task. This medium-sized knife with its curved tip gives you good control for a neater job; but any good sharp knife will do the trick.

I   Cut off any particularly big bits of fat: depending on the season and type of lamb, there may be some above the tail-bone at the thick end of the leg. (Note that trimming off the fat is more easily done while the joint is still whole.) Put the leg on a work surface with the bone facing towards you and the fat-side down. If necessary, cut off the gland on one side of the meat (your butcher may have already done this).

2, 3 & 4   Start at the thick end of the leg to cut out the thigh bone. There are two seams of fat running down the meat. Cut alongside the inner one to guide you to the bone. Hold your knife like a dagger and use a small, sawing motion with the tip of the knife to cut at an angle along both sides of the bone. You are not removing the bone at this point, just loosening and exposing it.

5   Put the knife underneath the knobbly end of the thigh bone and run the blade along and underneath the bone, following it with your knife on either side to continue to loosen it from the meat. Cut down between the two bones, wiggling your knife through the ball and socket joint, and cut away the thigh bone altogether.

6   Cut away the kneecap that remains on one side of the leg. To cut out the shank bone, run the blade down one side of the shank bone on the end of the leg to loosen the meat. Cut down the other side of the bone. To do this, it is easiest to position the leg so that the bone is vertical. Cut underneath the shank bone and remove it from the meat.

7   Cut out the triangular 7cm (3in) gland in the middle of the thick part of the leg; you don't have to do this, but removing it makes a neater job. Cut under the thick parts of the leg along the seams and open up the meat so it is spread out on the work surface.

8   Cut horizontally through most of the two thick parts of the meat and open them out, like wings. You can trim off any extra internal fat if you like, or leave it in for succulence.

9   What you've now got is a boneless piece of meat, roughly in the shape of a butterfly. You can flatten the meat further by placing a piece of clingfilm on top and tapping it firmly with a rolling pin.

Chicken wings are excellent value for money, and the tangy marinade used here makes them something really special. Threading wings on to two skewers in a 'ladder' turns them into a portion; it also makes them easy to turn and cook evenly, and ensures they won't slip through the grill-bars to fall on to the coals. Flat metal skewers are best, as the meat stays on more securely and doesn't slip around.

Chicken ladders

Serves 6

18 chicken wings

For the marinade
4 tablespoons olive oil
4 tablespoons Japanese soy sauce
5-cm (2-in) piece fresh root ginger, finely grated
2 garlic cloves, finely chopped
zest and juice of 1 lemon
4 tablespoons honey

Mix all the marinade ingredients together in a shallow non-metallic dish and set aside while the honey dissolves.

If necessary, cut off and discard the wing tips, or reserve for making stock. Place the wings in the marinade, turning to coat. Cover and place in the fridge, ideally overnight, but for at least 1 hour, turning occasionally.

Heat a barbecue until the coals are glowing hot. Alternatively, preheat a grill to its highest setting.

Meanwhile, set out 12 flat metal skewers: you need 2 skewers per portion. Arrange 3 wings in a column on the work surface, flat-side down. Push a skewer through one side of the wing, going through the flesh, over the bone and out of the skin the other side. Continue to push this skewer through the other 2 wings in the same way, spacing them about 3.5–5cm (1½–2in) apart. Push the second skewer through the opposite side of the wings in exactly the same way, keeping it parallel with the first skewer. You want to have the wings in a v-shaped ladder. Repeat this step with all the remaining wings.

Using a sharp knife, slash the fleshy top of each wing 4–5 times: this will help to speed up the cooking.

Barbecue or grill the chicken for about 12 minutes in total, turning every 3 minutes and brushing with the marinade. To test for readiness, slip a knife into the thickest part of the meat – it's done when the juices run clear.

Serve the ladders with a herby potato salad and a crisp green salad.

Lemon grass works well as a skewer, flavouring meat from the inside as it cooks. Our customers like this dish for a special barbecue when entertaining friends. When we first made it, we added grated dried shiitake mushrooms on top, which made a good finishing touch to the marinade – you can add that final flourish if you wish.

Chicken & lemon grass kebab

Makes 4 kebabs

4 skinless chicken breasts (about 160g/5½oz each)

4 lemon grass stalks

1 tablespoon finely chopped coriander leaves

1 lime, cut into quarters, to serve

For the marinade

150ml (¼ pint) coconut cream

1 teaspoon fish sauce (optional)

1 garlic clove, finely chopped

finely grated zest of 1 lime

2 tablespoons finely chopped coriander leaves

½ teaspoon sea salt flakes

First make the marinade by combining all the ingredients for it in a shallow bowl or dish.

If you want to be neat, remove the inner fillet of each chicken breast and trim off the pointed tip (you can use these another time, perhaps for a stir-fry). Cut each breast widthways to get 4 chunky pieces about 3.5–5cm (1½–2in) wide.

Toss the chicken in the marinade, then cover and chill, preferably overnight, but for at least 1 hour.

Run your thumbnail or a small sharp knife down each lemon grass stalk and pull off the outer skin.

Use the tip of a knife to cut a small hole through the centre of each piece of chicken. Push 4 pieces on to each lemon grass stalk so you have a complete chicken breast on each one.

Heat a barbecue until the coals are glowing hot. Alternatively, preheat a grill to its highest setting. Cook the kebabs for 7–8 minutes on each side, or until the meat is cooked all the way through.

To serve, scatter with the coriander and offer the lime wedges alongside.

Middle Eastern ingredients, such as cumin and thick yoghurt, work well on barbecue food. If you have it, use sumac – dried and ground sumac berries – to add an attractive red sprinkle and distinctive tart flavour to this dish. Chicken hearts can be ordered in advance from a butcher and are worth exploring. Like all poultry offal, they have a fine flavour and texture, making them easy to cook and eat. If you don't want to use offal, use chunks of chicken thigh instead.

Middle Eastern chicken hearts or thighs

Serves 8

500g (1lb) chicken hearts, or skinless, boneless chicken thighs, cut into chunks

3 tablespoons finely chopped coriander leaves

1 tablespoon finely chopped mint leaves

1 tablespoon sumac (optional)

salt and freshly ground black pepper

warm pittas or other Middle Eastern flatbreads, to serve

For the dressing

90ml (3½fl oz) full-fat Greek yoghurt

1 garlic clove, crushed

For the marinade

1½ tablespoons olive oil

juice and finely grated zest of 1 lemon

1 teaspoon ground cumin

2 garlic cloves, crushed

½ teaspoon chilli flakes

¼ teaspoon fine sea salt

Trim the chicken hearts (if using) by cutting off the tubes that stick out of the top. (They taste fine, but the hearts cook more evenly without them.) Wash the hearts and pat dry with kitchen paper.

Combine all the marinade ingredients in a non-metallic bowl or Ziplock bag. Add the meat, mix well, then cover or seal and leave in the fridge for a couple of hours, or overnight.

Just before you want to cook, set out 8 skewers. If made of wood, soak them in water for 30 minutes. Meanwhile, combine the dressing ingredients in a bowl and mix well.

Heat a barbecue until the coals are glowing hot. Alternatively, preheat a grill to its highest setting.

Thread about 8 hearts or 6 chunks of thigh on to each skewer. Don't cram them close together or the heat won't properly penetrate the meat. Season well with salt and pepper.

Barbecue or grill the hearts for about 4 minutes, then turn and cook the other side for 2–3 minutes, until cooked through. If using thighs, barbecue or grill for about 5 minutes on each side, then for a final minute or two on the first side. They are ready when the thickest part is pierced with the point of a knife and the juices run clear.

Serve the meat sprinkled with chopped coriander and mint, plus the sumac (if using), with the yoghurt dressing alongside for dolloping over the meat. Offer the warm pitta breads separately.

When making burgers for a barbecue, it's best not to use very lean mince as a decent fat content helps them to stick together. If lean mince is all you've got, though, add an egg to bind the mixture more firmly. Burgers made with good-quality mince can be left quite plain, but sometimes it's nice to add extras. Around the corner from Lidgate's, we've got some excellent Italian delis that give us inspiration for simple and tasty additions, like those below.

Italian beef burgers

Serves 4

500g (1lb) minced beef (not too lean)

1 red onion, finely chopped

2 garlic cloves, crushed

6 green olives, pitted and finely chopped

10 sunblush tomatoes, roughly chopped

25-g (1-oz) bunch of flat leaf parsley, leaves only, finely chopped

½ teaspoon fine sea salt

1 tablespoon olive oil, for cooking

freshly ground black pepper

To serve

4 ciabatta or other good bread rolls, cut in half

olive oil

1 garlic clove, cut in half (optional)

50g (2oz) hard goats' cheese, coarsely grated

1 red pepper, cut into thin strips

good handful of rocket

Put the mince into a large bowl with the onion, garlic, olives, tomatoes, parsley and salt, and season well with black pepper. Use your hands to mix thoroughly.

Dvide the mixture into 4 equal pieces. Lightly wet your hands – this makes the meat stick less to your fingers – and shape each piece into a burger about 9cm (3½in) wide and 2.5cm (1in) thick. Transfer to a plate, cover loosely with clingfilm and chill for at least 30 minutes, or up to 3 hours. The resting period helps the meat to stay together when cooked and improves the flavour.

Heat barbecue until the coals are glowing hot. When ready, brush the rack with the oil. Alternatively, heat the oil in a frying pan on the hob. Cook the burgers for about 2½ minutes on one side. Turn carefully and cook for another 2½ minutes. Turn back and cook for 30 seconds more. Transfer to warm plates and set aside for 1 minute. Meanwhile, lightly toast the cut side of the rolls. Drizzle with olive oil and, if you like, rub a cut clove of garlic over the surface. Check that the burgers are done to your liking. If not, barbecue or fry for a little longer.

Serve the burgers in the rolls, topping them with the cheese, red pepper and rocket.

Asparagus makes an unusual and delicious skewer for these kebabs. Our customers like to serve them as an elegant starter or a light lunch. Veal topside or, even better, rump are the cuts to use, but if you really want to push the boat out, use veal fillet, which will be incredibly tender. The kebabs can be oven-cooked or barbecued.

Veal & asparagus kebabs

Makes 4

4 x 150-g (5-oz) veal topside, rump or fillet steaks, about 2.5cm (1in) thick and 6cm (2½in wide)

4 asparagus spears

200ml (7fl oz) good-quality, thick tomato-chilli sauce

4 teaspoons finely grated lemon zest

4 teaspoons finely chopped flat leaf parsley

Trim the veal into a regular shape and cut into 4 equal pieces about 7 x 6cm (3 x 2½in). Trim the stalk end of each asparagus spear into a point. Push the tip of a sharp knife through the centre of the shorter side of each piece of veal. Cut sideways to enlarge the hole, then turn the knife over and cut the other way.

Push the pointed end of an asparagus spear through each piece of meat to thread the meat on to the spear. Place each spear of meat on a piece of foil large enough to wrap right around it.

Spread about 3 tablespoons of the tomato sauce over each kebab. Sprinkle with the lemon zest and parsley, then wrap tightly in the foil, making a good seal (especially if cooking on a barbecue). Place in the fridge until you're ready to cook.

Heat a barbecue until the flames have died down and you have hot coals, or preheat the oven to 180°C/350°F/Gas Mark 4. Cook the foil parcels for about 12 minutes, turning occasionally.

Barbecues are all about fragrant flavours that work well with smoke and chargrilled food. Rosemary is a natural partner for lamb, and its resinous quality makes it even better for robust outdoor dishes. Use the needles in a marinade, and the woody stalks as skewers. We tend to use shoulder steaks for these kebabs, or new season neck fillet when the meat is still reasonably tender (up to midsummer in southern Britain, but late summer or early autumn in northern parts and Scotland, where lambs are born later). Leg can also be used if you want to ensure the meat is really tender.

Lamb kebabs with rosemary, lemon & garlic

Makes 4 kebabs

400g (13oz) lamb shoulder or leg steaks or neck fillet, cut about 2.5cm (1in) thick

4 woody stems of rosemary, about 15cm (6in) long

4 tablespoons olive oil

finely grated zest of ½ lemon

2 garlic cloves, finely chopped

sea salt flakes and freshly ground black pepper

Cut the lamb into chunks about 2.5–3.5cm (1–1½in) wide. The shape will depend on your particular cut of lamb; what's most important is that they are roughly the same size and cook at the same rate.

Tenderize the meat by stabbing it lots of times with a small sharp knife (a butcher uses a special tenderizing mallet to do this).

Run two fingers down each rosemary stem to strip off the needles, but leaving a bushy flourish on top. Roughly chop some of the needles to give about 1½ tablespoons.

Put the chopped rosemary into a non-metallic bowl or dish, add the olive oil, lemon zest and garlic, season well and mix together. Add the meat and toss to coat. Cover and place in the fridge to marinate for up to 24 hours, turning occasionally.

Heat a barbecue until the coals are glowing hot. Alternatively, preheat a grill to its highest setting. Cook the kebabs for about 8–10 minutes on each side, until browned outside and done to your liking in the middle.

Serve with salads or as part of a barbecue.

At its simplest, a hotdog is a sausage in a bun. We love a good 'dog' and believe the best are made with quality sausages and served with interesting relishes. Of the three options given below, the onions go especially well with pork sausages, the guacamole with chicken or pork, and the tzatziki with lamb – we suggest making two of them to offer people a choice. We recommend you try the Australian technique for barbecuing sausages, which is to simmer them in boiling water for 30 minutes shortly before you barbecue them. They can then be browned as usual over the hot coals. This gives them the desired chargrilled taste and appearance, but avoids the problem of sausages burnt on the outside but raw within.

Hot Dog Heaven

Serves 6–12, as a main dish or as part of a barbecue

12 good-quality pork, lamb or chicken sausages

12 finger rolls, buttered

150g (5oz) rocket leaves

For the caramelized onions (for 6 hot dogs)
knob of butter

2 tablespoons olive oil

6 onions, sliced

¼ teaspoon sea salt flakes

pinch of caster sugar

½–1 teaspoon cider or balsamic vinegar

For the guacamole (for 6 hot dogs)
2 ripe avocados

½ small garlic clove, crushed

about 90ml (3½fl oz) olive oil

2 tablespoons roughly chopped coriander leaves

2 tablespoons finely chopped coriander stalks

2 tomatoes, chopped (optional)

½–1 red chilli, deseeded and chopped (optional)

¼–½ teaspoon sea salt flakes

For the tzatziki (for 6 hot dogs)
½ cucumber, diced

125ml (4fl oz) thick Greek yogurt

1½ tablespoons finely chopped mint leaves

2 tablespoons finely chopped chives

½ small garlic clove, crushed

¼–½ teaspoon sea salt flakes

First make the two relishes of your choice. For the caramelized onions, melt the butter with the oil in a frying pan. Add the onions and salt and cook over a medium heat, stirring occasionally, for 10 minutes, or until they start to soften. Lower the heat and cook very gently, stirring now and then, for another 30 minutes, or until soft and sweet. Stir in the sugar and vinegar and continue to cook on a low heat for another 5 minutes, stirring occasionally. Taste and adjust the seasoning if necessary.

To make the guacamole, roughly mash the avocado flesh in a bowl with the garlic and 50ml (2fl oz) of the oil. Mix in the herbs. Add the tomatoes and chilli if you like (this is a dressing rather than a salsa, so you may prefer it not to have chunks of tomato). Taste and season, adding as much more olive oil as you like to get the consistency you want.

To make the tatziki, combine all the ingredients for it in a bowl, seasoning to taste.

When you're ready to start cooking, light a barbecue or preheat the oven to 180°C/350°F/Gas Mark 4.

To barbecue the sausages, simmer them in boiling water for 30 minutes, then pat them dry with kitchen paper. Place them on a rack over the coals and cook until brown, turning frequently. This will take just 5 minutes as you have preboiled them.

To oven-cook the sausages, arrange them on a wire rack over a baking tray and place in the oven for 20 minutes. Turn and cook for another 20 minutes. Check they are piping hot all the way through and no pink remains.

Put the cooked sausages into your buttered rolls with some rocket and whatever relish you like.

8 Special Occasions

Meat has a special status on the table, and people tend to buy it for a celebratory meal. Every occasion throughout the year, from birthdays and anniversaries through to New Year's Eve, Burns Night, Easter, summer feasts and up to Christmas, has particular meats that fit the bill. We take great pride in providing the best possible meat for a special day, and these recipes show how to cook it well.

The pinnacle of Lidgate's year is the winter. From mid November onwards – we have a lot of American customers who celebrate Thanksgiving – the pace picks up, accelerating more and more until Christmas Eve. As Christmas approaches, the queues get longer and the back rooms are packed with all our butchers working at double speed as orders are fulfilled and boxed up to be dispatched all over the country. On Christmas Eve there's a line of 20 customers outside the door when we open up at 5am.

We take a great deal of pride in the window display at all times of year, but at Christmas it reaches its peak. Alongside deep red ribs of beef, some of them eight bones long, are pheasants crossed with streaky bacon, venison fillet wrapped in snowy white lardo, big white turkeys, golden geese, beautiful contrafillets, legs of lamb, three-bird roasts, pies-a-plenty and piles of pigs-in-blankets. It's a feast for the eyes that anticipates the feast on the table.

This chapter has the Christmas classics such as Roast Turkey (see page 250), including a step-by-step technique on how best to carve the bird, and a recipe for another festive meat, Roast Goose (see page 263). The recipe for Rib of Beef, another favourite, is in the Roasts chapter, on page 198. Other traditional dishes include Roast Ham and Spiced Beef (see page 261), great for serving cold at Christmas or any other time of year, when entertaining is at its peak.

For a crowd, there are dishes that can be made in advance, including the much-loved combination of salty pork and beans, both in our Bonfire Night recipe (see page 257), and our British butcher's version of the Brazilian classic Feijoada (see page 269), a great summertime party dish. We were guided through this fantastic recipe by Richard, the Brazilian who works in the shop, and have adapted it to what you might buy in a British butcher's.

Celebrations, though, are not just for large numbers. In this chapter there are recipes that feed two to four people, including a Valentine's Day Beef en Croûte and a Rack of Lamb with a pistachio crust (see pages 258 and 264). For Christmas in smaller households, no one has to miss out on the traditional meal – you can stuff a turkey breast and serve it with all the trimmings, and still have enough of delicious leftovers (see page 256).

At Lidgate's we favour traditional turkey breeds, such as Kelly Bronze. Descended from old-fashioned stock, they are more narrow-breasted and with a better fat covering than the modern, big-breasted birds. Not only do these turkeys have a better flavour and texture, but they also cook more quickly and are less likely to dry out.

Traditional roast turkey

Serves 7–8, with leftovers

5–5.5kg (11–12lb) free-range traditional-breed turkey with giblets

2 tablespoon olive oil

2 onions, halved

2 carrots, cut into large chunks

2 celery sticks, cut into large chunks

4–5 streaky bacon rashers, to cover breast (optional)

salt and freshly ground black pepper

For the chipolatas and bacon rolls

10–20 chipolatas

5–10 streaky bacon rashers, cut in half and rolled up

For the stock/gravy

1 onion, quartered

1 carrot, roughly chopped

1 celery stick, roughly chopped

1 bay leaf

1 tablespoon plain flour

good splash of red or white wine

For the roast potatoes

2kg (4lb) floury potatoes, e.g. King Edward

1 teaspoon sea salt

100g (3½oz) goose fat or beef dripping

1 tablespoon plain flour (optional)

To serve

1 quantity Stuffing of your choice (see page 280)

1 quantity Honey-roast Parsnips (optional, see page 291)

1 quantity Bread Sauce (see page 286)

steamed Brussels sprouts and carrots

cranberry sauce

→

Take the turkey out of the fridge 1½ hours before cooking so it isn't stone-cold when it goes into the oven. Untruss the bird and remove the giblets. Snip off the wing tips and set aside for stock.

Preheat the oven to 200°C/400°C/Gas Mark 6. Season the turkey breast with salt and pepper and rub all over with the oil. Put the onions, carrots and celery in a large roasting tray and sit the bird on top of them. Roast for 30 minutes, then lower the temperature to 180°C/350°F/Gas Mark 4 and continue to roast for around another 1½ hours or so, basting occasionally. If your oven is fierce, you might want to cover the breast with strips of streaky bacon to prevent the skin from burning.

Meanwhile, make the stock for the gravy by placing the reserved giblets and wing tips in a saucepan with 1.5 litres (2½ pints) water. Add the onion, carrot, celery and bay leaf. Bring just to the boil, then spoon off the froth and simmer, uncovered, until the turkey is cooked.

About 1 hour before the turkey is done, cut the potatoes into equal-sized pieces. Put in a large saucepan, cover with water and add the salt. Bring to the boil, simmer for 5 minutes, then drain. Put the fat into a roasting tray and heat in the oven for a few minutes. Meanwhile, sprinkle the flour over the potatoes. When the fat is very hot, carefully add the potatoes and roll them around in it. Season with black pepper and roast for about 1 hour, or until crispy around the edges, turning them after 35 minutes.

To make the chipolatas and bacon rolls, put them on a roasting tray or shallow dish, place in the oven with the turkey and cook for about 45 minutes, or until cooked through.

After the bird has been roasting for 1½ hours in total, you can start testing if it is done (this timing is for a narrow-breasted traditional turkey – a large-breasted bird will need longer in the oven). To do this, stick a knife into the thickest part of the thigh – the juices should run clear, not pink. If using a meatthermometer, stick it into the thickest part of the thigh, doing it first from the outside, then through the cavity from the inside: the temperature should reach 70–73°C/158–164°F.

Take the turkey out of the oven and transfer it to a large carving board. A butcher's trick for lifting the turkey is to slip two big knives into the bird under the breast, through the lower ribs between the wing joint and thigh joint. Lift, keeping the bird tilted slightly and neck up so that the juices don't run out of the cavity. Cover the bird loosely with foil and leave to rest for at least 30 minutes, or until ready to eat. It remains hot for a remarkably long time (up to 2 hours). You can also use hot gravy to warm it up when serving, and put the meat on to hot plates.

While the bird is resting, steam the sprouts and carrots. Cook the stuffing in the oven for about 30 minutes, or until hot all the way through and browned on top. If making the parsnips, roast them in a separate tray at the same time.

Meanwhile, strain the stock, discarding the solids. Discard the vegetables from the turkey roasting tray. Pour the remaining juices into a gravy separator or jug and pour off as much of the surface fat as you can into another jug. Place 2 tablespoons of the fat back in the roasting tray, place over a medium heat and stir in the flour, cooking it for 1 minute. Pour in the hot stock gradually, stirring as you do so. Add the wine, bring to the boil and bubble away until it reaches the thickness you like, adding some of the vegetable cooking water or more stock if necessary.

To carve the turkey, see steps on page 255. Serve with the roast potatoes and your favourite stuffing, plus bread sauce, steamed sprouts and carrots, and cranberry sauce.

→

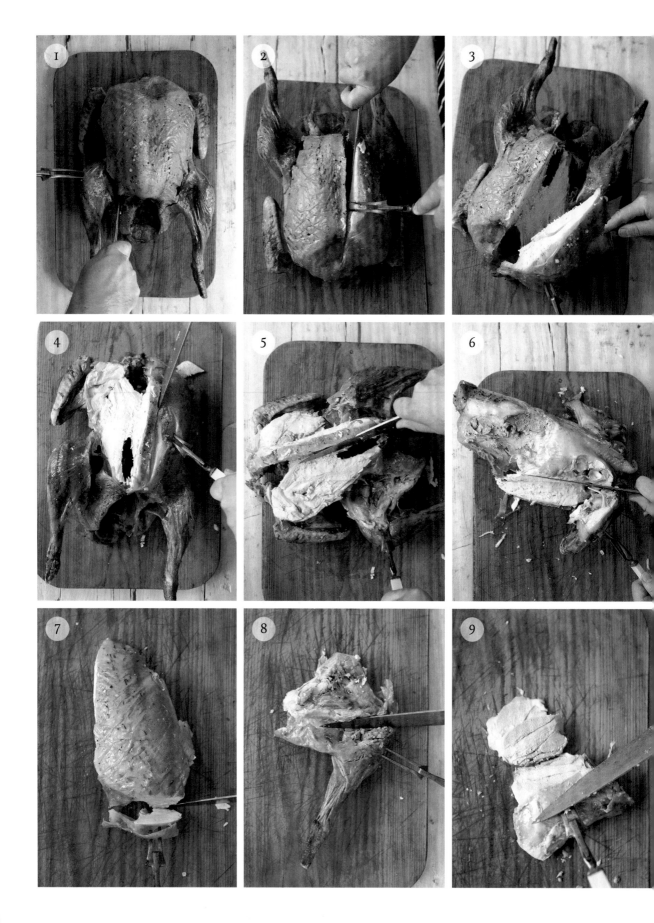

SPECIAL OCCASIONS **255**

How to carve a turkey

Many people find carving the turkey a bit of a challenge. But there is a straightforward and efficient method. By first removing the whole breast, you can cut it into neat slices across the grain to get tender and even-shaped pieces of white meat. After that, remove the leg and cut off the dark meat in slices. We've adapted this method from the one used by Paul Kelly, preserver and producer of the famous Kelly Bronze Turkey (www.kellyturkeys.co.uk).

I   Cut between the legs and the breast to loosen the legs – this will make the next step easier.

2 & 3   Cut along one side of the breastbone, using small strokes to ease the meat away from the ribs. Cut down to the bottom of the breast, using your free hand on the carving fork to add to the downward pressure. Remove the whole breast and transfer to a carving board.

4 & 5   Repeat steps 2–4 with the other breast.

6   Cut off the legs, using a carving fork to ease the drumstick and thigh away from the carcass. Cut around the 'oyster' on the base of the bird. Remove the leg and place on the carving board. Repeat these steps with the other leg. Cut just above the wing where the wing is connected to the carcass. Turn the bird over, cut around the little mini 'oyster', where the wing joins the carcass – you can wiggle the bone around a bit to help you put your knife through the socket. Put the wing on the serving platter. Repeat with the other wing.

7   Slice the breasts, including the skin, across the grain. Put on a serving platter.

8   Cut between the drumstick and thigh on each leg to separate them.

9   Slice the dark meat off the thighs and drumsticks. Put on the serving platter.

Traditional-breed turkey sizes & cooking times

To calculate the size of turkey you need, the general rule is to allow at least 500g (1lb) of the bird's weight per person. This is a generous amount, but there's nothing worse than running out of meat at a feast, and you need leftovers for sandwiches and the like. You can allow less weight per person if the bird required weighs more than 7kg (15lb).

Whatever the weight of the bird, cook it at 200°C/400°C/Gas Mark 6 for 30 minutes, then at 180°C/350°F/Gas Mark 4 for the remaining time. Birds up to 7kg (15lb) should be checked for readiness about 30 minutes before the end of the cooking time, and larger birds about 45 minutes before the end. If the skin is overbrowning – this can happen with large birds that have long cooking times – drape streaky bacon over the breast.

The timings below are for traditional-breed turkeys; bigger-breasted birds will take longer to cook.

For 6–7 people: 4–4.5kg (9–10lb); cook for 1¾ hours approx. length/width/height: 27 x 20 x 14cm (11 x 8 x 5½in)

For 7–8: 5–5.5kg (11–12lb); cook for 2 hours approx. length/width/height: 30 x 22 x 18cm (12 x 9 x 7in)

For 8–9: 6–6.5kg (13–14lb); cook for 2½ hours approx. length/width/height: 22 x 22 x 19cm (9 x 9 x 7½in)

For 10–12: 7–7.5kg (15–17lb); cook for 2¾ hours approx. length/width/height: 33 x 24 x 19cm (13 x 9½ x 7½in)

For 14–16: 8–8.5kg (18–19lb); cook for 3 hours approx. length/width/height: 38 x 28 x 19cm (15 x 11 x 7½in)

For 18–20: 9–9.5kg (20–21lb); cook for 3½ hours approx. length/width/height: 40 x 29 x 22cm (16 x 11½ x 9in)

For 20–22: 10–10.5kg (22–23lb); cook for 3¾ hours approx. length/width/height: 46 x 36 x 25cm (18 x 14 x 10in)

Small households who want to eat turkey on Christmas Day but would find a whole bird too much for their needs can buy just a breast and stuff it with this tangy stuffing flavoured with cranberries and lemon. It is excellent served with the traditional trimmings, such as chipolatas, bacon and roast potatoes (see page 250), which can be cooked in the oven at the same time.

Stuffed turkey breast

Serves 2–3 (with some leftovers)

1 turkey breast (625–750g/1¼–1½lb)

1 onion, halved

1 carrot, cut into chunks

1 celery stick, cut into chunks

olive oil, for drizzling

sea salt and freshly ground black pepper

For the cranberry and lemon stuffing
knob of butter

1 teaspoon olive oil

2 banana shallots or 1 large onion, finely chopped

1 garlic clove, finely chopped

50g (2oz) fresh white breadcrumbs

2 tablespoons cranberry sauce

juice of 1 lemon and finely grated zest of ½

3 tablespoons finely chopped flat leaf parsley

¼ teaspoon fine sea salt

For the gravy
1 tablespoon butter (optional)

½ tablespoon plain flour

500ml (17fl oz) hot chicken or turkey stock

90ml (3½fl oz) white or red wine

First make the stuffing. Melt the butter with the olive oil in a frying pan. Add the shallots or onion and fry over a medium-low heat until soft. Stir in the rest of the stuffing ingredients and season well with black pepper. Set aside to cool.

Place the turkey breast on a chopping board, skin-side down. Open it out by spreading the fillet to one side, making a heart-shaped piece of meat. Cut into the thick part of the breast to make a pocket, keeping your knife parallel with the chopping board and taking care not to cut right through the meat. Cut a little way into the other side of the breast, going towards the fillet, to increase the size of the pocket, again taking care not to cut right through the meat.

Pack the stuffing into the pocket in the turkey breast. Flip the fillet back over, turn the stuffed breast skin-side up and tuck the sides under slightly to give the meat a nice, plump shape. Using kitchen string or roasting bands, tie or fasten it at 4 regular intervals into a compact shape. This can be done up to 24 hours in advance, in which case cover and keep it in the fridge.

Preheat the oven to 180°C/350°F/Gas Mark 4. Weigh your stuffed breast and calculate your cooking time at 20 minutes per 500g (lb 2oz), plus 20 minutes.

Put the onion, carrot and celery in a roasting tray and drizzle over a little olive oil. Rub olive oil all over the turkey breast and season with salt and pepper. Place it on top of the vegetables and cook for the calculated time, checking it for readiness about 10 minutes before the end. It is done if the juices run clear when a knife is stuck into the thickest part, or when a meat thermometer put into the thickest part of the meat registers 70–73°C (158–164°F). Transfer the turkey to a carving board, cover with foil and set aside to rest whilst you make the gravy.

Discard the vegetables from the roasting tray. Add the butter if there's not enough fat remaining. When melted, sprinkle in the flour and cook for a minute, stirring constantly. Gradually pour in the hot stock, stirring as you go. Add the wine, bring to the boil and bubble away until it reaches the thickness you like, adding some vegetable water or more stock if necessary.

Cut the turkey breast into slices across the grain, making sure that each person gets a decent amount of stuffing. Serve with the gravy and trimmings.

Good sausages make all the difference in this hearty one-pot meal – essentially a meaty spin on American-style baked beans. This will keep everyone warm on Bonfire Night. Add chilli or not, according to your crowd.

Bonfire Night bangers & beans

Serves 6–8

2 tablespoons olive oil

100g (3½oz) pancetta, cubed

2 large onions, finely chopped

4 garlic cloves, finely chopped

2 celery sticks, finely chopped

500g (1lb) dried haricot beans, soaked overnight

1 litre (1¾ pints) water

2 bay leaves

200ml (7fl oz) good-quality barbecue sauce

1 tablespoon dark muscovado sugar, or to taste

700g (1lb 6oz) passata

½–1 red chilli, finely chopped

½ tablespoon smoked paprika, or 1 chipotle chilli (optional)

½ cinnamon stick

12 meaty sausages (about 1.25kg/2½lb)

lemon juice (optional)

Preheat the oven to 160°C/325°F/Gas Mark 3.

Place 1 tablespoon of the olive oil in a large, flameproof casserole dish and fry the pancetta over a medium-low heat until it starts to release its fat (about 5 minutes). Add the onions, garlic and celery and continue to cook over a medium-low heat, stirring occasionally, until soft (10–15 minutes).

Drain and rinse the beans in cold water, then add them to the onion mixture. Pour in the water and add the bay leaves, barbecue sauce and sugar. Tip in the passata, then fill the empty bottle with water and shake it to mix with the passata remnants. Measure this liquid and add enough water to make it up to a full litre. Add it to the pan and stir well, then mix in the fresh chilli, smoked paprika and cinnamon stick. If using the chipotle, tear it into 3 pieces, removing some or all of the seeds if you wish to reduce the heat, then add to the pan. Cover with a lid and cook in the oven for 1 hour.

Meanwhile, heat the remaining olive oil in a frying pan. When hot, add the sausages and brown them on all sides. After the beans have cooked for 1 hour, add the sausages to the casserole dish and cook for 30 minutes, then remove the lid and cook for another 30–60 minutes, or until the beans are soft and the sauce has thickened slightly. Cover with a lid if the mixture is thick enough, but don't let it get too dry. Add more water if necessary, and adjust the seasoning, adding some lemon juice or a little more sugar if the dish is too salty.

Before serving, discard the chipotle pieces (if using.) Serve with baked potatoes or crusty bread.

Serving beef fillet, the most expensive and tender cut, shows your beloved how much you care. We sell beef Wellingtons of many sizes, all made by Monika and her team in our kitchen. Make sure you use good-quality pâté to season the meat, and top-notch puff pastry.

Valentine's Day beef Wellington

Serves 2

375g (12oz) beef fillet
1 tablespoon olive or vegetable oil
100g (3½oz) mushrooms, finely chopped
100g (3½oz) chicken liver pâté, at room temperature
plain flour, for dusting
500g (1lb) butter puff pastry
1 egg beaten with 2 tablespoons milk, for eggwash
salt and freshly ground black pepper

Heat a heavy-based frying pan on the hob until it is really hot. Rub the beef with half the oil, then sear for about 1 minute on both sides in the hot pan until a good dark brown. Transfer to a plate to cool.

Lower the heat under the pan and add the remaining ½ tablespoon oil. Fry the mushrooms over a medium-high heat until they release their liquid and are reasonably dry, but do not brown (about 10 minutes). Set aside to cool, then mix with the pâté.

Preheat the oven to 200°C/400°F/Gas Mark 6, and insert a baking tray to heat up.

Dust a work surface with flour and roll the pastry into a rectangle slightly longer than the fillet and a little more than double its width.

Season the beef with salt and pepper and place it on the pastry. Trim the edges neatly, leaving a border of about 2.5cm (1in) all round. Spread the pâté mixture over the top and sides of the beef. Brush some of the eggwash around the perimeter of the pastry. Fold the pastry over the beef, pressing it around the meat, then run the rolling pin around the edges to make a tight seal.

Brush the top of the parcel with most of the remaining eggwash. Reroll the pastry trimmings and cut out a heart or two for the decoration. Stick them on top and brush with eggwash.

Put the beef Wellington on the hot baking sheet and bake for 35 minutes (this will give medium-rare meat) Set aside to rest in a warm place for 5 minutes, then cut into thick slices. If the beef isn't done to your liking, put it back in the oven for a short while until it is; your sweetheart will be in a tender mood and prepared to be patient.

Serve with dauphinoise potatoes and green vegetables or a sharply dressed green salad.

The amount of meat used in this recipe, and the process it goes through, might seem intimidating at first glance, but this traditional dish is easy to make and uses a cut that is relatively inexpensive. The recipe is based on one by the great food writer Jane Grigson, who noted that although spiced beef is traditionally served at Christmas, it is just as useful for summer entertaining. Saltpetre can be ordered online and helps to give the beef a better colour, but is optional.

Spiced beef

About 20 servings

100g (3½oz) dark muscovado sugar

1 heaped teaspoon saltpetre (optional)

125g (4oz) fine sea salt

25g (1oz) black peppercorns, cracked

25g (1oz) juniper berries, cracked

25g (1oz) allspice, cracked

2 bay leaves, snipped or crumbled into small pieces

1 x 3-kg (7-lb) piece of silverside, tied at 5–6 intervals to holds its shape

300ml (½ pint) water

Mix all the dry ingredients together in a bowl, then massage them into the meat. Put into Ziplock bag or a shallow non-metallic container, and leave in the fridge for 1 week, turning the meat and massaging in the marinade every day.

Preheat the oven to 140°C/275°F/Gas Mark 1.

Brush the coating off the meat, then rinse briefly under the cold tap. Put the meat in a deep ovenproof casserole dish and pour in the water. Cover the dish with a double layer of foil and then a lid. Place in the oven for 4½ hours. Set aside to cool for 3 hours without removing the foil and lid.

Drain off the liquid and pat the meat dry with kitchen paper. Wrap in foil, place in a dish and press it down evenly with a board and some weights on top (a couple of bags of sugar or some heavy cans will do the trick). Leave in the fridge for 24 hours.

Remove the foil, wrap the beef in greaseproof paper and store in the fridge for up to 3 weeks. Serve in thin slices with salad, potatoes and pickles.

Goose has come back into fashion in recent years as a winter and Christmas treat, even though it yields less meat than turkey and is more expensive. That's because its rich flavour – closer to beef than poultry – and copious amounts of crisp skin make it one of the best birds to put on the table. What's more, it generates plenty of fat, which can be saved for cooking other dishes. As a rough guide, a 4kg (9lb) bird comfortably feeds four people, a 5kg (11lb) bird feeds about six, and a 6kg (13lb) bird feeds about eight.

Roast goose

Serves 5–6

1 oven-ready goose, about 4.5kg (10lb)

1 onion, cut in half

2 carrots

2 celery sticks, cut in half

1.25kg (2½lb) floury potatoes, e.g. King Edward

1 tablespoon plain flour

salt and freshly ground black pepper

For the stock
goose giblets, plus the neck

1 onion, roughly chopped

1 carrot, roughly chopped

1 celery stick, roughly chopped

1 bay leaf

850ml (1½ pints) water

For the gravy
1 tablespoon plain flour

100ml (3½fl oz) red wine

Take the goose out of the fridge 1 hour before cooking so it doesn't go into the oven stone-cold, but keep the bag of giblets in the fridge. Remove any excess fat from inside the bird if this hasn't already been done. Prick the skin all over, especially on the fattiest parts. Season well with salt and pepper.

Preheat to oven to 190°C/375°F/Gas Mark 5.

Place the onion, carrots and celery in a roasting tray and sit the goose on top. Calculate the cooking time: 20 minutes per kilo (2lb), plus 20 minutes. Place in the oven for the required time, spooning the rendered fat over the breast and legs about every 30 minutes.

Meanwhile, make the stock. Put all the ingredients for it into a saucepan. Bring to the boil, skimming off the froth, then half-cover and simmer while the goose roasts. Strain, discarding the solids, and keep hot.

One hour before the meat is due to be ready, toss the potatoes with the flour and season with salt and pepper. Carefully spoon about 6 tablespoons of the rendered fat into another roasting tray. Roll the potatoes in it and place on the top shelf of the oven for about 1 hour, or until nice and crisp, turning them after 30 minutes.

As ovens vary, check if the goose is done about 20 minutes before the end of the calculated time: either insert a knife into the thickest part of the leg to see if the juices run clear, or insert a probe thermometer into the thickest part to see if the temperature is 70–73°C (158–163°F). When the goose is done, transfer it to a carving board or plate and cover loosely with foil while you make the gravy.

To make the gravy, skim off all but 3 tablespoons of the fat left in the roasting tray. Place it over a medium heat and sprinkle in the flour. Stir and cook for 30 seconds. Gradually pour in 500ml (17fl oz) of the hot stock, stirring constantly to prevent lumpiness. Pour in the red wine and bring to the boil, then simmer until slightly thickened.

Serve the goose with the roast potatoes and gravy, plus any other vegetables you like. The Apple & Cider Sauce (see page 284) is a good accompaniment with any leftovers.

Although expensive, rack of lamb makes a beautiful dish for a special occasion. This one has a green-speckled crust made from pistachios and scented with orange. You can buy small racks of lamb, but a large one looks magnificent on the table to carve before your guests.

Rack of lamb with a pistachio & orange crust

Serves 4

1 x 8-bone rack of lamb, chined and French-trimmed
1 teaspoon Dijon mustard

For the pistachio and orange crust
65g (2½oz) crustless white bread (about 3 slices)
leaves from a 20-g (¾-oz) bunch of basil
50g (2oz) shelled pistachios
finely grated zest of 1 orange
1–2 garlic cloves, finely chopped
30g (1¼oz) cold unsalted butter, cut into cubes
¼ teaspoon sea salt flakes
freshly ground black pepper

Trim any excess fat off the lamb so there is just a thin covering about 5–10mm (¼–½in) thick.

To make the crust, roughly tear up the bread and place in a food processor along with the basil leaves. Whizz briefly to get herby crumbs. Add the pistachios, orange zest and garlic and whizz until the nuts are roughly chopped. Add the butter, salt and a twist of black pepper. Whizz again, then tip the mixture out of the processor and knead it together.

Spread the mustard over the fat on the lamb, then press the stuffing evenly over it. Chill for 30 minutes to firm up. Meanwhile, preheat the oven to 220°C/425°F/Gas Mark 7.

Place the lamb in a roasting tray, crust-side up, and roast for 20–25 minutes (medium rare) or 25–30 minutes (well done), covering the meat with foil towards the end of cooking if the breadcrumbs are overbrowning. The timing depends on the size of the lamb, which varies according to breed and time of year. You can take the lamb out of the oven and cut into the middle to see how the meat is doing. (Don't worry – you can push it together again so it looks like a complete rack when you carve.) If it looks too rare, return it to the oven for another 5 minutes or so, then check again at the cut. If you prefer, you can you can use a meat thermometer about 10 minutes before the end of the cooking time to help get the meat to your liking:

> 60°C (140°F) for medium
>
> 70°C (158°F) for well done

Make sure the probe goes into the thickest part of the meat, and take the joint out of the oven when it is 5°C (40°F) under your target, as its temperature will continue to rise for a while.

When done to your liking, set the meat aside, covered with foil and a clean tea towel, and leave to rest for 10 minutes. (The resting time is crucial to redistribute the juices throughout the meat and make it evenly pink.)

Carve the rack between the bones. The cutlet on each end will be slightly more cooked than the central ones, so give these to anyone who likes their meat less rare.

Share out any stray bits of crust and pour the juices from the pan over the meat. Serve with dauphinoise potatoes or buttery mash, a saucy vegetable such as ratatouille, and a green vegetable or watercress salad. And don't forget to offer redcurrant or other fruit jelly.

Let's start by clearing up a common confusion: 'gammon' is the name for an uncooked hind leg of pork; the name changes to 'ham' only once it is cooked, or cured and ready to eat. Roast ham is always a great dish to have for Christmas feasts and summer parties – indeed, for gatherings of friends and family all year round. We've used the fillet end, without the bone, because it has more meat and is easier to carve. If you want a larger ham, include the knuckle end as well. You can also buy just the knuckle end, but make sure it weighs at least 2.5kg (5lb) to get enough meat. This recipe gives two options for flavouring the ham: a marmalade breadcrumb crust or a shiny lemon and honey glaze.

Roast ham with marmalade crust or honey glaze

Serves 8–10

1.5–1.75kg (3–3½lb) boneless smoked gammon (fillet end)
300ml (½ pint) apple juice
2 celery sticks, roughly chopped
1 onion, quartered
14 cloves

For the marmalade crust
juice of 1 orange (about 60ml/2¼fl oz)
2 tablespoons dark muscovado sugar
2 tablespoons thin-shred marmalade
100g (3½oz) dry white breadcrumbs

For the honey glaze
1 tablespoon honey
juice of 1 lemon
2 tablespoons water
1½ tablespoons soft brown sugar

If the gammon is very salty (it's uncommon these days, but ask your butcher), soak it in water overnight. Alternatively, place it in a pan of water, bring to the boil and simmer for 10 minutes. Drain and rinse it in fresh water.

Put the gammon in a large pan with the apple juice, celery, onion and 2 of the cloves. Add enough water to cover and put a lid on the pan. Bring to the boil, then simmer for 25 minutes per 500g (1lb). Transfer the ham to a roasting tray lined with baking parchment and allow to cool slightly. (This can be done a day in advance, in which case, cool completely, then wrap in foil and keep in the fridge.)

Strain the stock, discarding the vegetables. It's delicious, with a slightly sweet edge from the apple juice, so keep it to use for soup or risotto.

Preheat the oven to 220°C/425°F/Gas Mark 7.

Using a sharp knife, peel the rind off the ham, then cut off some of the fat, leaving a thickness of 1–1.5cm (½–¾in), or more if you wish.

To make the marmalade crust, put the orange juice and sugar in a bowl and stir to dissolve. Mix in the marmalade, then add the breadcrumbs, mixing first with a spoon and then with your fingers to combine well. Pat firmly on to the fat of the ham and put in the oven for 20 minutes, or until brown on top.

To make the honey glaze, mix the ingredients together in a bowl. Use the tip of small, sharp knife to cut a lattice pattern of 12 large squares in the fat of the ham. Brush both fat and meat with the glaze. Stick a clove in the centre of each square. Put the ham in the oven for 10 minutes, then brush with another layer of the glaze. Roast for another 10 minutes and brush again with the glaze. Return the ham to the oven until the outside is nicely browned and caramelized, giving it a final brush of glaze at the end.

Eat your ham hot, warm or cold.

A traditional Portuguese dish, feijoada has been raised to an art form in Brazil. Here, this thick pork stew contains various salty meats and black beans in a tasty sauce. Feijoada scales up easily to feed a crowd – just keep the meat and bean ratio at 3:1. The traditional accompaniments include farofa (a toasted cassava mixture) and Brazilian vinaigrette (part sauce, part salsa). In Brazil, a feijoada often includes trotters and other offcuts, but this version uses more familiar meats for a British butcher's version. If possible, start cooking the beans and meat the day before you're planning to serve them.

Lidgate's feijoada with farofa & Brazilian vinaigrette

Serves 8

500g (1lb) black beans, soaked overnight or for at least 5 hours

500g (1lb) salt brisket

3 bay leaves

1 x 250-g (8-oz) piece of smoked belly bacon with rind, off bone

1 tablespoon vegetable oil

1 x 250-g (8-oz) piece of fresh belly pork with rind, off bone

500g (1lb) fresh sausages, preferably spicy (some can be replaced with one or more pieces of salty meat, such as hot-smoked rack of pork rib, bratwurst, cooking chorizo or smoked loin of pork, and add a quartered pig's trotter)

2 oranges, each cut into 6 segments, to serve

For the sauce

1 tablespoon lard or oil

1 onion, finely chopped

3 garlic cloves, roughly chopped

1 red or green pepper, finely chopped

1 x 400-g (14-oz) can chopped tomatoes

1 tablespoon tomato purée

½ green chilli, deseeded (optional)

For the farofa

1 tablespoon unsalted butter

1 tablespoon olive oil

100g (3½oz) smoked streaky bacon, roughly chopped

1 onion, finely chopped

1 garlic clove, finely chopped

150g (5oz) carrot, coarsely grated

125g (4oz) mandioca (toasted cassava flour) or 65g (2½oz) dry white breadcrumbs

25g (1oz) good-quality pork scratchings (optional)

For the Brazilian vinaigrette

3 sweet peppers of different colours, cut into small dice

1 red or white onion, finely chopped

3 tablespoons finely chopped flat leaf parsley

3 tablespoons finely chopped chives

½ chilli, deseeded and finely chopped (optional)

1 tablespoon lemon juice

2–4 tablespoons olive oil

salt and freshly ground black pepper

Drain the beans, put them in a large pan and cover with water. Add the brisket and the bay leaves. Bring to the boil, then skim off the froth, cover and simmer for 1 hour.

Meanwhile, preheat the oven to 190°C/375°F/Gas Mark 5. When hot, put the smoked belly bacon in a roasting tray and place in the oven for 25 minutes.

Put the oil in a frying pan over a medium heat and brown the fresh belly pork on all sides.

When the beans have been cooking for 1 hour, add both the belly and the cooked bacon. Cover and cook for another 1 hour, stirring occasionally to check the mixture isn't burning or sticking on the bottom.

Lightly brown the fresh sausages (and bratwurst, if using) in the frying pan. Add to the beans and cook everything together for another 1 hour, until soft and tender.

Remove the meats and cut the rind off the pork and bacon and as much fat as you like, then cut the meat into large chunks about 2.5–3.5cm (1–1½in) square. Return the meats to the pan and stir well. The dish can be prepared up to this point a day in advance. Cover and chill until required.

Make the sauce at least 1 hour 15 minutes before serving. Heat the fat in a frying pan over a medium heat. When hot, add the onion and garlic and fry gently until soft (10 minutes). Add the chopped pepper and cook for another 10 minutes. Add the tomatoes, tomato purée and chilli (if using). Simmer, uncovered, for 10 minutes or so.

Reheat the beans and meat mixture if necessary then stir in the sauce. Cook, uncovered, for about 45 minutes over a medium-low heat, stirring occasionally so the beans don't stick to the bottom and the sauce reduces slightly. The stew can be left simmering until you are ready to eat or are ready for seconds, but make sure the beans don't catch on the bottom.

While the beans and meat are cooking in the sauce, make the ferofa and the vinaigrette. To make the farofa, melt the butter with the oil in a large sauté pan, then cook the bacon in it over a medium heat until crisp. Transfer the bacon to a plate.

Add the onion and garlic to the fat left in the pan and cook, stirring occasionally, until the onion is soft (10 minutes). Add the carrot and cook for a few more minutes, until slightly softened.

Stir in the cassava flour and cook for just a few minutes so that it absorbs the fat. Stir in the cooked bacon. Transfer to a serving bowl and garnish with pork scratchings, if you like.

To make the Brazilian vinaigrette, combine all the chopped vegetables and herbs in a bowl. Shortly before serving, season with salt and pepper, dress with the lemon juice and olive oil and mix well.

Serve the feijoada with rice, kale or cavolo nero, plus the farofa and Brazilian vinaigrette, putting an orange segment on each plate to refresh the palate. Also offer some chilli sauce on the side for those who like to spice things up.

Here is one of our most popular pies, with chunks of ham and mushrooms complementing the chicken. It suits any gathering, but is perhaps especially appropriate at Easter because in times past the first farmyard birds were ready for the pot at that time of year.

Easter chicken, ham & mushroom pie

Serves 6–8

1 tablespoon olive oil

1.25kg (2½lb) skinless, boneless chicken thighs, cut into 3.5-cm (1½-in) chunks

2 onions, finely chopped

1 tablespoon plain flour, plus extra for dusting

2 tablespoons tomato purée

1½ teaspoons mustard powder or 1 tablespoon Dijon mustard

½ teaspoon dried oregano

1 tablespoon finely chopped fresh sage

1 x 300-g (10-oz) piece of ham (preferably smoked), cut into 2.5–3.5-cm (1–1½-in) chunks

400ml (14fl oz) hot chicken stock

350g (11½oz) small button mushrooms

150ml (¼ pint) double cream

500g (1lb) puff pastry

1 egg, beaten

freshly ground black pepper

Pour the olive oil into a large frying pan and place over a high heat. When hot, fry the chicken in 2 batches for 2 minutes, stirring occasionally, until the meat is opaque. Transfer to a plate.

Add the onions to the pan, lower the heat and cook for 10 minutes, or until soft, stirring occasionally. Sprinkle the flour over the onions and cook for 1 minute, stirring. Add the tomato purée, mustard and herbs and stir well. Mix in the ham and the fried chicken. Pour in the hot stock and bring to the boil, then simmer for 5 minutes.

Preheat the oven to 220°C/425°F/Gas Mark 7.

Add the mushrooms to the pan and cook for 10 minutes, or until they are soft. Stir in the cream and let it bubble up briefly. Season with a few twists of black pepper. You shouldn't need any salt as the ham provides this. Tip the mixture into a 30 x 20-cm (12 x 8-in) pie dish.

Dust a work surface with flour and roll out the pastry so it is about 5cm (2in) larger all round than the pie dish. Cut 2.5-cm (1-in) strips from each edge of the pastry. Press these on to the lip of the pie dish, trim off any excess and brush with the eggwash. Press the pastry lid firmly on top of the pastry rim, then crimp the edges together to seal. Reroll the pastry trimmings and cut out shapes to decorate the pie, sticking them on with the eggwash.

Brush eggwash all over the pastry lid, then bake for 30 minutes, or until golden.

The Italian joint called porchetta is a magnificent roll of loin and belly pork flavoured with herbs and garlic, and good to eat hot or cold. We have a special way of making it at Lidgate's to get the best crackling on the outside and the tenderest meat within. You can ask a butcher to partly prepare the meat for you, using the step photos overleaf as a guide to where the meat should be cut. Alternatively, get adventurous with a saw and have a go yourself. You'll have to order a whole middle and trim off some pieces – a 10-cm (4-in) piece of belly, which can be used for a small roasting joint, and the ribs, which can be cooked as a starter or light meal – as these offcuts are too small for the butcher to sell separately.

Porchetta

Serves 10

1 x 9-bone pork middle
olive oil
sea salt flakes
about 8 sprigs of rosemary

For the herb and garlic paste
2 tablespoons roughly chopped rosemary
2 tablespoons dried thyme
2 tablespoons roughly crushed fennel seeds
¼–½ tablespoon coarsely ground black pepper
½ tablespoon sea salt flakes, plus extra for sprinkling
8 garlic cloves, finely chopped
about 90ml (3½fl oz) olive oil

Prepare the porchetta as shown in the steps overleaf, or ask your butcher to prepare it for you up to and including step 4.

Preheat the oven to 190°C/375°F/Gas Mark 5.

Combine all the paste ingredients, adding enough of the oil to make a loose paste. Open out the meat and spread the paste over it, then roll and tie it as described in steps 7 and 8.

Weigh the joint and calculate the cooking time, based on 20 minutes per 500g (1lb). Place it in a roasting tray and lavishly oil the external fat. Sprinkle generously with sea salt flakes and tuck rosemary sprigs under each piece of string.

Roast the meat for the calculated time, checking it for readiness about 10 minutes before the end. It is done if the juices run clear when a knife is stuck into the thickest part, or when a meat thermometer registers 70°C (158°F). (Make sure the probe goes into the thickest part of the meat, and take the joint out of the oven when it is 5°C (40°F) under your target, as its temperature will continue to rise for a while.)

Transfer to a carving board and set aside to rest for at least 15 minutes. Meanwhile, skim the fat out of the roasting tray and keep the juices warm.

Cut the meat into thick slices and serve hot with the reserved juices. It can also be served, hot or cold, with Salsa Verde (see page 285).

→

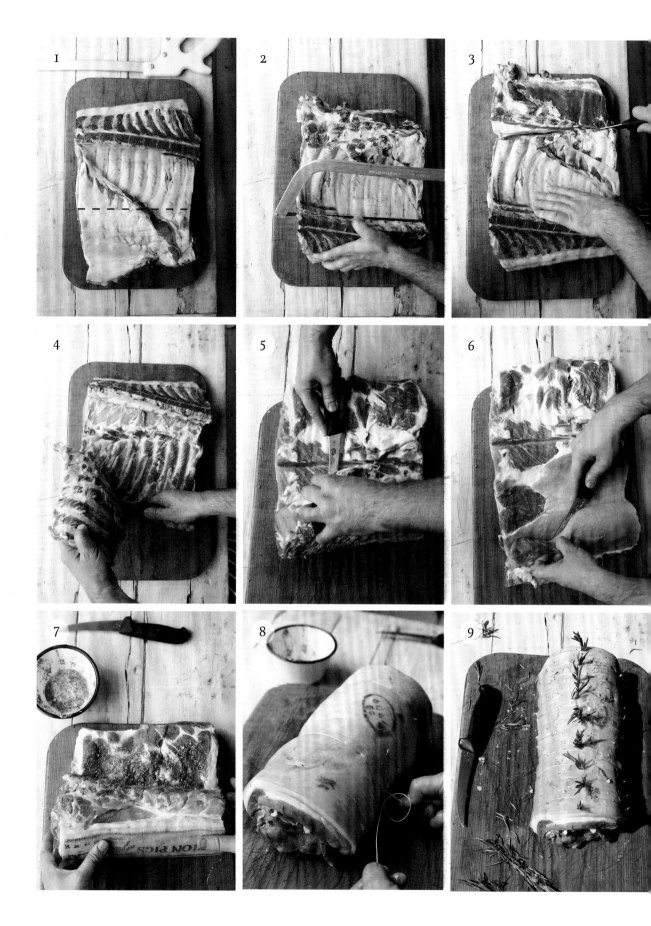

How to prepare porchetta

To prepare porchetta, you take out the sheet of ribs and backbone, then open out the thick, lean loin to get an even piece of meat. Then you cover the meat with the herby marinade and roll it up so the belly goes around the loin – you want each slice of the roll to have a good mixture of fat and lean.

At Lidgate's, we have a special way of preparing porchetta so that you get a neat and even roll. First, we remove part of the belly. We don't include this piece in the porcetta because it makes the roll much bigger, with too much fat into the middle that won't crisp up. Set this meaty piece aside for a roast, slow cooking or for use in Asian recipes.

Before you start, first score the skin – it is easier to do this while the meat is still on the bone. Hold your knife like a dagger to get pressure and control, and score making parallel lines about 5–10mm (¼–½in) apart.

I   Place the meat skin-side down on the work surface. Cut out the flare fat, the soft sheet attached to the bones (you can use this for making lard, see page 113). Saw straight down through the bones about 10cm (4 in) from the bottom of the belly. The saw shouldn't cut through the meat, just through the bone.

2   Turn the meat around and, lifting the backbone slightly to get a better slant for cutting, saw at a 30-degree angle down through the rib bones. Do this carefully because you don't want to go too much into the eye of the meat.

3   You now have the meat with the bones sawn through in two places. Now use a knife to cut through the meat at the first incision, squaring it into a block. Remove this meat and set aside for another meal.

4   Cut out the sheet of rib bones, keeping them also for another meal.

5   Cut halfway through the eye muscle meat (the thickest part of the meat).

6   Fold the cut meat back to open it up and create a flat, even surface.

7   Spread the herb and garlic paste over the meat.

8   Roll up the meat, pulling the skin right around the outside and cutting away any excess. Using kitchen string, tie the porchetta first in the middle and then at either end. You do these initial ties to get a straight cylinder shape, not a wonky cone. Ideally, use slipknots and get the strings parallel before tying them tight. Finish by tying in between the first ties so that the joint is tied at regular intervals about 2.5cm (1in) apart.

9   Tuck sprigs of rosemary under the strings. Place the porchetta in the fridge, but bring it out 1 hour before cooking so it isn't fridge-cold.

9

Stuffings,
sauces, stocks
& sides

In Britain, thanks to our lush pastureland, we have a long history
of raising excellent livestock, and a similarly long tradition of roasting
such meat, thanks to the woodland that supplied plenty of fuel.
Accompaniments, such as vegetables dishes, sauces and stuffings, have
always played an important role alongside such meat, partly to add
complementary flavours, and partly to make it go further.

This chapter includes some of the most populoar
vegetable accompaniments, including a number of
potato dishes, and a vegetable kebab that has become
a surprise bestseller after we developed it for a particular
customer. We've also given recipes for a range of
stuffings, another old trick for 'stretching' a meal, but
actually tasty dishes in their own right. These are
especially good with poultry, game and pork, and
we think they are definitely due a revival.

The Britsh have always had a great fondness for
sauces, and this chapter takes you through some
classics, ranging from Bread Sauce for game and
poultry, to Apple Sauce and even Salsa Verde for pork
(see pages 286, 284 and 285). Over time, we have
developed a taste for tangy accompaniments, though
they have not always originated on these shores. Mint
sauce with lamb, for example, is said to have been first
introduced by soldiers returning from the Crusades
in the Middle East between the 11th and 14th centuries.
Horseradish sauce, the traditional accompaniment for
beef – though mustard runs a close second – was
introduced to Britain during Renaissance times. Our
love for chilli sauces goes back a fair way too, with
recipes for them included in *Mrs Beeton's Book of
Household Management*, which was first published
in 1861. The popularity of these condiments is no doubt
due to the fact that they cut through some of the
rich fattiness of particular meats and add another
dimension to their flavour.

Like most butcher's, Lidgate's also sells a great array
of bottled sauces, and we focus on finding really tasty
products made from good ingredients. As well as being
great accompaniments, they can also be added to
recipes. In this chapter, we recommend using your
favourite bottled condiment in a Saucy Potato Salad
(see page 291). Elsewhere, we show how to use such
condiments to customize your own Sausage Rolls and
how to use barbecue sauce to pep up a potful of bangers
and beans (see pages 122 and 257).

Some of the best sauces to accompany meat – not least
gravy – can be based on stock. Good, fresh stocks can
be readily bought these days, but nothing beats the real
thing made at home. If you shop at a decent butcher's,
you are well on the way to making your own. Many
butchers will have bones going spare (or for a small
charge), but they don't hang around for long. To be sure
of getting what you want, ask in advance.

A good stock makes a subtle but significant difference to
recipes, boosting flavours, and even imparting a certain
silkiness, especially if you throw in a gelatinous pig's
trotter or veal bones. We spent a long time developing
the stocks that we sell in the shop, and have used this
knowledge in the recipes provided in this chapter.

STUFFINGS

The savoury mixture known as 'stuffing' is a great way of adding extra seasoning and flavour to a roast, as well as making the meat go further. At one time it was always cooked within a bird, which meant it was flavoured and lubricated by the meat juices and could have a delicious, very slight offal flavour. However, the advice is now to cook stuffing separately as it can otherwise become a medium for harmful bacteria, and also means the meat takes longer to cook.

The following stuffings are deliciously moist and offer a good contrast in taste. For a special occasion, it is worth making both and cooking them together in one dish. At Christmas, for example, you could make a full quantity of the apple, sage and onion stuffing, and a half-quantity of the chestnut. Put them side by side in a 23 x 18-cm (9 x 5-in) baking dish and cook as normal. To serve, slice across the stuffings so everyone gets a piece of each.

Here is a fresh, light stuffing that is excellent with chicken, duck, pork or game, and is substantial enough to act as a form of 'nut loaf' if someone at the table is vegetarian.

Apricot, thyme & almond stuffing

Serves 6–8

50g (2oz) butter, melted, plus extra for greasing
100g (3½oz) dry white breadcrumbs
30g (1¼oz) dried apricots, roughly chopped
100g (3½oz) flaked almonds, roughly chopped
1 tablespoon fresh thyme leaves
1 teaspoon sea salt flakes
1 egg
about 90ml (3½fl oz) water
freshly ground black pepper

Preheat the oven to 180°C/350°F/Gas Mark 4. Butter a loaf tin about 26 x 13cm (10 x 5in).

Combine all the dry ingredients in a bowl, then mix in the egg, butter and as much water as necessary to make a firm but pliable mixture.

Put the mixture into the prepared tin to form a layer about 3.5–5cm (1½–2in) thick. Bake for 20–30 minutes, until browned on top.

A looser style stuffing like this one is excellent with chicken, turkey, pork or game. The delicate flavour of the veal is good with the mushrooms, and the meat content helps make a roast more special and also go further. As veal mince can spoil quickly, order it from your butcher so that you can collect it when freshly minced.

Veal & wild mushroom stuffing

Serves 6–8

large knob of unsalted butter, plus extra for greasing

1 tablespoon olive oil, plus extra for drizzling

2 banana shallots, finely chopped

2 garlic cloves, finely chopped

1½ teaspoons finely chopped rosemary

250g (8oz) minced veal

25g (1oz) dried mushrooms, soaked in 150ml (¼ pint) water

¼ teaspoon ground mace or nutmeg

zest and juice of ½ lemon

3 tablespoons roughly chopped parsley leaves (optional)

50g (2oz) dry white breadcrumbs

1 egg

sea salt flakes and freshly ground black pepper

Preheat the oven to 160°C/325°F/Gas Mark 3. Generously butter a loaf tin about 26 x 13cm (10 x 5in), or line it with baking parchment.

Melt the butter in a frying pan over a medium-low heat, then pour in the oil. Add the shallots, garlic and rosemary and cook until soft (about 10 minutes), stirring occasionally. Add the veal and cook for another 10 minutes, stirring once or twice.

Drain the mushrooms, reserving the water. Chop them quite finely and add to the pan. Cook for 5 minutes, stirring occasionally. Turn off the heat.

Add the mace, lemon zest and parsley (if using). Season with about ½ teaspoon or so of salt and a generous twist of pepper. Stir well, then set aside to cool slightly.

Add the breadcrumbs and lemon juice to the meat mixture and stir to combine. Finally, add the egg and reserved mushroom water and mix thoroughly.

Press the mixture into the prepared tin to form a layer about 3.5–5cm (1½–2in) thick. Drizzle a little more oil on top and, if you like, a sprinkling of salt. Put in the oven for about 30 minutes, until brown on top and cooked through.

Turkey, goose and chicken go well with a richer stuffing, and this one is both traditional and tasty.

Chestnut stuffing

Serves 10–12

75g (3oz) butter, plus 15g (½oz) for the top and extra for greasing

150g (5oz) shallots, finely chopped

150g (5oz) smoked streaky bacon, finely sliced

400g (13oz) chestnut purée

200g (7oz) cooked chestnuts, roughly chopped

200g (7oz) fresh white breadcrumbs

50g (2oz) melted butter, plus a little more for greasing

¼ teaspoon fine sea salt

¼ teaspoon ground nutmeg

leaves from a 40-g (1½-oz) bunch of parsley

2 tablespoons finely chopped chives

2 eggs

freshly ground black pepper

Use a little butter to grease a rectangular baking dish about 23 x 18cm (9 x 7in). Melt about 25g (1oz) of the remaining butter in a sauté pan. Add the shallots and bacon and cook gently over a medium-low heat for 15 minutes, until soft.

Add the chestnut purée and stir for 30 seconds or so. Stir in the chopped chestnuts, then transfer the mixture to a bowl.

Melt 50g (2oz) of the remaining butter and add to the chestnut mixture along with the breadcrumbs, salt, nutmeg, chopped herbs and a good seasoning of black pepper. Add the eggs and mix well.

Press the stuffing into the prepared dish to form a layer about 3.5–5cm (1½–2in) thick. Dot the surface with 15g (½oz) butter and cook in the oven with the turkey or joint for 25 minutes, or until brown on top and cooked through. The stuffing can be cooked up to 2 days in advance if you wish. Simply cool the mixture, then cover and store in the fridge until needed. Cover in foil and reheat in the oven, or cover in clingfilm and heat in a microwave, until piping hot.

This slightly sharp stuffing is good with a fatty roast, such as duck or pork. Reduce the lemon juice by half to serve it with chicken or turkey.

Apple, sage & onion stuffing

Serves 6

10g (¼oz) unsalted butter, plus 10g (¼oz) for the top and extra for greasing

2 large or 3 medium red onions, finely sliced

65g (2½oz) dry white breadcrumbs

30g (1¼oz) dried apple, chopped

3 tablespoons finely sliced fresh sage leaves

¼ teaspoon sea salt flakes

juice and finely grated zest of 1 lemon

150ml (¼ pint) apple juice

1 egg

freshly ground black pepper

Use a little butter to grease a loaf tin about 26 x 13cm (10 x 5in). Melt 10g (¼oz) butter in a frying pan. Add the onions and cook over a medium-low heat until softened (about 10 minutes), stirring occasionally.

Meanwhile, put the breadcrumbs, dried apple, sage and salt in a bowl. Season with plenty of black pepper and mix well. Add the cooked onions, the lemon zest and half or more of the lemon juice (see introduction above). Finally, stir in the apple juice and egg.

Press the mixture into the prepared tin and dot with the remaining butter. Cook with the roast for about 20–30 minutes, or until brown on top and hot all the way through.

SAUCES

Fresh apple sauce can be made in advance and kept in the fridge for a couple of days. It's magic with cold roast pork as well as hot. This version has the extra twist of a simple cider and thyme reduction, which makes it good enough to turn plain pork chops into a dinner party dish.

Mint is a traditional partner for lamb, and this refreshingly sharp sauce cuts nicely through its rich fat. It can be made up to two hours before serving.

Apple & cider sauce

Serves 6

200ml (7fl oz) medium or dry cider
½ teaspoon fresh thyme leaves
2 Bramley apples
½ tablespoon honey
salt and freshly ground black pepper

Pour three-quarters of the cider into a medium saucepan and add the thyme. Bring to the boil and let it bubble for 3–4 minutes, until much reduced and sticky. Stir in the remaining cider, then set aside off the heat.

Meanwhile, peel and core the apples and chop into small pieces. Add them to the cider reduction and stir well. Season with a pinch of salt and some pepper, then stir in the honey. Bring to the boil, then cover and simmer until the apples have collapsed, stirring once or twice to help them on their way.

Taste and adjust the seasoning and honey content according to taste. Serve with roast pork.

Fresh mint sauce

Serves 6

2 tablespoons white balsamic or cider vinegar
4 tablespoons water
3 teaspoons caster sugar
1½ tablespoons finely chopped fresh mint
fine sea salt and freshly ground pepper

Put the vinegar and water into a small bowl and stir in the sugar. Add the mint, then taste and season. Set aside for at least 10 minutes so that the sugar dissolves. Whisk again just before serving.

While it's possible to buy good-quality horseradish sauce, homemade is superior, even if it does mean having to cope with the eye-watering task of grating fresh horseradish root.

Horseradish sauce

Serves 6–8

2 tablespoons finely grated fresh horseradish

1½ teaspoons cider vinegar

½ teaspoon English mustard powder

about 75ml (3fl oz) double cream or crème fraîche

¼–½ teaspoon caster sugar

fine sea salt and freshly ground pepper

Put the horseradish in a bowl and mix in the vinegar and mustard. Stir in enough cream to make a saucy consistency. Add sugar and seasoning to taste.

A fresh and strong herb sauce flavoured with anchovies, salsa verde goes especially well with steaks and cold meats, including the porchetta on page 272. It can be made in a small blender or by hand.

Salsa verde

Serves 8

1 or 2 small garlic cloves

30g (1¼oz) drained anchovy fillets

2 tablespoons capers

½ teaspoon red wine vinegar

200ml (7fl oz) extra virgin olive oil

20 mint leaves

50g (2oz) basil leaves

50g (2oz) flat leaf parsley leaves

freshly ground black pepper

If using a blender, whizz the garlic with the anchovies, capers, vinegar and 2 tablespoons of the olive oil to a coarse paste. Add the herbs and remaining olive oil, plus a twist of black pepper. Whizz to a sauce texture. Taste and adjust the seasoning if necessary (you probably won't need any salt as the anchovies are already salty).

If preparing the salsa by hand, finely chop the garlic, anchovies, capers and herbs. Place them in a bowl and stir in the vinegar and olive oil. Season to taste.

STOCKS

To make good bread sauce, you need to infuse the milk with a decent amount of seasoning, you must get the right consistency – neither too firm nor too sloppy, and it's essential to add some butter at the end. This sauce can be made the day before and kept in the fridge. Simply reheat when required.

Game stock adds magic to a game stew, soup or gravy. Here, we tell you how to clarify stock from frozen, a tip picked up from Catherine Phipps' book *Chicken*.

Bread sauce

Serves 10

1 onion, cut in half

2 cloves

750ml (1¼ pints) milk

1 bay leaf

150g (5oz) fresh white breadcrumbs (whizz crustless bread in a food processor)

freshly grated nutmeg

75g (3oz) butter, cut into small pieces

fine sea salt and freshly ground black pepper

Cut the onion in half through the root, then push a clove into each half. Place in a small pan with the milk, bay leaf and breadcrumbs. Season with a good grating of nutmeg and some salt and pepper. Bring just to the boil, then turn off the heat and leave to infuse for 1 hour.

Discard the onion and bay leaf. Return the mixture to a simmer and cook for a couple of minutes. Stir in the butter, then taste and adjust the seasoning if necessary.

Game stock

Makes 1.5 litres (2½ pints)

1kg (2lb) bones (venison bones and/or bird carcasses)

1 tablespoon oil

2 onions, quartered

2 carrots, roughly chopped

2 celery sticks, roughly chopped

2 bay leaves

1 small bunch of thyme

stalks from a handful of flat leaf parsley

1 teaspoon black peppercorns

2 litres (3½ pints) water

Put the bones in a large saucepan and add the rest of the ingredients. Bring just to the boil, skimming off any scum that rises to the surface, then simmer, uncovered, for 2–3 hours.

Strain into a bowl, discarding the solids. If you like, you can return the stock to the pan and boil it hard to reduce it and concentrate the flavour. Cool the stock as quickly as possible (ideally, sit the pan in a bowl of iced water). When cold, store in a covered container in the fridge.

To clarify the stock and get it sparkling clear for a special soup, freeze it hard, then place in a colander lined with a double thickness of muslin or cheesecloth. Set the colander over a deep bowl, then place in the fridge and allow to defrost (this takes 1½–2 days). Discard the contents of the muslin, and use the stock as required.

Chicken stock is excellent for adding flavour and nourishment to stews and soups. You can use the leftover carcass of a roast, or ask your butcher if he has carcasses from jointing chickens. Alternatively, use chicken wings.

Beef stock is a great ingredient to have in the fridge to add body and taste to soups, stews and sauces.

Chicken stock

Makes about 1.2–1.5 litres (2–2½ pints)

chicken bones or 12 chicken wings

1 onion, quartered

1 celery stick, roughly chopped

1 carrot, chopped

1 leek, white and green parts, roughly chopped

stalks from a bunch of parsley

1 bushy thyme sprig

1 bay leaf

½ teaspoon black peppercorns

2 litres (3½ pints) water

125ml (4fl oz) white wine (optional)

If using raw bones or wings, you can roast them first to get a different flavour. Preheat the oven to 220°C/425°F/Gas Mark 7. Put the chicken bits in a roasting tray and place in the oven for 15–20 minutes, or until browned.

Put the bones, roasted or unroasted, in a large pan with the onion, celery, carrot, leek, parsley stalks, thyme, bay leaf and peppercorns. Add the water and wine (if using). Bring just to the boil, then simmer, uncovered, for 2–3 hours, skimming off any froth that rises to the surface.

Strain, discarding the solids. Return the stock to the pan, bring to the boil and boil for 10 minutes or so, to reduce slightly and concentrate the flavours.

Cool quickly by transferring the stock to a cold bowl and sitting it in a sinkful of cold or iced water. Cover and store in the fridge for up to 4 days, or freeze in small amounts for future use. Smell the stock before using, and if it has a sourish odour, throw it away. Always boil chicken stock before use to avoid the risk of food poisoning.

Butcher's beef stock

Makes 1.5 litres (2½ pints)

1 tablespoon olive or vegetable oil

1kg (2lb) beef bones

2 onions, unpeeled and cut in quarters

2 carrots, cut into large chunks

2 celery sticks, cut into large chunks

2 leeks, green parts only, roughly chopped

200ml (7fl oz) red wine

2 litres (3½ pints) water

2 bay leaves

1 bushy sprig of thyme

1 teaspoon black peppercorns

1 teaspoon juniper berries, roughly crushed

1 star anise

Preheat the oven to 220°C/425°F/Gas Mark 7.

Pour the oil into a roasting tray. Add the beef bones, onions, carrots, celery and leeks and roll them around to coat well. Roast for 30 minutes, until brown. Transfer the bones and browned vegetables to a large pan.

Pour the wine and about 300ml (½ pint) of the water into the roasting tray and place over a medium heat. Bring to the boil, scraping up any tasty bits stuck in the bottom with a wooden spoon. Add this mixture to the bones.

Add the remaining ingredients and water to the pan and bring just to the boil. Skim off any scum that rises to the surface, then simmer slowly, uncovered, for 4 hours.

Strain into a bowl, discarding the solids. If you like, return the stock to the pan and boil it hard to reduce it. Cool the stock as quickly as possible by sitting the pan in cold or iced water. Store in a covered container in the fridge. You can lift off the fat that solidifies on top and use it for cooking. Alternatively, freeze the stock in ice-cube trays.

Side dishes

The best chippies, particularly in the north of England, traditionally use beef dripping for their frying because the flavour is superb. The method below of making oven chips with dripping is adapted from a canny method devised by the food writer Patricia Wells, and means you can do most of the work in advance.

Beef dripping oven chips

Serves 4

1kg (2lb) floury or baking potatoes, such as King Edward, peeled and cut into thick chips (approx. 2.5cm [1in] square x 7.5cm [3in] long)

3 tablespoons beef dripping

fine sea salt

Preheat the oven to 220°C/425°F/Gas Mark 7.

Put the chips in a steamer and steam for 8–10 minutes, until tender to the point of a knife, but not cooked through or breaking up at the edges. You can do this up to 2 hours in advance and leave the chips at room temperature until needed. If you are going to use them straight away, pat dry with kitchen paper.

Spoon the dripping into a large non-stick baking tray. Place in the oven until melted and hot.

Put the chips in the dripping and carefully turn them to coat in the hot fat. Return to the oven for 20 minutes, turn them over and continue to cook for another 10 minutes, or until golden brown.

Season with salt and serve piping hot.

This mash is rich, so you don't need much more than a large dollop on a plate. The French chef Joel Robuchon uses a proportion of 2:1 potatoes to butter, but you don't need to go quite that far. Add more or less butter as you wish, and double cream or milk, according to how luxurious and soft you want your mash to be.

Buttery mash

Serves 6

1.25kg (2½lb) floury or all-purpose potatoes (e.g. King Edward or Maris Piper)

150–200g (5–7oz) unsalted butter, chopped

¼ teaspoon finely grated nutmeg (optional)

125–150ml (4–5fl oz) double cream or milk

salt and freshly ground black pepper

Peel the potatoes either now or after cooking, as you prefer (cooking them in their skins retains more of their nutrients and flavour). Cut them into large pieces of roughly the same size and place in a large pan of salted water. Cover with a lid and bring to the boil, then simmer until tender.

Drain the potatoes and set aside in the colander for a few minutes to dry off and cool slightly. Chop them into smaller pieces, then tip them back into a dry pan.

Add the butter and the nutmeg (if using). Season with black pepper. Mash well to ensure there are no lumps, adding enough cream or milk to get the consistency you like. Taste and adjust the seasoning if necessary. If the cooking water was well salted, or you are serving the mash with a well-seasoned accompaniment, you might not need to add any more. Serve hot.

Sarlat, a town within the Dordogne in southwest France, is famous for its potatoes, and this recipe, which cooks them in duck fat, herbs and garlic, is justly famous too. The version given here is from Thomas Maieli, who supplies Lidgate's with his duck products. It's a rich dish and makes a lovely accompaniment, but is also a tasty lunch if combined with chopped smoked duck breast and served with a salad.

Pommes sarladaises

Serves 6 as a side dish or 4 as a light lunch with smoked duck

50g (2oz) duck fat

1 onion, finely sliced

625g (1¼lb) floury or all-purpose potatoes (e.g. King Edward or Maris Piper), unpeeled

½ small garlic clove, crushed

1–2 tablespoons finely chopped flat leaf parsley, or 6 basil leaves, roughly torn

sea salt flakes and freshly ground black pepper

Melt half the fat in a sauté pan. When hot, add the onion plus a pinch of salt to prevent burning, and cook very gently for about 30 minutes, until soft and sweet. Stir occasionally to prevent sticking. Transfer to a plate.

Meanwhile, put the potatoes in a large pan of salted water. Bring to the boil, then simmer until nearly cooked. Drain and set aside for a few minutes. When just cool enough to handle, peel off the skin and cut the flesh into large chunks (about 3.5–5cm [1½–2in]).

Melt the remaining duck fat in the sauté pan, then add the garlic. Add the potatoes and cook over a medium heat, stirring occasionally, until they are glossy, crisping in parts and cooked through. Stir in the onion and warm through. Finally, season with black pepper and more salt, as needed, and the chopped herbs.

Everyone loves potato salad, but here we ring the changes by using a mixture of yoghurt and double cream instead of mayonnaise, which gives a lighter, fresher taste. To pep it up, buy one of the range of high-quality bottled condiments that butchers often sell. The great thing about this recipe is that it's adaptable to any number of people and can be made with whatever sauce and herbs you like.

Saucy potato salad

Serves 1

125g (4oz) firm-textured potatoes (e.g. Charlotte), peeled

1 teaspoon sea salt flakes

1 tablespoon thick natural yoghurt

1 tablespoon double cream

1 tablespoon finely chopped fresh herb leaves (e.g. mint or parsley), plus extra to serve (optional)

½–1 teaspoon of your chosen sauce (e.g. barbecue, ketchup)

freshly ground black pepper

Put the potatoes and salt into a pan, cover with water and bring to the boil. Simmer until tender, then drain and set aside to cool.

Mix the yoghurt and cream together in a large bowl. Stir in your chosen herb and sauce, then season to taste with pepper and more salt if you wish. Add the cooled potatoes and mix gently to coat in the mixture. Transfer to a serving bowl and sprinkle with a few more chopped herbs if you wish.

Parsnips are especially good with honey, and delicious roasted with butcher's dripping. The trick is not to let them dry out by leaving them in the oven for too long or cooking them too far in advance. Cook them towards the end of the joint's roasting time, and while it is resting. They are a great accompaniment to beef, pork or turkey. Alternatively, shave flakes of hard salty goats' cheese over them and serve as a supper dish for four.

Honey-roast parsnips

Serves 6–8 as a side dish

3 tablespoons dripping, or olive or vegetable oil

750g (1½lb) parsnips, peeled and cut into batons 1.5–2.5cm (¾–1in) thick

2 tablespoons honey

salt and freshly ground black pepper

Preheat the oven to 190°C/375°F/Gas Mark 5 (or leave it at 180°C/350°F/Gas Mark 4 if you're roasting a turkey at that temperature, see page 250).

Put the dripping or oil in a medium roasting pan and place in the oven until hot. Add the parsnips and season well with salt and pepper. Drizzle the honey over them, then roll the batons around so they are well coated.

Roast for 30–40 minutes, until nice and brown, turning them twice during cooking and watching out that they don't burn towards the end.

Down the road from Lidgate's is one of the best greengrocers in London – Michanicou Brothers – and every day we get top-quality produce from them. Head butcher Alan devised this dish at the request of a customer, and it has been a bestseller ever since – ironic, given that we're butchers, but we're happy to sell good food that isn't raw meat.

Michanicou vegetable kebabs

Makes 4

2 medium-large yellow courgettes

8 cherry tomatoes

1 medium-large red onion

2 orange peppers, cut into 8 square-ish pieces about 7 x 5cm (3 x 2in)

8 tubby mushrooms, peeled and stalks cut off

½ aubergine, cut into chunks about 3.5 x 3.5cm (1½ x 1½in) thick

4 tablespoons Caribbean or Chinese sauce (optional)

olive oil, for brushing (optional)

sea salt and freshly ground black pepper

Preheat the oven to 200°C/400°F/Gas Mark 6.

Trim the ends off the courgettes, then cut in half widthways. Use an apple corer to hollow out each half from one end to the other so you're left with tubes. Cut each tube into 2 chunks about 5cm (2in) long. (If you don't have a corer, cut the courgettes into chunks and use a small sharp knife to hollow out each piece.)

Push a tomato into the centre of each courgette chunk. Cut the onion in half through the root and peel off 8 of the outside layers.

Get a skewer about 30cm (12in) long and push pieces of the vegetables onto it in the following order: orange pepper, mushroom, onion (curved over the mushroom), tomato-stuffed courgette, aubergine, mushroom with onion curved over it, tomato-stuffed courgette, orange pepper. Make 3 more kebabs in the same way.

Brush the whole kebabs with sauce if you wish, or just brush generously with olive oil and sprinkle with salt and pepper.

Place the kebabs on a baking tray (lined with baking parchment if you've coated them with sauce). Roast for 30–35 minutes, or until brown on the outside and soft in texture.

These kebabs can also be cooked on a barbecue, in which case turn them often, for about 15–20 minutes, or until tender.

Homemade herb jelly makes a real difference to roasts and cold meats. This one, flecked with chilli and herb, has a slight kick and looks wonderful.

Spiced herb jellies

Makes 3 x 350-ml (12-fl oz) jars

1kg (2lb) cooking apples (about 4 large ones)

1.2 litres (2 pints) water

2 large bushy sprigs of mint, sage or rosemary

about 750g (1½lb) granulated sugar

juice of 2–3 lemons

2 tablespoons finely chopped mint, sage or rosemary

1 red chilli, deseeded and finely chopped (use a Scotch bonnet chilli if you like heat)

Quarter and roughly chop the apples, discarding the stalks and any blemished parts. Place in a large pan (skin, core, pips included), and add the water and herb sprigs. Bring to the boil, then simmer for 45 minutes.

Ladle the mixture into a jelly bag or muslin cloth suspended over a large bowl and leave it to drip through without squeezing. (Recipes often say to leave it overnight, but 3 hours is enough.)

Measure the liquid and pour it into a pan. For every 500ml (17fl oz), add 400g (13oz) of sugar and the juice of 1 lemon. Bring the mixture to the boil, stirring occasionally to ensure the sugar has dissolved by the time it is boiling. Meanwhile, put a saucer in the freezer.

Boil the jelly mixture for about 10 minutes, then put a teaspoon of the liquid on the cold saucer and place in the fridge for 1 minute. If the mixture then wrinkles when you push it with your finger, it has reached setting point. If not, continue to boil the mixture and test it every few minutes, cleaning and chilling the saucer between each test. It can take 15 minutes or so.

While the jelly mixture is boiling, preheat the oven to its lowest setting and thoroughly wash the jars and their lids. Put them on a baking tray and place them in the oven for 10 minutes to sterilize.

Once the jelly has reached setting point, turn off the heat and stir in the chopped herbs and chilli. Leave to cool for 10 minutes, stirring occasionally to distribute the herbs and chilli throughout the jelly. When they stay within the jelly rather than floating to the top, you can pot up.

Skim any scum off the surface, then ladle the jelly into the hot sterilized jars, filling them almost to the top. Put the lids on immediately and set aside to cool. Store in a cool, dark place. Once opened, keep in the fridge.

INDEX

Glossary of UK & US terms

UK	US	UK	US
aubergine	*eggplant*	escalope (chicken)	*scallop*
autumn	*fall*	greaseproof paper	*wax paper*
		flaked almonds	*slivered almonds*
bacon		floury potato	*mealy potato*
back bacon	*Canadian bacon*	frying pan	*skillet*
rashers (bacon)	*slices*	full-fat milk	*whole milk*
streaky (bacon)	*lean*	full-fat yoghurt	*whole yoghurt*
		grill (oven)	*broiler*
baking tray	*baking sheet*	grill (verb)	*broil*
		jug	*pitcher*
beef		kitchen paper	*paper towel*
brisket	*plate*		
featherblade	*flat iron*	**lamb**	
fillet (beef & pork)	*tenderloin*	best end lamb	*rack of lamb*
fillet-tail beef	*tenderloin-tail beef*	scrag end	*no equivalent in US*
sirloin/silverside	*round*		
rump	*sirloin, tenderloin & top sirloin*	mangetout	*snow peas*
		mince	*ground meat*
rump-tail (beef)	*sirloin-tail*	mince (verb)	*grind*
topside	*round*	muscovado sugar	*brown sugar*
		natural yoghurt	*plain yoghurt*
black pudding	*blood sausage*	offal	*variety meats*
button mushrooms	*white mushrooms*	pastry case	*pastry shell*
caster sugar	*superfine sugar*	plain flour	*all-purpose flour*
chestnut mushrooms	*cremini mushrooms*	prawns	*shrimp*
chicory	*endive*	pudding basin	*ovenproof bowl*
chips	*fries*	rocket	*arugula*
chopping board	*cutting board*	shin	*shank*
clingfilm	*plastic wrap*	spring onions	*scallions*
coriander (fresh)	*cilantro*	swede	*rutabaga*
courgette	*zucchini*	tea towels	*dishtowels*
demerara sugar	*raw brown sugar*	tomato puree	*tomato paste*
double cream	*heavy cream*	trotters (pig)	*feet*
dry cider	*hard cider*		

Authors' Acknowledgements

This book is a gathering of knowledge from generations of Lidgates and the many people who are now part of the shop. Thanks to all the Lidgate's staff, past and present, for their ideas, energy and many contributions. Everyone in the shop is part of these pages, both butchers and cooks, and special thanks to Alan Shires for step-by-step guidance.

Our loyal and knowledgeable customers are always commenting on what we sell and giving us ideas. Thanks to all who come through our doors, and in particular to Kimiko Barber for her recipe.

We are fortunate to be linked to some of the best farmers in the country, many of them named in this book, and their superb meat is always a joy to work with. Thanks, too, to the makers of the other high-quality products we sell, especially chef Thomas Maieli of Mr Duck's Delicacies, who kindly provided three recipes.

Thanks to all at Octopus who have made this book a pleasure to put together, particularly Eleanor Maxfield, Juliette Norsworthy and Alex Stetter, and to Elly James of HHB Agency. We're so glad to have had the eye of Andy Sewell on our meat and recipes. Thank you, Andy, and thanks to Laura Fyfe for her beautiful styling and cooking.

Our last and largest thanks go to David Lidgate, Danny's father: a man of vision, great knowledge and an unshakeable and questing belief in the qualities of good meat.

C. Lidgate
Butcher Charcutier
110 Holland Park Avenue
London W11 4UA
020 7727 8243
www.lidgates.com
Mail order around the UK and free delivery
to London and surrounding areas

Q Guild
www.qguild.co.uk
High-quality butchers around Britain

Danny Lidgate is the fifth generation of Lidgate butchers, taking over as managing director in 2009.

Hattie Ellis is an award-winning food writer with an interest in British food and good meat.